THE CANALS OF
YORKSHIRE AND NORTH EAST ENGLAND

Volume II

THE CANALS OF THE BRITISH ISLES

EDITED BY CHARLES HADFIELD

British Canals. An illustrated history. By Charles Hadfield
The Canals of Eastern England. By J. H. Boyes
The Canals of the East Midlands (including part of London). By Charles Hadfield
The Canals of the North of Ireland. By W. A. McCutcheon
The Canals of North West England. By Charles Hadfield and Gordon Biddle
The Canals of Scotland. By Jean Lindsay
The Canals of the South of Ireland. By V. T. H. and D. R. Delany
The Canals of South and South East England. By Charles Hadfield
The Canals of South Wales and the Border. By Charles Hadfield
The Canals of South West England. By Charles Hadfield
The Canals of the West Midlands. By Charles Hadfield
The Canals of Yorkshire and North East England. By Charles Hadfield
Waterways to Stratford. By Charles Hadfield and John Norris

OTHER BOOKS BY CHARLES HADFIELD
Canals of the World
Holiday Cruising on Inland Waterways (with Michael Streat)
The Canal Age
Atmospheric Railways

THE CANALS OF YORKSHIRE AND NORTH EAST ENGLAND

by
Charles Hadfield

WITH PLATES AND MAPS

VOLUME II

DAVID & CHARLES : NEWTON ABBOT

ISBN 0 7153 5975 4

Printed in Great Britain by
Latimer Trend & Company Ltd Plymouth
for David & Charles (Holdings) Limited
South Devon House   Newton Abbot   Devon

CONTENTS

VOLUME I

VOLUME II

PART TWO—1790–1845 (*continued*)

PART THREE—1845–1972

APPENDICES

ILLUSTRATIONS

Volume II

PLATES

TEXT ILLUSTRATIONS AND MAPS

PART TWO—1790–1845
(continued)

CHAPTER XI

The Sheffield Canal

IN the late 1780s business was brisk between Sheffield and the Don's wharf at Tinsley. In 1787 the agent there got a salary increase because of the 'great Increase of Business at Tinsley',[1] in 1788 a surveyor was appointed for the first time to look after the company's road thence to Sheffield, and in 1790 certain Sheffield collieries were exempted from the road toll. There was also an adjoining private wharf at Tinsley, which in 1796 was described as having 'five limekilns, four stables each for four horses, and six houses'.[2]

On 4 July 1792 a public meeting at Cutlers Hall favoured extending the Don navigation upwards from Tinsley to Sheffield[3] and £8,450 was subscribed. The Don company informed their shareholders and had an estimate made, and at their 9 August annual meeting these decided themselves to build a canal to Sheffield, and also that a branch 'into the Coal Country towards Beighton and Eckington would be of utility to the Navigation, and of great Advantage to the Town of Sheffield': that is, towards the Chesterfield Canal.

Three weeks later the company agreed to make a canal from Sheffield, not to Tinsley, but by Brinsworth to the river near Rotherham, with a branch to Renishaw near Eckington.[4] At the end of October the committee were rather doubtful whether the branch was still necessary now that the Dearne & Dove Canal project (see p. 280) promised ample supplies of coal to Sheffield, but their engineer John Thompson having said that it might be difficult to supply the Sheffield canal with enough water without it, they decided it should run to a point east of Eckington, and that they would approach the Duke of Norfolk and other land and millowners.

At a Sheffield canal committee meeting on 6 December, a representative from the Chesterfield Canal Company[5] attended to object to the Eckington branch. He said his company considered they had a prior claim to the coal round Eckington, 'and that it wo^d be injurious to their Navigation to have it taken away by any other Line'.[6] The Duke of Norfolk was also there. He agreed on terms, but these were 'much higher than was before thought of by the Committee',[6] so that the estimate was now £46,292 for a canal 4 miles long from Sheffield to Rotherham with a 10-mile branch to Eckington and another of 2 miles to the Duke's Attercliffe Common colliery.

After this, a newspaper reported that, 'In consequence of the opposition of the Land Owners . . . the business is entirely quashed for the present.'[7] This was not so. The committee did feel that in view of the likely cost the Don shareholders should consider the situation later that month. Robert Mylne gave a report 'very favourable to the undertaking',*[8] and in January the committee recommended the shareholders to carry out the full scheme 'notwithstanding any opposition that has yet been suggested to them'.[10] Alternatively, they thought there would be no opposition to 'a compleat Navigation from Sheffield to Rotherham, and that they ought at all Events to undertake the making of the same'. To conciliate landowners on the Eckington line, they suggested it should be built by a separate subscription, three-eighths from landowners, three-eighths from Sheffield people, and a quarter from Don shareholders.

The project now took off semi-independently at a public meeting in Sheffield on 15 January chaired by Dr John Browne, which agreed to build a Sheffield Canal, that to Eckington, needed to supply water, to be separately financed. However, a second meeting a few days later thought coal might be got more cheaply than from Eckington, and asked the Don to postpone a Bill to the next session of Parliament, promising to produce an alternative plan by 24 June. They certainly did not want the Sheffield canal dropped, however, and said that those present would open a subscription should the Don company abandon their scheme.

Benjamin Outram was then asked to report, and did so on 19 August 1793. He proposed a level canal 12¾ miles long from the Eckington–Beighton road via Attercliffe, 'to a close behind the Hospital Chappel at Sheffield', with a 770 yd tunnel and a fair

---

* His visit was a brief one on one of the shortest days of the year. His diary records: 'Dec. 26 (1792). Bad day, in a chaise to Sheffield; viewed line, lands and brooks to that place. Viewed the termination and place for bason. Attended a Committee—made a report viva voce to the meeting on this Canal.'[9]

amount of cutting. The section from Attercliffe to Sheffield would be 'navigable for the River Bargers', as would a branch from Attercliffe to the Don and the making navigable of that river to Tinsley wharf, with 7 canal and 3 river locks. The rest, together with an extension with 5 locks to the Chesterfield Canal, would, like that canal, be narrow. This extension, he thought, 'would open a cheap conveyance to the Iron works near Chesterfield, the Markets of Worksop and Retford, and the Lime works on the Chesterfield canal', which would make cheap lime available at Sheffield.

His estimate was £45,041 for the main line and Tinsley branch, plus £4,175 for the Chesterfield Canal connexion and £3,000 for reservoirs, £52,216 in all. His estimate of revenue was £4,000 p.a., £2,500 of which would be from coal, though 'a Canal thro' a Country, full of Coals, & Manufactories, with ye Town of Sheff^d at its head, cannot fail to have many sources of commerce that are not foreseen'.[11]

There was no enthusiasm in a difficult time, and the project then lay dormant until 1801, when William Jessop, in a letter to the Don committee, included an extension to Sheffield as possibly to make part of a Don improvement Bill. He probably did so because the idea was being talked about in Sheffield. In March the Don committee received an 'application from the Inhabitants of Sheffield for extending the Navigation from Tinsley to the Town of Sheffield', which required 'mature consideration and the Consent of the Proprietors'.[12] Jessop had only done a quick survey, because of 'rainy weather, and want of Time'. He worked on a level line from Sheffield to Tinsley where, he thought, locks must be grouped because water would have to be back-pumped from the Don, there being none to be obtained in Sheffield. His conclusion was: 'I am afraid the execution of such a Canal, with the maintenance of a Steam Engine, will cost more than will be thought prudent to expend', but recommended a further study.

About the end of 1801 the Cutlers' Company took the initiative in reviving a canal scheme, now to Sheffield only, and Joseph Bailey the Master Cutler pressed William Dunn, then completing the Oakham Canal,[13] to survey the line: 'We are anxious to have A Survey of the Navigation from Tinsley to Sheff^d as soon as pasable. I did expect you before this time you would have had An Opertunity to do it as I am Contineley Questioned about Request your answer at what time we may expect you to make the survey.'[14] Early in July 1802 Dunn agreed to do the job, seemingly working

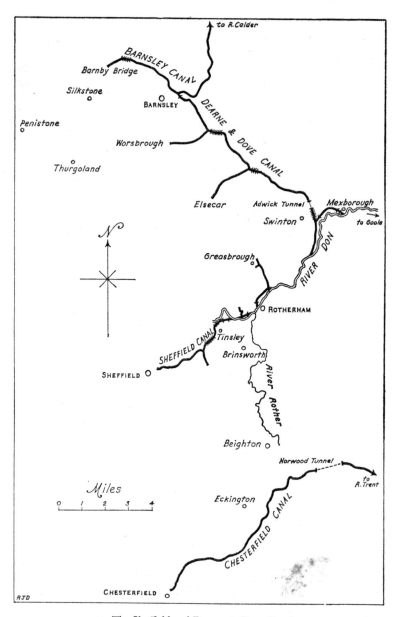

23. The Sheffield and Dearne & Dove Canals

with William Fairbank, and later proposed a line similar to Outram's, up the Don from Tinsley with 4 locks, then a canal from Brightside with 5 locks, the summit to be $7\frac{1}{2}$ ft deep for water storage, with one or more reservoirs as well. The fair copy of his report[14] gives no figures, but his draft[15] notes engineering expenses of £16,348. A plan was deposited and Parliamentary petition sent in.[16] The Cutlers' Company then having asked Dunn to produce some traffic figures, he consulted the Don, and came up with 11,000 tons and a revenue of £1,800 p.a.[17]

At the end of January 1803 the Don company learned that the Cutlers had given Parliamentary notice of a Bill, and that £29,400 had been subscribed in a week,[18] Dr John Browne being still a moving spirit. They were pardonably annoyed, for they had been asked for their assent or dissent to the Bill 'without any offer to satisfy the River Dun Company for the Loss of their Wharfs and other Damages they may sustain'.[19] They decided to oppose until compensation and relief from the maintenance cost of the Tinsley–Sheffield road had been agreed, estimating their loss by the new canal at £600 p.a., or £15,000 at 25 years' purchase, plus road costs. They hoped locks would be made 70 ft × 16 ft 6 in, with 5 ft on the sills, and the canal 5 ft deep. A few days later they were taken aback to learn that the promoters thought the Don company would be benefited, not harmed, and would make no offer. So they decided to oppose. A Bill was introduced in 1803, but made no headway against the Duke of Norfolk, and in July a meeting at Cutlers' Hall wound the scheme up, having spent £250.[20] In 1804 the Don company were wondering whether to include either a railroad or a canal in their own proposed scheme, and got Jessop to report on the railroad possibilities. To a public meeting at Cutlers' Hall on 26 April 1804 they proposed a lock charge of 6d ($2\frac{1}{2}$p) per vessel for coal when capital cost and interest had been paid off.[21] One would have thought it a bargain for Sheffield, but they also had to drop their Bill, and the project slumbered.

Late in 1810, at a time when there was some support in Sheffield for possible links with other canals that edged the Peak district,[22] Richard Gresley, who favoured them, wrote to tell the Don company about 'the propriety of making a canal from Rotherham to Chesterfield Canal and from thence to the Cromford Canal'.[23] This, the North Eastern Junction Canal, had created very little interest when proposed at a public meeting at Rotherham in October,[24] and now, in January 1811, was of no more to the Don committee, though its first part resembled their own earlier

Eckington scheme. However, from 1811 to 1814 talk continued upon links between Sheffield and the Cromford and Peak Forest Canals that might be extended to Rotherham to form a Sheffield–Don waterway. These paralleled others upon a possible branch from the Don at Rotherham or Tinsley to join the proposed High Peak Junction Canal[25] from the Peak Forest to the Cromford Canal. William Fairbank surveyed this in 1813.[26]

Then, on 20 July 1813, on the initiative of the Cutlers' Company, a meeting was held to consider building a canal from Rotherham to Sheffield, though extensions to Eckington or the Peak Forest Canal were mentioned as possibilities, and were reported on by William Chapman.[27] For the Rotherham–Sheffield canal, the engineer surveyed lines to the north and to the south of the river, he himself preferring the northern as cheaper and shorter. His estimate was much higher than Dunn's had been, but so also was his forecast of traffic, now 150,000 tons. For extensions beyond Sheffield, whether to the Chesterfield or the Peak Forest Canals, Chapman preferred tramroads.

In November a deputation from the promoters, which included the Master Cutler, met the Don committee. They offered the Don company the option of building the canal Chapman proposed. These declined, considering that:

'if a Canal is made it should be on the North side of the . . . River, but that a Conveyance from Sheffield to Tinsley by means of a double Iron Rail road (to join which other Rail Roads may be made into the Coal countries) and the improving the present Navigation from Tinsley to the River Ouse so as to insure the more regular Conveyance of Goods . . . will be of much greater advantage to the Town of Sheffield than making the said proposed Canal'.[28]

They offered to call a shareholders' meeting if the canal promoters would approve of a railroad, and get coalowners' support for it at reasonable tolls. But the promoters wanted a canal, and after considering Chapman's report, and alternative routes to the north and south of the Don, the river shareholders in April 1814 decided against it. Their own figuring was that the gross revenue would be £1,988, against which expenses and interest on capital, less savings on the road, would be £3,390, leaving a net loss of £1,402.

In November the Don committee warned the promoters, who had sent them a route plan, that they would want compensation for wharfage and buildings at Tinsley, and freedom from all road repair liabilities. After bargaining that continued into the Parliamentary committee, they settled for £11,000, and then decided to sell their property 'above the present Lock (Except the two Locks, Lock House and Bridges at Tinsley aforesaid and the navigable Cut with the banks with which the said Canal is intended to communicate)',[29] to the canal company, who would take over responsibility for repairing the upper lock, as well as the road to Sheffield. Because the company would now control Tinsley Cut, they could charge toll on traffic coming from Jordan Dam into the Don.

Now that negotiations with the Don were out of the way, another public meeting was held at Cutlers' Hall on 15 July 1814, which recommended the south side line in spite of Chapman's preference for the northern, partly because it would serve the Handsworth colliery of that thorn in the promoters' flesh, the Duke of Norfolk, and partly, so it was said later, though from an interested source, 'the Southern side of the River was adopted, and a higher level chosen for the Line of the Canal, at a considerable pecuniary sacrifice, for the express purpose of affording facility, at a future period, of communication with the Chesterfield Canal'.[30]

Chapman then did another report especially on the south side line.[31] Slightly altering his earlier ideas, he now provided for three reservoirs, a steam engine to pump colliery water, and a branch canal towards Darnall. His Parliamentary estimate was £55,510. Some £24,000 was allowed for land, Parliamentary expenses and the compensation payable to the Don. The Act,[32] passed on 7 June 1815, authorized the company to raise £80,000, and another £20,000 if necessary: the Duke of Norfolk (£2,000) and Earl Fitzwilliam (£1,000) led the 182 subscribers, most of whom had their names down for one or two shares only. Reservoirs were to be built, because water rights were restricted in the Act in the interests of industrial users, and the Tinsley road had now to be maintained by the canal company, who could charge 1d a ton toll. There was also to have been a cut and cover tunnel some 100 yd long near Attercliffe,[33] but a cutting was substituted.

Hugh Parker of Woodthorpe laid the foundation stone of the basin on 19 June 1816,[34] and Henry Buck as resident engineer took charge of construction. Seemingly, canal cutting was used by the local overseers of the poor as a means of giving the unemployed work.[35]

The canal was opened on 22 February 1819, 3⅞ miles long with

B

12 locks, taking craft 61 ft 6 in long × 15 ft 3 in wide, and drawing 6 ft. The first craft into the basin was *The Industry*, whose name still remains as that of a public house a hundred yards away. It was 'the most beautiful spectacle ever witnessed in Sheffield',[36] and an onlooker wrote, 'I subscribed for a share in the adventure at its commencement, rather because I thought it proper than from any expectation of profit; but there is a fair prospect even of pecuniary advantage. . . . Never was a greater concourse seen in Sheffield.'[37] Indeed, 'The oldest man in Sheffield never saw such a day.'[38] The branch, ⅜ mile long from a point about half a mile short of the top lock south to the Greenland Engine road near the reservoir at Darnall, was opened at the same time, a boat with Handsworth coal being in the opening procession. An existing tramroad to the Duke of Norfolk's colliery at Handsworth joined the end of the branch, and became a public line. The cost had been £104,719,[39] £70,400 having been raised from 704 £100 shares and £22,500 borrowed on mortgage, the balance being presumably owed. Much of the excess overestimate was said to be due to the high prices paid for land. The takings for the first 13 months to end-March 1820 were £4,808, the expenses £1,954:[40] as for the town, 'The markets already feel the effect of a free communication with distant places which can supply their demand.'[41]

Tramroads were soon afterwards opened from the basin to Manor Laithes and Manor Pits collieries, and from the junction of the Greenland arm to Tinsley Park collieries.[42]

In 1824 a revival of the earlier High Peak Junction Canal scheme appeared as the Grand Commercial Canal, to link the Sheffield with the Cromford, Chesterfield and Peak Forest Canals,[43] the last named giving access to Manchester. Thomas Telford was asked to report on the scheme, and a Sheffield meeting in August raised money towards his fees. The Sheffield branch of the proposed canal network, now called the Sheffield & Manchester Canal, was surveyed for Telford by William Fairbank.[44] Some discussion took place on the respective merits of this scheme and the older North Eastern Junction line of 1810, but by the time Telford reported early in 1825, the proposal that became the Cromford & High Peak Railway, connecting the Peak Forest and Cromford Canals and dropping the other links, had overtaken it. Nevertheless, in 1827 a meeting with the Master Cutler in the chair revived ideas of a canal from Sheffield to the Peak Forest, but the Don company at any rate were not interested enough to send representatives to a promotion committee.

The company paid its first dividend of 2½ per cent in 1826, and in the following year the shares stood at £95.[45] Dividends were paid thereafter each year until 1841. For the year ending 31 March 1831, gross receipts had reached £8,015, against £7,249 for the previous year.

In the autumn of 1830 a group of mainly Sheffield men proposed a railway from Sheffield via Rotherham and Doncaster to Goole. This frightened the company, who immediately appointed a subcommittee to oppose the railway project, and halved their grain toll, from 4d to 2d a quarter, having got a 2d concession also from the Don on the river to Doncaster. For the moment the project went no further.

In June 1832, a Sheffield meeting once more discussed a possible Sheffield & Chesterfield Junction Canal. A committee was appointed, and Joseph Burke, who described himself as one of the Sheffield Canal's original engineers, laid it out as a 7¾ mile long canal with 2 locks from the head of the Sheffield's locks (originally from the Greenland branch) to below Killamarsh forge on the Chesterfield. His estimate of cost was £46,204, and of revenue a meticulous £4,999, just over half of which would be derived from coal. The prospectus,[46] naming a capital of £50,000, said the proposed line would unite the Don and the Trent by a route alternative to the Stainforth & Keadby Canal. Running through a large coalfield, it would also reduce the price of corn, and carry malt from Worksop and Derbyshire lime and limestone from Ashover. George Leather was then asked to report on the line, and did so on 22 October. He broadly approved Burke's route, but now estimated the cost, with some improvements of his own, at £75,870, more than the subscribers had thought, though he did refer to a possible trade in coal from new collieries on the line to Sheffield and down the Don to compete with coal from Silkstone. The Don company took no interest, being themselves more attracted to building railroad branches to new collieries round Sheffield. Only £13,000 came in, and the project dropped.

A newspaper, reporting the general meeting held on 2 May 1833, says that a 4 per cent dividend was declared. Gross receipts had nearly doubled in the previous years, from £4,633 in 1822 to £8,263 in 1832. In these years nearly £14,000 of debt had been paid off, and dividends declared.[46] Shares now stood at £105. A year later the company paid 5 per cent.

In the autumn of 1833 a railway, first from Wortley to Rotherham, soon from Sheffield to Rotherham, was being promoted so vigorously that a Bill was in the House in March. At the beginning of May the Don put it to the Sheffield Canal Company,

> 'whether the most effective opposition they could offer to the intended Railway would not be to reduce their dues on Coal at least one half as this would take away the most important ground urged by the promoters of the Railway for the necessity of that Measure'.[47]

The Bill passed the Commons, but was thrown out in the Lords on the preamble not being proved—that is, that the necessity of the line had not been established, a decision as satisfactory to the canal company as to the Don.

The canal's water supply came mainly from mines, and in 1834, due to mine pumping deficiencies, the canal had been badly short, the normal 6 ft depth being down to 4 ft 6 in. Given the danger from railways, this could not be allowed to happen again, so an agreement was made with the Sheffield Water Works Company to supply water for ten years from March 1836.[48]

In October 1834 a prospectus appeared for a Sheffield & Rotherham Railway, mainly designed to bring coal from Earl Fitzwilliam's Greasbrough collieries as a counterpoise to the Duke of Norfolk's Sheffield mines, to terminate at a basin and wharves at Masborough near Rotherham. It referred to the unfortunate choice of the south side of the Don for the canal, resulting in many locks and a high cost, so 'that from this unhappy choice of line and level, and the consequent sacrifice of capital, the Canal never has been nor ever it can be, of much public benefit'. It said that 1,800 tons of coal a week passed through the Sheffield Canal, and also 1,000 tons from Tinsley Park and Darnall collieries; and that 1,500 tons a week passed over the Tinsley road. The prospectus alleged that the canal charges for tolls and freight from Rotherham to Sheffield were half those for the whole distance from Hull to Rotherham.[49] The canal company's view was ambivalent. They were of course bitterly opposed to the Sheffield & Rotherham line as competing directly with their own, and welcomed the cut the Don company were then making to improve the navigation between Rotherham and Tinsley (see pp 218–19). But they would not have minded a railway from Rotherham towards Goole or Hull. As they told their counsel in confidence about the Don, 'below Rotherham and particularly at Doncaster and in the Dun and below Stainforth Dutch River there are occasionally . . . formidable stoppages which afford a reason why the Rail Road should be continued to the Ouse or the Humber'.[50]

In opposing the railway Bill, the canal officials gave the 1834 traffic as 159,000 tons of coal; there were also 14,126 tons of limestone, 10,152 of bar iron, 7,323 of corn, 5,108 of timber, 953 of pig metal, and 19,694 of sundries: 216,356 in all. Fly-boats took 3½ to 4 hours to work through the canal, sloops 5 to 6 hours. The locks would take 70 ton craft, but so far 64 tons had been the limit, though the Don company were then widening some of their upper locks to give the greater capacity. The first Bill of 1835 failed, but the second passed in 1836, and the line opened on 31 October 1838, the Greasbrough Canal basin branch becoming operational early in 1840. This railway wharf connected the railway to the Don and so enabled the Sheffield Canal to be by-passed. A notice of February 1840 announced a transhipment service from Sheffield, goods transferring at Greasbrough twice a week into 'Fly Boats in connexion with the Hull and London Steamers'.[51]

In May 1837 the canal company had paid a dividend of 5 per cent, in 1838 of 4 per cent, 1839 of 5½ per cent, 1840 of 5 per cent, and 1841 of 3 per cent. In this year of 1840–1* the takings at Sheffield, the bulk of the company's income, had been £6,428; the figure then fell as follows:

	£
1841–42	4,575
1842–43	3,276
1843–44	3,776

The profits of £706, £259 and £714 allowed no dividends.[52] The 1842–3 report summarizes their position. Income, totalling £4,262, was made up of tolls, £3,319; rents £475; warehouses £235; and wharfage and weighing, £233. Heavy items of expenditure were interest on mortgages, £1,252; the Tinsley road, £837, and the supply of water, £700.

Sheffield directories of 1839, 1841 and 1845 give us a composite picture of the available carrying services, which were extensive. There were two direct services without transhipment to London, by the sloops of the London & Sheffield Union Company or the contract vessels of the London, Hull & Sheffield concern. Richard Pearson & Co's fly-boats ran twice a week to Thorne for onforwarding goods to Goole, Hull and Stanton's wharf, London 'twice a week by their Regular Sailing ships; and by Steam

* The company's financial year ended on 31 March, and the dividend was paid in May.

Vessels, three times a week, to and from Custom-House Quay, London,'[53] and in 1839 and 1841 the Humber Union Steam Company's fly-boats ran twice a week to Hull.[54] Other services served points down river and to Hull, including those daily from the Don Navigation Company's wharf, but others more specialized were set out in 1841: once a fortnight by one and every three weeks by another carrier to Manchester and to York; fortnightly to Gainsborough; every three weeks to Leeds. But in 1845 there was one significant change: William Cobby, previously agent of the Humber Union concern, was now offering water transport from London to Hull and Selby, for onforwarding to Sheffield by rail.

In 1840 the North Midland Railway from Derby via Rotherham to Leeds was opened; in 1843 it was said, 'The Canal Company . . . are poor, partly from law suits, partly from failures, but principally from decay of traffic. Bad trade has been one cause of this and the N. Midland Railway another, for it has lowered the dues greatly.'[55]

One grievance the company had against the Sheffield & Rotherham Railway was that company's refusal to pay £100 a year towards maintaining the Tinsley–Sheffield road, which the canal company said had been decided in 1836. A law suit about it was still going on in 1843. At the same time they had it in mind to promote a Bill in 1842 to get rid of this liability, transferring it to the parishes.[56] But their report of 4 May 1843 blamed national depression of trade as much for the poor results as railway competition. They admitted that rail rates were very low, but thought there were 'already signs that the Railway Companies are returning to a sounder System of charging'.[57]

In 1844, when shares were reported as selling for £25,[58] the company cannot have welcomed an agreement between the Sheffield & Rotherham Railway and the Don company covering 'Terms or Propositions for the Conveyance of Traffic upon that Railway to and from this Navigation'.[59]

In early 1845 the Don heard that the Sheffield Canal Company were promoting a Bill seemingly concerned with their liability to maintain the Tinsley–Sheffield road.* Then, in August, at a time when the Don were moving to acquire the Barnsley and Dearne & Dove Canals, the river company's shareholders' meeting asked the committee to find out 'whether a more intimate connection cannot be formed with the Sheffield Canal than at present exists'.[60] However, the following month saw the beginning of their in-

* This Bill is mentioned again at the beginning of 1847.

volvement with the South Yorkshire Coal Railway promoters, and approaches to the Sheffield Canal were laid aside.

In 1844 the Sheffield & Lincolnshire Junction Railway was proposed from Sheffield to Gainsborough. They got their Act on 3 August 1846 with the support of the Sheffield, Ashton-under-Lyne & Manchester Railway, and almost at once heard that the Sheffield, Rotherham, Barnsley, Wakefield, Huddersfield & Goole Railway Company were trying to acquire the Sheffield Canal.[61] The Sheffield & Lincolnshire Junction therefore themselves approached the canal company, and later in 1846 agreed to take over the canal, paying a perpetual annuity of 50s (£2·50) a share to the canal's shareholders.[62] This news decided the Don company to buy land and buildings, 'it appearing desirable that an independent Communication betwixt the Dun Navigation and the Town of Sheffield should be obtained'.[63] By the end of the year they were able to say that they had agreed, or were about to agree, to buy estates 'which together extended a great portion of the intervening space betwixt the Dun Navigation and the Town of Sheffield'.[64]

Meanwhile on 1 January 1847 the Sheffield & Lincolnshire Junction Railway amalgamated with the Sheffield, Ashton-under-Lyne & Manchester and another to form the Manchester, Sheffield & Lincolnshire Railway. They went ahead with a Bill to acquire the canal, so that in October 1847 the Don company decided to seek a Bill to extend their own navigation to Sheffield,[65] and quickly drafted it. The shareholders approved it on 28 February 1848, on the same day receiving a deputation from the Sheffield town council headed by the mayor. This explained that the council had already sent them to find out whether the railway company would agree to clauses being inserted in the Transfer Bill 'for the protection and security of the Town of Sheffield', or whether:

'some arrangement could not be made for vesting the Canal in the River Dun Company who in the opinion of the Committee of the Town Council was the proper party to hold the same with the greater prospect of advantage and accommodation of the public'.

The council committee had gone on to tell the railway company that they would not, however, oppose the Transfer Bill if clauses were included to ensure 6 ft depth, tolls limited to twice those the Don company would take on their own proposed extension, and the abolition of the road toll. But were these conditions to be accepted, they had still refused to commit themselves to support the Transfer Bill and oppose the Don extension. The council representatives then inquired the terms on which the Don would negotiate with the railway for the canal, and were told the river company were willing to buy it at 50s (£2·50) a share so long as the railway did not require too much land for their station, which 'would render inefficient the Wharfage accommodation'. They would also reduce the canal tolls to their own navigation's level. In return for this offer, the town council pledged themselves to support the Don extension Bill.[66]

The railway replied refusing the Don's offer, but assuring the town council that they 'have no intention to obstruct the traffic on the Canal or to charge that traffic at rates unduly high'.[67] The Don thereupon withdrew their offer, and decided instead to oppose the Transfer Bill. By May 1848, however, the Don company and the Manchester, Sheffield & Lincolnshire Railway had come to an agreement. The canal would be transferred to the Don at cost, plus cash for some land needed by the railway, and leased under the Carriers' Act until the purchase took effect. In exchange, the Don extension Bill would be withdrawn. When the agreement had been executed, the Don promised to reduce the canal's coal toll to ½d per ton/mile. A little later the Don company arranged to put the road in good condition and then transfer it to the Doncaster & Tinsley turnpike trustees together with £1,000, and in December, as they had promised, they reduced coal tolls. They also took steps to increase the canal's water supply from collieries and from their own river.

It was, however, too late to stop the railway's Bill, and by it the canal company was vested in the M.S. & L.R. on 22 July 1848.[68] Shareholders were to receive a perpetual annuity of £2 10s (£2·50) per £100 share. The railway company were to take over the canal's £25,500 mortgage debt, and keep the canal open and in good repair.

A year later, another Act[69] of 28 July 1849 transferred the canal from the railway to the River Don company. The latter were to take over the mortgage debt, and pay the railway company £1,760 p.a. in perpetuity, equivalent to 2½ per cent on the £70,400 capital of the canal company, out of which the annuities to the former canal shareholders would be paid. Authorized tolls were reduced by the Act, to ½d on coal and limestone, 1d on iron, and 1½d on grain, timber and general merchandise, with maxima also for discharging, porterage, wharfage and warehousing rates.

Separately, the railway bought part of the canal basin's land for £5,000. The canal now passed to the River Don company, whose amalgamation with the South Yorkshire, Doncaster & Goole Railway took effect a year later. The Sheffield Canal Company was not dissolved until the Manchester, Sheffield & Lincolnshire Railway (Additional Powers) Act[70] of 1886, which also extinguished the current annuities to shareholders and substituted $4\frac{1}{2}$ per cent railway debenture stock. (*To continue the history of the Sheffield Canal, turn to Chapter XVIII.*)

CHAPTER XII

Satellites of the Don

+++++++++++++++++++++++++++++++++++◆+++++++++++++++++++++++++++++++++++

THE Dearne & Dove and Stainforth & Keadby Canals were simultaneously promoted by the Don. Both were built, both were useful, both profitable, though the Dearne & Dove was much more so.

Dearne & Dove Canal

Soon after the Don Navigation had been opened, Swinton became a transhipment point for road transport to and from Barnsley. In 1770 the Don company complained that the road between the two places was 'almost impassable with Carriages in many parts thereof to the great Impediment in the Carriage of Goods',[1] and threatened to indict the seven responsible townships. The work seems then to have been patchily done, but in 1775 the Don company were again threatening to indict three townships. About 1773 also, the Marquess of Rockingham interested himself in the possibility of making the river Dearne navigable upwards from the Don to Barnsley and the coal and iron producing areas nearby, and a possible line to Cawthorne with a branch to Haigh bridge (see p. 79) was surveyed.

In February 1791 the Don company appointed an assistant at Swinton wharf because of the increase of business, and at their shareholders' meeting in August 1792, having agreed to make a canal from Tinsley to Sheffield, they went on to resolve that:

'the making the River Dearne navigable, from its Junction with the River Dun, up to Barnsley and that neighbourhood, would also be of great public utility: not only to the Trade carried on in and about Barnsley, but also on account of the great Quantity of Coal which might be got in that neighbourhood, and which would afford a regular Supply (now very much wanted) to the Trade upon the River Dun'.[2]

It was to be recommended to the next shareholders' meeting. One assumes they knew that the Aire & Calder also had their eye on Barnsley, having a month earlier told their manager to get a survey and estimate made for a canal from near Barnsley to near Wakefield (see p. 169).

The meeting was held three weeks later. Don shareholders agreed that a navigable cut from the river 'up to Barnsley' would be valuable, and that they should 'use their best Endeavour to forward the making of the . . . Canal'[3] at a cost of about £50,000. Their object was to open up the coal and iron districts near Elsecar and Worsbrough, and the coal field round Barnsley. They thought of it as a subsidiary, proposing that Don shareholders should subscribe £30,000 pro rata to their holdings in the river company, and landowners or others who wished to support it, the balance. Eight shareholders, together with the Don committee, were appointed to manage the affair, William Jessop to be asked to survey the various possible lines and make an estimate.

Jessop seems to have been too busy, and Whitworth to have been asked instead, but under Jessop's supervision. Surveys were started by John Thompson of the Don and William Fairbank, and hopeful subscribers told to come back later. On 24 September the committee were told that wet weather had impeded surveying, but that a line from Swinton to Barnsley and Haigh bridge, and also Barnby bridge, had been approved by landowners, who themselves were asking for a bigger proportion of the subscription. As, however, the Aire & Calder company had called a meeting at Barnsley for 15 October to present their plan for a canal to Wakefield, they thought it wiser to send representatives to the meeting and then wait and see what it brought forth. Meanwhile, a 'skilfull Engineer' to report on the line was urgent; they asked Robert Mylne, who was described as the canal's engineer in October.[4] Mylne did his survey on 22 and 23 December, and later gave evidence on the Bill.[5]

It soon became clear that two canals would be built to Barnsley, one from the Aire & Calder, the other from the Don. The Don committee therefore instructed their representatives who were to meet the Aire & Calder that they must if possible get for the Dearne & Dove the building of the vital length from Barnsley upwards to the coalfield at Barnby bridge and Haigh bridge. If they could not, then they were to arrange 'the most beneficial System of Tonnage for Boats passing and repassing to and from the River Don'.[6]

The meeting was held on 20 October. The Aire & Calder refused to give way on getting the coalfield section for their protégé, but agreed to add a Haigh bridge branch to the plan that had been approved on the 15th for the Barnsley Canal, and also to the Don's plan to build a canal from the latter to the Don. A junction lock on the level was to be planned jointly by Jessop, the Barnsley's engineer, and Mylne so that neither canal would lose water, and the Barnsley agreed not to take any water that ran into the river Dearne and so into the Don. The two parties also agreed that the tolls already proposed at the meeting on the 15th for the Barnsley should apply to the Dearne & Dove, neither company to reduce these without the other's consent. Finally, the Don and Aire & Calder agreed that if in the future either the Barnsley or the Dearne & Dove shareholders 'shall be disposed to continue a Navigation from the terminations of the said intended Canals towards Manchester, each Party agrees with the other not to oppose such Extension'.[7] On the 22nd the Dearne & Dove's first subscribers' meeting was held, and settled the capital at £60,000, one-third to be allotted to landowners of ground cut through, one-third to gentlemen and merchants 'resident within seven Miles of the Canal', and one-third to Don shareholders 'who have brought forward so useful an Undertaking, to be held by them in like Number as they possess Shares in the River Dun',[8] any deficiency to be made up by the last named. The existing Don promotion committee was continued as that of the Dearne & Dove. Shares were quickly taken up in the exciting atmosphere of the canal mania: the extensive coalfields to be developed guaranteed that money would be made. The 'gentlemen and merchants' came smartly forward, the '£20,000 was instantly filled, and five times the sum would then have been subscribed by them, if they could have been permitted to do so'.[9]

Another scheme, for a canal from the Don near Conisbrough up the Dearne valley to join the Horbury–Haigh Bridge line being projected as a rival of the Barnsley Canal (see p. 172), hardly got off the ground. Its chief promoter, T. R. Beaumont, did, however, organize opposition to both the Dearne & Dove and Barnsley Canal Bills.

Nevertheless, an Act[10] was passed in June 1793, on the same day as that for the Barnsley Canal. It authorized the company, which included the Duke of Leeds, Earl Fitzwilliam, Sir L. Copley, Bt, Sir G. Wombwell, Bt, and Sir F. Wood, Bt, all land and mineral owners on the line, to raise £60,000 in £100 shares, and a further

£30,000 on mortgage if necessary. In July, a month later, the mania now left behind, 62 Dearne & Dove shares not taken up were ballotted for by Don shareholders who wanted to participate. Don Navigation influence was therefore considerable. On the one hand, the canal was burdened with exemptions from tolls on manure (except lime) and road materials. On the other, the Act not only authorized reasonable tolls, but provisions that a boat passing any lock should pay for six miles, that the minimum charge should be for 30 tons,* and that fractions of a mile should be charged as a whole mile, all of which were important on a short canal. Locks were to be big enough to admit vessels commonly using the Don, and a depth of 4 ft 6 in was to be maintained.

John Thompson, the Don's engineer, took charge of construction, and in July was offering contracts for cutting and for prepared stone.[11] As often on other jobs in this time of rising costs, the navvies working on the Dearne & Dove became restless:

'On Saturday night last, a riotous affray took place amongst the navigators at Wath upon Dearne, in consequence of which the Rotherham Troop of the Yorkshire West Riding Cavalry were ordered to hold themselves in readyness; but some of the ringleaders being secured by the constables, peace was soon restored.'[12]

Robert Whitworth surveyed the works in the spring of 1795 and, Thompson having died that year, became engineer until his own death in 1799. One of his sons, Robert or William, probably finished it.

In November 1796 a special meeting considered extending their branch from Cobcar Ing* to Elsecar. It seems not to have taken action, for another was summoned the following May to consider how to raise more money, and also a notice given them by Earl Fitzwilliam that he intended to make the branch from Cobcar Ing to his new colliery workings at Elsecar, on condition that it would be supplied from the company's Elsecar reservoir.[13] If the Earl was manoeuvring to get action, he succeeded, for in September 1797 the company announced they would continue the branch, the Earl lending them the money to do it, and allowing them to pass through his estate.[14] On 3 December 1798 the company announced that the Dearne & Dove was open from the Don at

* There were variations.
* About ¼ mile. Cobcar lock is the one below the top lock of the Elsecar branch. However, the deposited plan shows a lockless branch, which would have involved deep cutting at the Elsecar end.

No. *71.*

DEARNE AND DOVE CANAL.

(1st CALL.)

Received of Oct. 11: 97 of Richard Greaves Esq.
the Sum of fifteen Pounds being the seventeenth Call of
Five per Cent. on his Subscription of £300
towards the said undertaking.

FOR WALKERS, EYRE AND STANLEY, Treasurers.

£. 15.

D. Hirst

24. Subscription call receipt of the Dearne & Dove Canal

Swinton to Elsecar colliery, and would be navigable to Aldham mill, less than three miles from Barnsley, by 1 January.[15] On the same date Lord Fitzwilliam announced the colliery's opening, 'where Coals will be sold at 9s per Waggon, for Ready Money'.[16] By 1800 720 tons a week were being boated from the colliery.[17]

By August 1797 £60,000 had been spent, and the company then tried to borrow £30,000. Quickly finding this to be difficult, they said in September they intended to seek a Bill to authorize higher tolls. They must then have decided to get the Elsecar branch open first, and some trade going. That done, some of the shareholders lent the company £2 per share, which enabled them to pay for the Act[18] of 1800. This enabled the company to raise another £30,000, not by mortgage as in the original Act, but by additional calls or issuing new shares, and to borrow £10,000 as well. The reasons given for needing the money were: 'the great Advance in the Price of Timber, Labour, Deep Cutting, Extra Banking, and Puddling, where first thought unnecessary; the making of the Tunnel, and the mistaken Idea of the Value of Land cut through'.[19] Should the additional money be raised from new shares, it was to be in half-shares of £50. Authorized tolls, wharfage and other charges were all increased by 50 per cent, except flag paving stones, limestone or lime which had come up the Barnsley Canal from Wakefield.

Cutting continued on the main line to Barnsley and on the Worsbrough branch. It stimulated the appetite:

'A few days ago 25 bankers* . . . had a supper provided in commemoration of peace, at the Red Lion Inn at Worsbrough Bridge . . . where they eat and drank as follows, 40 lbs of beef,

* A local name for excavators or navvies.

36 lbs of potatoes, 20 lbs of pudding, 18 lbs of bread, and a quantity of ale equal to 150 lbs weight, which amounted to 10½ lbs to each man.'[20]

On 12 November 1804 water was let into the stop-lock at the junction with the Barnsley Canal, and the Dearne & Dove was open. A local newspaper said proudly that the canal 'in respect of locks, bridges, aqueducts &c all built of the best Ashler stone, is equal if not superior to any canal in the kingdom'.[21] It was 9⅝ miles long, with two branches, to Elsecar (2⅛ miles) and Worsbrough (2⅛ miles). There were 19 locks on the main line, including the junction lock at Barnsley, rising 127 ft from the Don at Swinton, with flights of 6 at Swinton, 4 at Elsecar junction and 7 at Worsbrough junction.† There were also 6 on the Elsecar branch, rising 48 ft. The canal took craft 58 ft × 14 ft 10 in, drawing 4 ft 6 in and carrying 50 to 60 tons, slightly smaller than those of 61 ft 6 in × 15 ft 3 in that could pass the Don and later the Sheffield Canal locks. There was one cut-and-cover tunnel, 472 yd long, 18 ft wide and 18 ft high, at Adwick near Swinton, and two reservoirs at Elsecar and Worsbrough. At Elsecar basin tramroad inclined planes ran to the colliery and two local ironworks. The cost had been something under £100,000. A number of shares must have been forfeited, for though £150 had been called on each, the amount received was only £89,000. In addition, £5,000 had been borrowed from Earl Fitzwilliam and toll receipts had been ploughed back.

The line's completion coincided to a month or two with that of the Rochdale Canal, thereby opening a line from Liverpool, Manchester and Rochdale to Sheffield, Rotherham and Doncaster by way of the Barnsley and the Dearne & Dove, and so to the lower Trent. In March 1805 Tofield & Co advertised to 'Corn Factors & Others' that their market boats would leave Doncaster every Saturday evening, arrive at Barnsley on Tuesday, and return the same week.[22] In 1813 the Rochdale Canal company gave a drawback on goods from their line passing over the Barnsley and the Dearne & Dove,[23] and in 1824 were offering a bonus on all trade between Manchester and Sheffield or Rotherham, if the Calder & Hebble, Barnsley and Dearne & Dove companies would also contribute.[24]

In 1804 the company agreed to supply the Barnsley, then very short of water, from their Worsbrough reservoir between December and February so long as it was surplus to their own

† Making, with one at Aldham, the flight often called the Aldham 8 locks.

needs. But in the summer of 1805 and 1806 the Dearne & Dove itself was stopped for lack of water.

In the first decade of the nineteenth century, about half the small quantity of coal then being mined on the upper section of the Barnsley Canal went down the Dearne & Dove for the Lincolnshire market. In 1808, when the Barnsley Canal were seeking an Act to raise both money and tolls, the Dearne & Dove got a clause inserted to prevent the Barnsley from giving a preferential rate on coal carried the whole length of their own canal. However, the Barnsley found a way round that by charging 1½d a ton on coal from Barnby to the Dearne & Dove junction, and 1d below.

In 1810, out of a coal tonnage of 73,384 carried on the Dearne & Dove, 22,395 came off the Barnsley Canal, against 26,462 from Elsecar and 20,312 from Worsbrough, but thereafter the proportion from the Barnsley increased to about half. On the other hand, some coal mined above Worsbrough went up the canal to the Barnsley and so to the Calder. This traffic became more important in the late 1820s, when the excellent Silkstone coal found its main market in London. Therefore the upper section of the Dearne & Dove could be found carrying loaded coal boats both ways.

In 1829 the Don and the Dearne & Dove cut coal tolls, forcing the Aire & Calder to report that: 'the greatest part of the Coals from Worsborough and the Barnsley district are diverted into that line, instead of passing . . . into your Navigation for exportation from Goole'.[25]

Trading had begun on 3 December 1798, but little business was done until the junction was made with the Barnsley Canal at the end of 1804: for 1803 only 17,867 tons of coal were carried, and toll receipts were £931. Thereafter the canal became steadily busier. A first dividend was paid for 1810, eighteen years after the company had been promoted, and by the end of the decade the rate was averaging 6¾ per cent. In that year 2,334 (presumably loaded) boats were recorded as using the canal.

Coal carryings first exceeded 100,000 tons in 1817. Coal was the predominant traffic, but for 1805–21 inclusive the following were other average tonnages: lime and limestone, 15,610; merchandise and sundries, 9,630; pig iron, 4,862; timber, 909. The limestone was mainly going to Elsecar and Worsbrough for the furnaces there, and upwards into the valleys for agricultural purposes, the pig iron coming from Elsecar. Corn averaged 8,195 quarters, but this figure disguises a great increase, from 993 in 1805, the first year of through access from the Don, to 26,651 in 1821. The growth of Barnsley and of other places on the line is pulling in corn brought from Lincolnshire via the Trent, the Stainforth & Keadby Canal and the Don; this was competing with supplies also carried to Barnsley from east coast ports via the Aire & Calder and the Barnsley Canal. For the period 1825–30 inclusive averages had risen to 20,830 tons for lime and limestone, 5,850 tons for merchandise, and 31,330 quarters for corn.

Here are averaged figures:[26]

Years	Coal tons	Total tolls £	Dividends on £150 shares per cent £ s d	
1800–02	24,066	1,112		
1803–05	26,290	1,441		
1806–08	45,999	3,026		
1809–11	72,532	5,167	4 9 4	(4·46½)
1812–14	86,047	6,698	5 7 4	(5·36½)
1815–17	95,438	7,116	6 1 4	(6·06½)
1818–20	106,337	7,630	6 15 4	(6·76½)
1821–23	106,284*	7,485*	7 9 4	(7·46½)
1824–26	138,500†	10,430†	8 8 0§	(8·40)
1827–29	159,667	10,686		
1830–32	181,000‡	11,715‡		

* 1821 only   ‡ 1830 only
† 1825 and 1826 only   § 1825 only

In late 1820 the company were thinking of building a tramroad inclined plane from the end of the Worsbrough branch 'to Tomroyd in Thurgoland', where there was promising coal land, and also providing more reservoirs.[27] The Barnsley company (see p. 180), supported by the Aire & Calder, opposed the idea, and also surveyed for a line of their own from the Silkstone tramroad or from their summit level to the same area. A year later the Dearne & Dove again gave notice of a Bill for a tramroad, this time past Thurgoland to Oxspring bridge towards Penistone,[28] again met opposition, and went no further. In the end, the company dropped the scheme, which was partially replaced by a private line from the Worsbrough branch by Rockley to Top Pit Wood, with a branch to Pilley. Later, in October 1828, the owners of the Heck & Wentbridge Railway thought briefly of extending their line to Barnsley, Thurgoland and the Worsbrough valley.

The shareholders' meeting of July 1823 decided to promote a Bill for a new reservoir at Law Dam near Wentworth Castle, above their existing Worsbrough reservoir. But in Parliament the

C

House of Lords committee refused to allow it to proceed 'unless the Company would consent to the repeal of all the powers contained in the original Dearne & Dove Act for making Railways towards Collieries, which powers extend to 2000 yards in the Parish of Wath, and 1000 yards in other places'.[29] This opposition may well have been the work of the Aire & Calder and the Barnsley, trying to get a hold in Dearne & Dove territory. The company refused to agree and withdrew the Bill. George Leather, called in, then recommended raising Worsbrough reservoir by 4 ft 6 in to add 20 acres to its existing 42, at a cost of £3,150 and the price of the land. This the shareholders approved, the work being finished in 1826. Leather also criticised the canal's locks as having been too lightly constructed, and it was agreed to rebuild them, two or three each year.

Coal was now mined along much of the canal: at the end of 1828 the coal viewer Andrew Faulds gave the quantities sent to the tideway from the area as follows:[30]

	Tons
Down the Barnsley Canal and into the Aire & Calder	90,000
Down the Dearne & Dove Canal and through the Don	147,000
Got in the Don valley	60,000
Sent to the tideway	297,000

In 1833 Birks of the Dearne & Dove wrote to the Don company, who replied:

'while this Company are anxious to fall into the wishes of the Dearne & Dove Company as far as practicable this Company beg to suggest to the Dearne & Dove Company the importance and necessity of making considerable improvements in their Canal either by raising the Banks or deepening the Channel so as to enable Vessels to navigate on a greater depth of water, otherwise it is evident, that Coal coming down the Dearne & Dove and Dun Navigation must ultimately go down the Barnsley and the Aire & Calder on account of the greater depth of water in those Canals. Provided the dues on those two lines of Navigation are equal'.

They went on threateningly:

'unless the Dearne & Dove company do seriously enter upon some improvement of this nature the Dun company will themselves be obliged to undertake and enter upon plans for bringing beds of Coal of excellent quality in the neighbourhood of Sheffield by means of Rail Roads and the Dun River'.[31]

This last sinister remark may have been an indirect result of the unsuccessful promotion a few months earlier of a possible canal from the Sheffield to the Chesterfield Canal to open up new collieries (see p. 273), George Leather's report upon which had specifically referred to its coal competing with that coming from Silkstone and down the Dearne & Dove. The canal had proved too expensive, and probably a railroad had also been talked about as an alternative.

Three months later the company asked the Don to receive a deputation, and received the snub direct: that unless they had

'some Communication to make respecting Improvements on the lines of their Canal . . . this Company should be sorry at present to give the Dearne & Dove the trouble of Meeting the Company'.[32]

Silkstone coal seems about this time to have lost its market on the Witham Navigation in Lincolnshire,[33] for a letter written to the Don in 1833 says that the Dearne & Dove have given a drawback that reduces their toll from 3s 9d (19p) to 2s (10p) a waggon. The Don, too, agreed to reduce, as did the Stainforth & Keadby. The coal must have travelled by the Trent and Fossdyke. A similar reduction was made on coal entering the Witham Navigable Drains through Anton's Gowt lock. About 1841 a general reduction of one-third was made in coal tolls.

The building of the North Midland Railway in the late 1830s (it was opened in 1840) enabled the canal company to divert their line alongside the railway and so both by-pass Adwick tunnel and provide interchange facilities.

On 21 August 1845 the committee of the Don Navigation recommended that company's shareholders to buy the Barnsley Canal and lease, and then buy, the Dearne & Dove. Given the excitement of the time over railways, this was a sensible precautionary move to safeguard their coal supplies from the Silkstone area. A month later the Don company themselves had agreed in principle to amalgamate with a railway, the proposed South Yorkshire, that itself intended to build a line to connect the 'Silkstone, Elsecar, Worsborough and Barnsley Coal Fields'[34] with various railway systems then being planned or built.

This made it still more necessary to make sure the canals did not fall into other hands, and the Don had by mid-October agreed with both the Barnsley and the Dearne & Dove companies to buy them, and to give their shareholders an opportunity of subscribing for railway shares. The agreement to lease and then buy the

Dearne & Dove was dated 30 December, and on 1 January 1846 the Don company took possession. The Don failed, however, to hold the Barnsley. The agreement provided for a lease, followed on 2 January 1857 by purchase for £210,000 (£350 per share), a sum that was eventually paid by the South Yorkshire & River Dun Company. It was then said that for some years past the company had been paying £16 dividend per £150 share, or 10⅔ per cent.

In 1846, by agreement with Earl Fitzwilliam and other coal-owners on the line of the Dearne & Dove, coal tolls were reduced,[35] from 1¼d to ½d a ton. The result was to take traffic off the Barnsley Canal when that company had provisionally agreed to sell themselves to the Don and therefore considered themselves protected.[36]

In 1847 the new owners decided not to charge empty boats going up the canal.

In that year also the South Yorkshire, Doncaster & Goole Railway got its Act,[37] this providing for amalgamation with the River Dun Company and the Dearne & Dove, as soon as half the authorized railway capital had been subscribed and expended. It happened on 19 April 1850, when the Railway Commissioners certified that this had occurred. (*To continue the history of the Dearne & Dove Canal, turn to Chapter XVIII.*)

Stainforth & Keadby Canal

The idea of connecting the Don Navigation with the Trent (partly to obtain the trade of the Idle to and from Sheffield) took practical form as early as 1763, when Brindley was paid five guineas for helping William Martin, the Don company's manager, to estimate the cost of a Trent connexion to the Don below Thorne.[38] It came up again in August 1772, perhaps because of the canal to the Barnsley coalfields then proposed (see p. 79), when the company thought that 'a new Cutt or Canal was to be made out of the River Dun at or near Stainforth . . . to the Trent near Althorpe would be of great advantage to the Trade of the River Dun'.[39] Their engineer John Thompson was told to survey and estimate a line from Stainforth lock to Althorpe (on the Trent, 1½ miles on the Gainsborough side of Keadby). Helped by ThomasTofield, he reported in October, proposing a line to take 40 ton craft drawing 4 ft, and a branch to the Don at Hangsman Hill. With three locks, it would cost £14,614.[40] In October the shareholders agreed in principle to make the canal, but took no further action, though Doncaster corporation in December agreed to subscribe £1,000.[41]

In 1782, however, when the Trent navigation Bill was being planned,[42] the Don company tried to get the stretch of river from Gainsborough upwards to Dunham exempted from tolls except for a towpath, on the grounds that it was a good navigation and needed no improvement.[43] Then, excited by the canal mania, the Don shareholders on 14 September 1792 revived the idea of a canal from Stainforth to near Althorpe to avoid the difficult route to the Trent by way of the Dutch River and Trent Falls, recommending that they themselves should undertake it, subscribing half the capital and leaving landowners the opportunity to put up the other half. Thirty-three Don shareholders immediately offered to subscribe £100 per Don share held, and a committee was appointed to push the project forward. The following day a Parliamentary notice appeared, for a line to Althorpe or Keadby, with a branch to the Don at Hangsman Hill, and another from Crowle through the Isle of Axholme to Epworth.[44]

A meeting was called for 17 October at Thorne, and a survey ordered, either to Althorpe or Keadby. The previous day a Don shareholders' meeting thought an Althorpe–Stainforth canal, with a branch to the Don at Hangsman Hill, 'essentially necessary' and 'of the greatest advantage to the River Dun'. These shareholders had already subscribed £9,200, and it was decided to leave the remaining £15,000 of the estimated cost of £24,200 to be provided by local landowners and residents if they wished, and the Don shareholders if they did not.

On the 17th, with Richard Ellison of the Don in the chair, the project was approved, and the £10,000 offered at the meeting immediately subscribed, the remaining £5,000 being reserved for those with a claim to participate who had not yet done so. The 'present acting Committee of the River Don for managing the said Canal' were appointed to manage the Bill, with John Thompson as engineer.[45] In November Robert Mylne was asked to survey the line with Thompson.[46] He did so on 19 and 20 December, and then went on to the Dearne & Dove. He seems not to have done any more work for the Stainforth & Keadby; it was John Thompson who with William Fairbank as surveyor appeared before the Parliamentary committee.

An Act[47] of 1793 empowered the Company of Proprietors of the Stainforth & Keadby Canal Navigation to raise £24,200 in £100 shares and a further £12,100 if necessary, to build a canal from the river Don navigation cut near Stainforth to the Trent near Keadby, and also a collateral cut (never constructed) from Thorne to the river Don again at Hangsman Hill. The authorized tolls were low—that for coal being ¾d per ton per mile. The Don's engineer John Thompson took charge of construction until he died in 1795, after which Daniel Servant became engineer. Robert Whitworth inspected the canal in 1795.

Cutting contracts were advertised in August 1793,[48] and building from the Keadby end went on for two years. Then the company seem to have become involved in a Chancery lawsuit, which may have delayed construction, for little money was called in 1796, 1797 or 1798. A second Act of 1798[49] repealed the authority to raise an additional £12,100, and replaced it by one to raise £20,000 from the shareholders, and £10,000 more on mortgage. It also gave powers to vary the line near Thorne. It had also been intended to get powers to make a branch to Crowle, but this fell through.

It is curious that the canal's opening seems not to have been advertised in the local press: it probably took place early in 1802. This seems to be implied by the incidence of calls, and by a notice of meeting given in May 1802 to consider how to raise the canal's water level and the construction of warehouses and other buildings.[50] The canal was 12¾ miles long, with a lock at Thorne and one at Keadby. Following Mylne's report, this lock and the lower pound of the canal had been made 81 ft × by 22½ ft, big enough to take 200 ton craft.[51] It had two pairs of canal gates and two pairs of river gates, for use when the tide in the Trent ran higher than the canal level. Bridges were all of swivel type, to take sailing keels.

A third Act of 1809[52] stated that the shareholders had raised almost the whole of the additional £20,000; it repealed the authority to raise £10,000 by mortgage, and substituted one to raise that sum by calls from the proprietors 'for the Discharge of their Debts, and to finish and complete the said Canal', and to borrow £5,000. Calls of £157 12s 6d (£157·62½) seem to have been made on the 229 shares. If the *Doncaster Gazette* carried all the call notices, then some £36,100 was raised from those shares, and perhaps £1,000 from those forfeited, giving a total cost of about £57,000[53] to that time. The House of Lords Committee was told in 1809 that for the three previous years receipts had averaged £1,226 p.a.

When the canal opened, Keadby became a calling place for the sailing packets that ran from Gainsborough down river to Hull, and sometimes further, as to Newcastle. These were mainly carriers of fast goods: one such was advertised in 1803 as being carefully fitted with platforms for cheese.[54] Steam came in 1815 with a vengeance, and by 1818 a Hull news item of August can read: 'Owing to the spirit of rivalry, which now subsists among the owners of steam conveyances, between this port and Gainsbro', passengers are conveyed . . . (being a distance of 50 miles) at the rate of *six-pence* each.'[55] The rivalry included occasionally risky racing. One of the craft used was a 24 hp passenger-carrying tug, *Maria*, put on by Henry Smith of Gainsborough (who also ran vessels to London) to tow his sloops in one day to and from Hull.[56] Thereafter there were regular steam services, up to Gainsborough and for a time through to Nottingham from Hull, though a Nottingham steam packet service was taken off in 1825.[57] One also finds the occasional day return excursion from Hull to Gainsborough advertised. In 1815 a horse packet was put on from Thorne to Keadby to connect with the Trent steam services,[58] in rivalry with those from Thorne down the Dutch River to Hull: it was still there in 1839.[59]

The first dividend seems to have been paid about 1816. In about 1836 a canal company document[60] said that subsequently dividends were at most from £6 to £8 per share on shares of about £157⅝, or some 4 to 5½ per cent, though in 1837 they were said then to have reached £10 (6¾ per cent approx.)[61] and in 1841 to 'have for many years averaged 5 per cent'.[62] In 1822 a share sold at £98;[63] in 1834 prices were £152–£160.[64]

In 1828, two years after the completion of the Aire & Calder's Goole Canal, a Trent & Balby Canal was projected, to run from Stockwith on the Trent to near Doncaster on the Don. This unlikely scheme, needing at least 20 locks, was to by-pass the Stainforth & Keadby for traffic between the Trent above Stockwith and the upper Don and also to and from the Dearne & Dove. At the same time the Don company were discussing with the Stainforth & Keadby a new cut to by-pass the lower Don and run direct to the Goole Canal. The Stainforth & Keadby welcomed this plan, and offered either to help make it or to pay a special toll for access for their traffic. George Leather did a good deal of work on plans for it, but when in October 1828 it was clear that the Trent & Balby would not get to Parliament that session, the Don suggested to the Stainforth & Keadby that the proposed Stainforth–Goole Canal cut, which seems now to have gathered a group of its own supporters, might also be postponed. The Stainforth & Keadby sought and got provisional Aire & Calder consent to a line in November,[65] and issued a Parliamentary notice for this and the Hangsman Hill cut,[66] but went no further. In April 1834 they asked the Aire & Calder to make a cut about half a mile long with a lock above Newbridge, to connect the Don and the Goole Canal; the navigation company refused.[67] In 1836, however, the Aire & Calder themselves told George Leather to report on a similar junction,[68] and actually bought land for it.[69]

Galvanized by the Trent & Balby scheme, the company had in 1829 improved the Keadby end of their canal so 'that loaded brigs can now enter';[70] in July they proposed to build a deep water jetty in the Trent at Keadby Roads, and suggested the cost of some £450, which was to include pilots' accommodation, should be shared with the Don and Dearne & Dove companies. The Don agreed to pay £150 if the others would also. The jetty was completed early in 1833.

In the autumn of 1833, together with the Dearne & Dove and Don, the company gave a drawback on Silkstone coal passing the canal on its way to the Witham Navigation and beyond.

The lower Don and Dutch River were unsatisfactory navigations, difficult to use at neap tides, liable to shoaling, and with three awkward bridges. More and more craft from the Humber tended to reach the Don by way of Keadby, especially after the improvements. However, this trade was threatened with extinction when in February 1836 a meeting of Don shareholders agreed by a two-thirds majority to go ahead with a Bill to build a new cut from Stainforth to Swinefleet on the Ouse below Goole —a canal equivalent to the Knottingley–Goole line the Aire & Calder already had, at a cost of £66,000. Stainforth & Keadby shares slumped from £200 to £130 on the news. To do so, the Don thought they would be helped by buying two miles of the Stainforth & Keadby at the Stainforth end, to incorporate in their new cut, and opened talks with our company about it, while at the same time proceeding with their Bill.

By end-February 1836 this was in the House. The Stainforth & Keadby naturally opposed it, bitterly pointing out that their own company owed its origin to the Don's promotion, and contrasting what they alleged to be the much higher per mile tolls of the river company with their own, to the point where it seemed to the Don company simplest to buy the whole canal and work it as an alternative to their proposed cut.

In April, the Stainforth & Keadby launched a strong attack on the Don, saying that company, having initiated the Stainforth & Keadby, 'have since parted with most of their shares, and left the other shareholders, whom they had thus misled, to bear the loss', and that 'no good reason can be assigned for making this third outlet from the Dun Navigation, whilst two thirds of that Navigation remain so bad, except the cupidity of the Dun Company, who, not content with the immense tolls they are at present dividing among themselves, seek to monopolize the whole navigation; at the same time neglecting to provide the accommodation the public is entitled to, by improving their Navigation from Stainforth to Tinsley'.[71]

At the end of May, therefore, agreement was reached. The Don company would pay £45,800 plus £700 Parliamentary expenses for the Stainforth & Keadby (later raised to £48,000 in all), and withdraw their Bill. A draft agreement was made in December, and in early 1837 a Bill introduced to authorize the sale. And then was thrown out in the Lords committee, the preamble not being proved because 'a portion of the Shareholders . . . objected to the sale and had petitioned against the Bill'.[72] Not surprisingly, the Don company were very annoyed, and seem to have growled some threats, for in June they received a resolution from the Stainforth & Keadby that they heard the Don intended to make a new lock at Stainforth, above the entrance to their canal, and lower the water there. The Don replied that nothing had been decided.[73]

The episode left some irritability behind. In October 1837 the company removed the bridge over the entrance to their canal at Stainforth that formed part of the Don's towing path. The Don company told them to restore it within a month, or they would do it at their expense. Taking their time, the Stainforth & Keadby agreed to do so. A year later the Don found that the canal company had put a swing, not a fixed bridge as before, and wrote to say that they either wanted a fixed bridge, or control over the swivelling one. It was sixteen months later before the Stainforth & Keadby agreed in writing that their swivel bridge would not prejudice the Don,[74] and another four before the matter was settled.

In 1841 the Don must have been thinking of the Trent–Ouse line of waterway, for they asked the Stainforth & Keadby whether they had any intention of making their authorized branch from Thorne to Hangsman Hill.[75] Three years later, in June 1844, the Don company minuted that they were willing to lease the Stainforth & Keadby for seven years (the maximum allowed by the latter's Act), at £2,290 p.a. or £10 a share on condition that the Don could buy land necessary for the authorized cut, make it, and also make any other improvements the Stainforth & Keadby's Acts authorized. If a further lease on the same terms were given them by the Stainforth & Keadby, the latter were to repay all capital expenditure incurred on buying land and making improvements.[76]

The Stainforth & Keadby made a counter-proposition, whereupon the Don suggested amalgamation instead, 'upon the principle of a future division of Profits in the same proportion as the Profits of each have borne to the other for the last seven years'.[77] Finally, it was agreed in July that the canal company would lease itself to the Don for 1,000 years at £2,290 p.a. The Don company were left to work out how to effect the lease, on condition that if they went to Parliament they would not agree to charge more for coal on the canal than the current toll. In December, however, the Stainforth & Keadby shareholders had not yet approved the agreement, though the Don were told they could take possession on 1 January 1845.

However, once more the elusive canal company started to argue. Having agreed to leave the method of implementing the agreement to the Don, they now insisted on an Act, at a time when the Don were reluctant to go to Parliament. So matters remained in abeyance through 1845, during which eventful year the Don absorbed the Dearne & Dove Canal and agreed to amalgamate with the South Yorkshire Coal Railway. When in June 1846 the Stainforth & Keadby woke up to their dangerously isolated position and wrote to ask the Don the situation about completing the lease, the Don replied that they 'consider the Agreement therein referred to to have terminated twelve months ago by the Canal Company refusing to adopt the mode of carrying out the same elected by the Company'. They added: 'this Company are not at the present time in a situation to renew the negociation'.[78]

In 1847 the Stainforth & Keadby opposed the South Yorkshire, Doncaster & Goole's Bill, and used the opportunity to reopen talks with the Don. A meeting was held in April which included railway representatives. After much bargaining, an agreement was reached that the Don would take an absolute lease for 21 years at £10 per share* for the first three years and £7 per share thereafter.

* There were then 299 shares in issue. The offer was therefore for £2,290 p.a. for three years, and £1,603 thereafter. The cash offer was £34,350.

Should the South Yorkshire's Bill pass, they, or the Don if they desired and obtained powers, would buy outright at £150 per share at the end of ten years, and could do so sooner. Whereupon the lease would end. The South Yorkshire agreed if possible to insert an authorizing clause into their current Bill; if not, to promote a new one. The Don were to have possession on 1 July 1847.

Yet once more the Stainforth & Keadby backed out, this time refusing to seal the agreement—after the agreed vesting date—on the grounds that the South Yorkshire had not yet got an Act authorizing them to complete it. The Don replied that the 'reasons assigned . . . for the completion of the contract for sale to the South Yorkshire Railway do not in the slightest degree apply to the Lease to the Dun company',[79] and asked the canal company to complete the lease. They seem not to have replied.

A year later Isaac Hill, the Stainforth & Keadby's manager, told the Don his company intended to make the collateral cut, and asked whether they could buy some Don land. The latter replied brusquely that they would not sell any land in the neighbourhood. This led to one more agreement, this time that the Don would lease the canal for seven years at £7 per share, and then buy at £150 (£34,350)—worse terms than before, and much worse than those of 1836. The Don to have possession on 1 January 1849. But on 26 December the Stainforth & Keadby had not sealed the agreement, so the Don sent forward precautionary Parliamentary petitions to extend their Stainforth cut. This time the canal company sealed. The canal was transferred on 1 January, a Bill was introduced to authorize it, and this passed in 1849,[80] though not before the Stainforth & Keadby's committee had, early in 1849, actually offered to negotiate with the Aire & Calder.[81] That company refused the offer, regarding the canal as a natural outlet for the Don which held no threats for them. A year later the amalgamation already arranged between the Don and the South Yorkshire, Doncaster & Goole Railway became effective, and the Stainforth & Keadby became part of the South Yorkshire Railway & River Dun Company. (*To continue the history of the Stainforth & Keadby Canal turn to Chapter XVIII.*)

CHAPTER XIII

Hull and Humber

+++◆+++

THE Hull River, relieved of surplus water by the building of catchwater drains and cleaned of obstructions during the 1790s,[1] continued to carry keels and other craft upwards from the Humber to Beverley Beck and the Driffield Navigation, to which the Leven Canal was added, probably in 1804. At this time the stretch nearest the Humber was becoming very congested, 'being blocked up by the Ships to and from Foreign Voyages, Coastwise, River Craft, and Rafts of Timber', so much so that in 1794 the manufacturers of Beverley and elsewhere petitioned for dock enlargement with a separate entrance.[2] Congestion was to persist for a long time, the result of Hull's rapid growth, itself related to the expanding trade of the West Riding.

Further inland, the Market Weighton Canal continued its ambivalent way, half navigation, half drainage channel, but other navigation schemes in the area, at Cottingham, Hedon Haven and Keyingham, came to nothing.

Beverley Beck

Grovehill, normally a falling lock at the Beck's junction with the Hull River, was put in towards the end of 1802. William Chapman was engineer to the Beverley & Barmston Drainage, whose new drain was to be passed in a tunnel beneath the Beck. He therefore advised the Corporation that in order to maintain sufficient depth in the Beck, they should build the lock. He designed it, the cost being met by a corporation loan for £1,000 at 5 per cent.

The Beck lessees were usually traders. John Webster, for instance, lessee for many years from 1825, was a coal merchant. In 1837 the corporation decided to appoint an official at £48 p.a. to collect the Beck dues themselves: William Tindall began work on

Beverley BECK.

PERSONS DESIROUS

Of Contracting

FOR THE

Cleansing & Bottom Scouring

OF

Beverley Beck

are requested to send in their **PROPOSALS**, in writing, sealed up, to Mr. JOHN WILLIS, at the GUILD-HALL, in BEVERLEY, on or before SATURDAY, the 27th day of June instant, at Ten o'Clock in the Forenoon.

The Beck must be scoured to the depth of Seven Feet below the present level of the water. The Contractor will have to provide all Materials—to make and maintain all necessary Dams and Drains during the continuance of the Work ; and to remove or make good the same when finished.

Beverley, 19th June, 1835.

25. Contractors are sought to dredge Beverley Beck

1 June. A committee was also appointed to oversee Beck affairs, and this in 1839 decided that Tindall's salary was extravagant, and advertised the post as to be paid 5 per cent of takings, an alteration that became effective from 1841. The total takings for the year ending 31 May 1838 were £594, and for 1839 were £620. The tonnage carried in 1838 was 31,185.

Average figures of the rental received for the Beck are:

Years	£	Years	£
1793–97	190	1818–22	362·50
1798–1802	190	1823–27	405
1803–07	314	1828–32	435
1808–12	372	1833–35*	435
1813–17	330		

* Three years.

(*To continue the history of Beverley Beck turn to p. 429.*)

Driffield Navigation

The 1790s saw a brisk increase of trade. More dredging was done, two more warehouses were built at Driffield, the coal wharf being used to make room for them, a new factory started by Sheepshanks, Porter & Co between Skerne and Driffield† was given similar terms to Bainton, Boyes, and two or three lighters were bought, which the toll-collector, who acted as manager, was to 'lett and use . . . to the best advantage for this Navigation'.[3]

Then in 1796 a proposal for improving the navigation was put to the commissioners by George Knowsley, partner of J. R. Pease, one of the two principal mortgagees, in a Hull banking firm which in the same year had become treasurers to the navigation. William Chapman, called in, put up plans and estimates. But these were considered too expensive, and for the time laid aside, for the commissioners were too busy asking Hull's M.P., William Wilberforce, to help them get protective clauses into the Beverley & Barmston Drainage Bill, before Parliament in 1798. This was the first of many conflicts with drainage authorities, these naturally wanting to lower water levels that the navigation bodies wanted to maintain or increase. However, agreement was reached with William Jessop, who was engineer to the drainage authorities for the purpose of their Act.

Another problem of the time was Hull bridge below the naviga-

† These, the Bell mills, wove carpets and textiles.

tion limits, with its arch so low that when the water level rose, 'frequently every year Vessels are prevented from passing through the same'.[4] Liability for maintenance was with Beverley corporation, who got 4d toll for each passing vessel. The commissioners met in November 1799 to consider means 'for avoiding the very great losses, injuries and inconveniences sustained by this Navigation, from the stoppage of the Vessels (using the said Navigation) at Hull Bridge'.[5] They asked for the bridge to be raised, offering £100 towards the cost, but got no encouragement, the corporation saying they had no intention of altering it in any way.

In July 1800 an improvement committee was appointed. This went back to Chapman's report, and recommended parts of it to the commissioners: that Hull bridge be raised, a towpath made from Beverley Beck to Fisholme, a lock built on the Hull River, which should be straightened and the canal deepened, and river access to Corps Landing and Frodingham bridge improved, these at Chapman's estimated cost of £8,491 exclusive of the Act. Meanwhile the financial position had improved, 4 per cent interest having been paid from 1791 to 1794, 4½ per cent for 1795 and 1796, and from 1797 the full 5 per cent. At this time £15,175 had been borrowed, on which some £8,000 of interest arrears were owing: of this sum, £6,434 had been lent by Richard Langley, and £3,812 by J. R. Pease.

So the commissioners agreed, and after successful negotiations with Beverley corporation, which seem, however, to have included the condition that, in the interests of Beverley Beck, no horse towing path should be built between the Beck and the bridge,[6] in July 1801, with William Wilberforce's help, an Act was passed.[7] This set up a separate body to administer what was to be called the new navigation, the original line becoming the old navigation. The two bodies were separate administratively rather than physically. With separate tolls, accounts, bank balances (till 1882), and minute books, they shared officers, offices and meeting rooms.

Power was given to take over and rebuild Hull bridge, and charge 2s 6d (12½p) per vessel passing it; make a towing path from the bridge to Fisholme and on to Frodingham bridge, and also to Corps Landing; and make a cut and lock on the main river, and a cut to Corps Landing. Additional tolls, and also separate towpath tolls, were granted for the use of the new works. Arbitration was arranged to settle tolls for the use of the branch to Frodingham bridge, to be paid by those using Foston corn and flour mills, whence a private cut exclusive to the mill occupiers and able to take 'small lighters'[8] led down Foston Beck to Frodingham Beck at the bridge. Private landowners were empowered to make navigation cuts, and, finally, a maximum height was established for the water level above the new lock in the interests of drainage.

Chapman was appointed engineer, Thomas Atkinson of Driffield contractor for the river works, the mortgagees of the old navigation put up more money, and by 1805 the work was done, except that to Corps Landing. Hull bridge had been rebuilt for £500, half the cost being paid by Richard Bethell, who was concerned that bigger craft could at all times reach the Leven Canal, on condition that the bridge toll should be reduced to 1s (5p). The work was done by April 1804, and the bridge tolls were then let annually. Higher up, Struncheonhill lock* had been built downstream from Fisholme, and between the two a ¾ mile cut made to by-pass a big river loop. Finally, the navigation to Corps Landing, though without the authorized cut, was completed in 1811, when tolls began to be taken on it. It seems, however, that towing paths were not made on the Frodingham bridge or Corps Landing branches, though the former may eventually have been built about 1838. The new works had cost £6,143.

The old navigation was now doing well and the full 5 per cent interest could be paid (in 1801 also the 3½ per cent owing for 1774). The new navigation quickly paid its way, and by 1808 was starting to pay off debt. Then in 1817 the old and new concerns combined after some argument to obtain an Act[9] to settle their financial affairs. At that time the old navigation still owed £15,175 and £8,195·50 arrears of interest, but the new concern had paid off £4,300 of its debt, and only owed £1,843. The Act provided that after the new navigation's debt had been extinguished, tolls should be continued to pay 50 per cent more on the original debt of £6,143 i.e. £3,071·50, and after that were (except for the Hull bridge toll) to be reduced to cover expenses only. When this happened, automatic benefit to the old navigation would follow.

By 1820 the new navigation's original debt had been repaid, and by 1823 the additional 50 per cent, tolls then being cut to very low figures, and eliminated altogether for merchandise and for traffic

---

* There is no clear evidence whether Struncheonhill was built as a staircase pair, or whether the second lock was added later. I think it probable that the lower lock was added within two or three years of the first one. They are referred to in the plural in a minute book entry of 8 March 1810.

PLAN

FOR ESTABLISHING

A SINKING FUND;

By which in the course of 34 Years the Capital advanced
for making the DRIFFIELD OLD NAVIGATION
with the present existing Arrears of Interest
may be paid off and the Navigation
become TOLL FREE.

It is sufficiently known to the Commissioners under
the Driffield Navigation Acts, that the Driffield New Navigation has been Toll free for some Years past, by which the
Proprietors of the Lands situated on that Navigation have
obtained very considerable advantages, as the produce of their
possessions is removed to and fro without any payment except the Freight and a mere trifle towards keeping the Works
of the said Navigation in repair ; while those who have to
frequent the Old Navigation cannot do so without paying
heavy Tolls. It is also equally well known that the Subscribers to the Old Navigation have for a number of Years
not received full Interest for the Sums they advanced, from
which cause the present Arrears of Interest have accrued,
and it appears therefore absolutely necessary the Commissioners should take such measures as would in time place
the Landholders on the Old Navigation in the same favor-
able situation as those on the New Navigation ; and create
also some Security to the Subscribers by which they will be
in future sure to receive the full Interest for the Capital
they have advanced and the Arrears already due to them.

26. The Driffield Navigation Commissioners consider a plan for a sinking fund

D

from Foston mills on the Frodingham bridge branch. Coal tolls came down also on the old navigation in 1819, when that concern started to pay off its interest arrears, a few per cent in most years. In 1834 a plan for combining payments of interest arrears with capital debt repayments chosen by lot was adopted (based on J. B. La Manche's *Plan for Establishing a Sinking Fund*, printed in 1826). By 1844 all interest arrears had been paid off, but sinking fund payments continued almost to the end.

In 1817 a steam packet was advertised as running three times a week between Driffield and Hull.[10] She seems to have been too slow, and failed, for in 1825 another advertisement[11] said that the *Express* steam packet would recommence running on 21 March, her engine having been altered and improved to produce more speed. She was to leave Driffield at 7 a.m., fares being 3s (15p) best cabin and 2s (10p) fore-cabin to Hull. Packages would be carried for 9d cwt, grass seed for 6d, light goods for 3d. She was not advertised again the following year. In 1823 Baines's *Yorkshire* notes three craft, *Progress*, *Hope* and *Speedy*, which belonged to the Randall family, as 'regular traders to Hull every other day for goods'.

In 1824 the commissioners noted that public wharves had not yet been built at Frodingham bridge or Corps Landing, 'whereby the Public is debarred from free enjoyment of those advantages which were contemplated by the Acts'.[12] After counsel's opinion had confirmed their powers to provide these, that at Corps Landing was opened in 1825, that at Frodingham bridge in 1826. On the old navigation another warehouse went up at Driffield in 1826, where additional trade was in 1828 promised from a new whiting manufactory.

Trade steadily increased on the Hull River and the new navigation, especially after the toll reductions. One indication of this is the average yearly rental figure for which Hull bridge's 1s (5p) toll was let, though we must remember that this included traffic to the Leven Canal.

Years	Rental £	Years	Rental £
1810–12	77	1828–30	92·67
1813–15	63	1831–33	94
1816–18	70·33	1834–36	104·67
1819–21	70	1837–39	100
1822–24	65	1840–42	100
1825–27	93·33	1843–45	100

Here are averaged traffic figures for the new navigation:

Years	Coal chaldrons	Wheat quarters	Oats quarters	Barley quarters	Flour sacks
1821	7,732	7,858	15,700	small	1,915
1822–24	8,599	17,170	22,414	small	2,688
1825–27	9,357	24,679*	14,723	10,467	3,196*
1828–30	7,418	14,231†	4,815	13,156	3,629†
1831–33	7,394	18,173‡	7,745	19,396	4,555‡

* Plus an average of 535 quarters of wheat to and 4,513 sacks of flour from Foston mills in 1826 and 1827.

† Plus an average of 735 quarters of wheat to and 6,392 sacks of flour from Foston mills in 1828–30.

‡ Plus an average of 1,564 quarters of wheat to and 8,194 sacks of flour from Foston mills in 1831–33.

The old navigation shows a drop in receipts in the later 1820s, followed by a levelling out. This seems to have been due to a fall in coal carryings and in the high-rated wheat traffic, Driffield being at that time a sizeable corn market.§ The following averaged figures are interesting as showing the extent to which barley growing replaced oats and to some extent wheat in the navigation's area at the time:

Years	Coal chaldrons	Wheat quarters	Oats quarters	Barley quarters	Flour sacks	Toll receipts* £
1821	5,027	7,553	13,634	small	301	1,125
1822–24	5,445	14,634	17,070	small	1,150	1,494
1825–27	5,888	20,621	11,715	8,610	983	1,616
1828–30	4,599	12,054	3,873	12,546	1,495	1,218
1831–33	4,181	13,191	5,884	17,933	2,164	1,355

* Year ending 31 March.

The uneventful life of the navigation went on, interrupted only by such events as the Beverley & Barmston Drainage Commissioners complaining that the river water was kept too high, 'whereby injury was occasioned the Drainage of the adjoining Lands',[13] the Hull Dock Company refusing to insert into their 1840 Bill protective clauses to:

'insure to the Driffield Navigation a free and unobstructed passage for Vessels through the Mouth of the Hull River called the Harbour or Old Haven and also to withdraw the Toll of Three pence per Ton now charged on Vessels passing through the said Harbour although not using the Hull Docks',[14]

and the inhabitants of Driffield asking that the fishing in the canal

§ Wheat traffic was in both directions. Most was downwards from Driffield, but some imported wheat came up to be mixed with home-grown at the mills, and e.g. in 1836 wheat from Beverley to Wansford mills is recorded.

might be regulated and preserved. And so they came to the railway age. (*To continue the history of the Driffield Navigation, turn to* p. 430.)

Leven Canal

The Holderness drainage parallel to, and eastward of, the river Hull towards Leven had been made by Smeaton and Grundy in the 1760s. In 1786 the commissioners decided to take a new look at it, and asked William Jessop 'to take a View of the Works of the Drainage, and of the River Hull, and to report what Measures (in his Opinion) ought to be pursued to give the best Effect to the Undertaking; what will be the probable Expence of those Measures, Whether a Navigation be Compatible with the Drainage, and if it be, what additional Expence would be required to Effect a Navigation (as well as a Drainage) from the Outfall to Monk bridge'.[15] Monk bridge is a mile south of Leven. Jessop, reporting in July 1786, said that a navigation 'will by no means be incompatible with Drainage, but rather an advantage to it, if properly executed'. With two locks and a number of passing places, the drains could be made navigable for craft drawing 4 ft 6 in to Monk bridge at an extra cost of £5,136. But the trustees do not seem to have taken the idea further.

In September 1791 a group of promoters proposed to seek an Act for a canal from the Hull River near the Holderness drain outfall to Monk bridge or Leven, with a capital of £7,000, half of which was reported subscribed in October.[16] As Jessop had probably been consulted on the idea—he was later to be engineer of the canal as built—and was also employed by the drainage trustees, the latter in February 1792 called in John Hudson of Louth 'to take a view of the line of the proposed navigation from the Holderness sluice near the river Hull to the town of Leven, and to report . . . whether [it] will in any degree be injurious to the drainage'.[17]

A petition reached Parliament in March,[18] but the Bill went no further. In August the promoters talked of a Bill for a line now to run further eastwards, by Marfleet,[19] but by the time Hudson reported in October the scheme, like others of the mania period, had faded away.

When the idea of a canal to Leven was revived in 1801, there were two schemes. One, with what support I do not know, was for a line from the river Hull below Hull bridge to Skirlaugh bridge south-east of Leven, with a branch to Monk bridge below the town.[20] The other was Mrs Bethell's,[21] for a privately-made cut from the Hull River just below the beginning of the Driffield Navigation at Aike Beck mouth. The Bethells,[22] considerable landowners, were active locally in agricultural improvements and land drainage, and in support of turnpike roads. Richard Bethell and his mother Mrs Charlotta Bethell were concerned in the Beverley & Barmston Drainage Act of 1798, and it is likely that their interest in this, and also in the Driffield Navigation's plans for improvement, especially for rebuilding Hull bridge lower down the river, encouraged them to build the Leven Canal.

Mrs Bethell employed William Jessop about the end of 1799 to do her survey, probably because he had previously worked for the Holderness Drainage who would need satisfying that their drains would not be affected. He reported in March 1800. The drainage trustees then asked Mrs Bethell in the autumn to pay for the opinion of a second engineer; she agreed 'in order that the Trustees may see that her Object is to do a general good of promoting a measure which will tend to the Improvement of the Agriculture of the Country, without injury to the drainage'.[23] James Creassy was then employed; he agreed with Jessop that no damage would be done, and the drainage trustees then approved Mrs Bethell's plans.

Mrs Bethell obtained the Act[24] of 1801, passed six weeks before that to improve the Driffield Navigation. The purposes were stated as the exchange of trade between Leven and Hull, and the import of lime and manure for use on the land. She was granted tolls of 9d a ton on coal, 6d (2½p) on lime and limestone, and 1s (5p) on everything else, including corn and merchandise.

Jessop had estimated the canal at £4,041.[25] The Act required him and James Creassy to agree before work began on the canal's width, depth and size of lock 'to the Intent that the said Canal . . . may be constructed so as not to be injurious to the Drainage'. If they disagreed, Rennie was to arbitrate. In any case, Mrs Bethell indemnified the drainage body against damage from the canal.

The line was then built and opened, it is said in 1802.*[26] It was 3¼ miles long, nearly in a straight line from the river. At the junction a single lock to take keels 64 ft × 14 ft 10 in was built. Originally it seems to have had three sets of gates, two pointing to the Hull and one inland, so that it could only be passed on the level or at high tide. Later the masonry lock was extended by

*More likely in 1804.

brickwork to provide an upper set of inland pointing gates. A basin was built at its termination beside the road at Leven.

In June 1805 Mrs Bethell got a second Act[27] which, because 'much more Expence hath been incurred in completing the . . . Canal and Works than the same was originally estimated at', authorized her also to charge an additional 7s (35p) a boat for wharfage on many goods carried, and also mooring fees after 48 hours.

Before this, however, Richard Bethell had paid half the cost of rebuilding Hull bridge, on condition that the Driffield Navigation's toll of 2s 6d (12½p) a boat was reduced to 1s (5p), to which the commissioners agreed (see p. 302). Traffic to the Leven Canal was therefore relieved of this extra charge. No horse towpath was made down river beyond the bridge; this was always a disadvantage to the traffic of the three branching canals, including the Leven.

Baines[28] tells us that in 1823 Robert Thompson carried to Hull by water every Tuesday: he competed with three land carriers also working every Tuesday. In 1840 Hugh William Jackson is described as wharfinger and carrier from the canal.[29]

In 1847 the York & North Midland Railway obtained power to buy the Leven Canal, but did not exercise it, presumably because their York–Beverley line did not then get further than Market Weighton. In October 1849 it was said the purchase 'will most probably not be required'.[30] (*To continue the history of the Leven Canal, turn to p. 433.*)

Aike Beck (Lockington Navigation)

About 1798–1800 the Hotham family made the Aike Beck[31] navigable from the river Hull at the point where the Driffield Navigation began, by the stream and then by a short artificial cut to a landing place and coal wharf (at 027469) immediately southeast of Lockington station. There were two pound locks taking craft of 40 ft × 8 ft 10 in maximum.[32] William Chapman, reporting to the drainage commissioners in 1809,[33] complained that the locks had raised water levels and caused flooding.

Judging by the first edition of the 6 in OS plan, surveyed in 1851–2, the navigation was out of use by then, though Sheahan & Whellan's *History* of 1856[34] refers to it as if it were still used.

Cottingham & Hull Canal project

In December 1802 a group of landowners in and around Cottingham, then a large village of 2,000 people about four miles north-west of Hull, called a meeting on the 22nd to consider making a canal to that port.[35] The leading spirit seems to have been George Knowsley of Cottingham Grange, a Hull banker who had recently brought about improvements in the Driffield Navigation (see p. 300). The meeting asked him to have the scheme estimated, and after consulting Thomas Dyson who worked as engineer for the Driffield and also the Keyingham Drainage, he produced a figure of £14,322 including land, or £20,000 to cover contingencies. The canal was to run to Paragon Street, Hull, and on to the Humber, with a river lock and one other, and beside it a 12 ft wide gravelled footpath for the use of which a toll or annual subscription would be charged.

Knowsley saw it as bringing up lime direct from Knottingley on the Aire & Calder for land improvement: 'the heavy expence of land carriage confines the application of this valuable article within narrow limits', and also coal, taking down agricultural produce from the district. There was to be a twice-daily passage boat taking passengers and milk.

His estimate of income was £1,231. The meeting under Thomas Williamson's chairmanship accepted the proposal unanimously, but decided that because raising money and public affairs generally had recently become so difficult with the resumption of the war, the scheme should be postponed to a better time or until it ended.[36] They however asked Knowsley to make the plan public, which he did in an enthusiastic pamphlet:

'To persons in business at Hull there can be no doubt, that when the Canal shall be compleated, Cottingham will become the most eligible country residence in its vicinity, no other village can present equal advantages; whether we consider the cheap conveyance of coals . . . or the safe and easy passage to and from Hull, an accommodation of which the inhabitants may avail themselves, at a very trifling expence, at different periods of the day . . .'[37]

He suggested a company should be formed, and told his readers that he would go ahead when £10,000 had been subscribed. But it never was, probably partly at any rate because the financial prospects offered were poor, and the plan died.

Hedon Haven

In the late eleventh century Hedon was founded as a harbour for Holderness, using the natural creek. When trade expanded, two artificial cuts totalling about 1,480 yd were dug to extend the quays. As Hull grew, Hedon decayed, and these cuts were disused by Henry VIII's reign, though they can still be traced.[38] The natural haven remained in decreasing use, until an Act[39] to restore and improve the navigation of Hedon Haven from the Humber east of Hull to the little town of Hedon was passed in 1774, commissioners being empowered to carry it out and take tolls. It was then an estuary improvement scheme. It was reported complete towards the end of 1775.[40]

In 1781, however, it must have been found unsatisfactory, for an advertisement offering the letting of the tolls said preference would be given to those willing to build a lock.[41] Evidently nothing happened, for in 1803 Hedon corporation and others petitioned Parliament saying the original Act's powers were defective and tolls insufficient, and seeking powers 'for making a new Cut or Canal, with a new Lock, Pen or Wier, and proper Towing-paths' from the Haven near the Ferry House to it again 'above Newfield Clough'.[42] This was not, however, followed by a Bill, dan the Haven remained a tidal one. It was used to ship corn until 1855, and occasional boats visited it even in this century.

Keyingham Navigable Drains project

In the 1790s the landowners south-east of Hull were planning to improve the old drainage line that ran down past Keyingham to the Humber at Stone Creek. Joseph Hodskinson had done a preliminary report in October 1795, and said that if the drains were to be rebuilt, the outfall, 'Clough may be so constructed as to admit such vessels as usually navigate to the collieries through the upland rivers', and that the main drain might easily be made navigable for about three miles to Keyingham bridge to carry coal and lime inland and bring corn down. A subsequent meeting on 3 October 1796 commissioned William Chapman to make a survey, and he reported on 30 June 1797.[43]

One question he had been asked was, 'Can a navigation be united with this drainage: how far up the country, and at what additional expence?' Answering it, he proposed that small 8 ton craft, double-ended, 28 ft long × 7 ft wide, drawing 2 ft 6 in and working in pairs, should be able to move further inland by one fork from the main drain to Roos bridge south of the village, and by the other to near Owstwick, each terminus being about nine miles from the Humber. A transhipment quay and basin should be built beside the Humber. The drain boats, he thought, should each be fitted to carry 24 containers on the lines of the Duke of Bridgewater's mine boats.[44] These could be loaded from the Humber craft with coal or lime, swung on board by a horse crane, and eventually be used to discharge their contents into carts through trap-bottoms. His estimate for extra navigation work was only £1,500, and of probable tonnage 8,000 p.a.

These navigation proposals were accepted by a meeting of 18 September 1797, but the scheme then remained in abeyance until 20 August 1800, when another meeting rescinded them, presumably to placate opposition,[45] and a Parliamentary petition of March 1801 does not mention them.[46] The landowners then seem to have come to terms with those who were against this aspect of the scheme,[47] for the eventual Act of 1802 authorized the drainage commissioners generally to carry out Chapman's recommendations, by using the drains from Stone Creek by Keyingham to Roos bridge and Owstwick for navigation 'for the Purpose of conveying Corn, Lime, Coals, and other Goods, in Boats and Barges; and by and out of any Money which shall come into their Hands by virtue of this Act, to cause to be made and constructed so many Boats, Barges, and Vessels, and of such Form and Dimensions, as shall be suitable and proper for the Carriage and Conveyance of such Goods upon the said Drains'. They could also build a wharf and basin at Stone Creek with a crane, and take such sums 'for the Carriage and Conveyance of such Goods', as they should decide. The deposited plan of 1801,[48] surveyed by Robert Stickney, shows a new canal being cut for about 1½ miles from the Humber to join the existing drain, which, apart from three shortening cuts, would then be utilized to the junction. The existing Roos Bridge drain would then be used, but that to Owstwick would be extended by a short cut to the Roos–Burton Pidsea road.

However, the following section of the Act laid it down that the navigation was not to be used until a majority of four-fifths in value of the proprietors of the low lands had agreed, and this they presumably did not do. There is no evidence that the drains were ever so used.

Market Weighton Canal

From the early 1790s to 1850 the Market Weighton Canal went its quiet way, carrying coal and some merchandise upwards, corn, timber and other produce down. The coal came mainly from the Aire & Calder, that company claiming in 1792 that they carried 'very considerable Quantities towards the Supply of . . . Market Weighton'.[49] At Newport, where the Hull–Howden road crossed the canal, a large brick, tile and earthenware industry grew up in and after the turn of the century. Baines[50] tells us that in 1823 there was a fortnightly service to Hull for goods and passengers by Thomas Dudding's packet. Financially, its position slowly improved, as the following averaged dividend figures show:

Y.e. 31 March	Dividend per cent	Y.e. 31 March	Dividend per cent
1795–99	5·15	1825–29	4·9
1800–04	2	1830–34	4·5
1805–09	4·1	1835–39	6·2
1810–14	2	1840–44	6·8
1815–19	3	1845–49	7·2
1820–24	6·8		

For the rest, its problems were those of reconciling navigation and drainage interests, of dredging—for a drainage channel was especially liable to silting yet had to be kept dredged to maintain the drainage fall—and of lock repairs. Beyond those, Ann Whitworth, the first lock-keeper's widow, opened a shop at Weighton lock in 1800, and there was a pub there by 1819; the trustees considered such minor matters as 'That the Pig Styes on the Towing Path are to be immediately removed'[51] or less minor, as 'no Vessel (except Laden with Corn) shall be allowed to go out of the Canal on Sundays until after six o'Clock in the Evening' and 'no Vessel coming in be allowed to be hailed until after six o'Clock'[52] on penalty of £1 fine, arranging to lay a buoy outside Weighton lock, or in 1835 making a turning point for sloops above Newport bridge, and a public wharf there in 1842. William Chapman, writing in 1797,[53] thought the principle of trying to combine drainage and navigation inherently uneconomic: 'wherever they are . . . attempted to be combined, as . . . below Market Weighton, it is attended with more charge than making them separate, because the increase of width and depth of a deep drain, to render it fit for the navigation of large boats, is more expensive than the forming of a parallel canal'.

In 1834 a special general meeting considered extending the canal to Market Weighton itself, but no action followed. It may have been now that Sir Edward Vavasour's or the Holme Canal was built privately under the powers of the Market Weighton Act from the Market Weighton a little below River Head for ¾ mile to the Holme-Market Weighton Road.

The trustees assented to the Hull & Selby Railway's crossing of their line at Newport subject to protection, and indeed found it did them more good than harm. On 17 May 1845 the York & North Midland Railway shareholders approved a line from the York–Scarborough line past Pocklington and Market Weighton to Beverley, and got their Act in 1846. This was likely seriously to affect the canal's trade, and must at once have led to talks that went unminuted, but which produced railway agreement to buy the shareholders out, while preserving the rights of the trustees. The result was the York & Midland's 1847 Act,[54] which authorized 'the purchase . . . of the Interest of the Shareholders in the Market Weighton Canal, and the purchase of the Canal connected therewith, called Sir Edward Vavasour's Canal', as well as the Pocklington and Leven Canals. The railway was opened from York to Market Weighton in 1847, but not on to Beverley until 1865. A shareholders' meeting of 23 November 1847 unanimously approved the sale, and the purchase of the shareholders' interest took place on 1 January 1850, but the trustees continued to run the canal along with the drainage. The company also agreed to buy Sir Edward Vavasour's Canal for £847,[55] but it appears the powers were not exercised. (To continue the history of the Market Weighton Canal, turn to p. 433.)

CHAPTER XIV

The Ouse to York

THE half-century to 1845 saw great changes upon the Ouse. In 1804 the Foss Navigation was completed as far as Sheriff Hutton bridge, after which it maintained a precarious existence until the opening of the York to Scarborough railway in 1845. Soon afterwards the Stainforth & Keadby Canal was opened, so making it unnecessary for craft moving between the Trent and the Don to work round by Trent Falls and the Dutch River. Lastly, the first steamer reached York. It was to have been the *Caledonia* in 1815 but she could not get through Naburn lock; then the *Waterloo* began a service between Hull and York on 25 April 1816,[1] taking 8 to 9 hours, followed in 1820 by the *Countess of Scarboro'*, on a twice-weekly York to Gainsborough run.[2] Steam was, however, exceptional in 1834, when Thomas Rhodes wrote his report: he attributed this to the size and shallowness of Naburn lock and the river below it.[3]

River trade improved, and the trustees felt confident enough to build in 1823 their banqueting house near Naburn lock, at the time of the inquiries that led to the Municipal Corporations Act somewhat of a scandal; to us, perhaps, an interesting example of business done in style. And then, in 1826, the Aire & Calder's Knottingley & Goole Canal was opened. Quickly the pattern of river trade changed. Craft from the Aire & Calder for the Derwent or York still used the Selby Canal, but all that for down river moved to Goole, followed by most of the steamer services. Selby declined, the tendency only briefly arrested during the short time between the opening of the Leeds & Selby Railway in 1834, and that on to Hull in 1840.

Average toll figures show the Ouse getting steadily busier as the new century advanced, especially after steam packets began to encourage the Hull trade, only to fall away after the opening of the

Goole Canal and York's inability to match it as a port for seagoing ships:

Years	Tolls £	Years	Tolls £
1794–96	470	1815–17	1,389
1797–99*	569	1818–20	1,434
1800–02	656	1821–23	1,401
1803–05	722	1824–26	1,612
1806–08	777	1827–29	1,573
1809–11	955	1830–32	1,362
1812–14	1,258		

* 1797 and 1799 only.

The rise of Goole of course affected York also; so much so that a meeting of traders on 19 September 1833 demanded river improvements that would 'admit Steam Vessels of sufficient magnitude to navigate direct between this City and London'.[4] A steam dredger was bought, and Thomas Rhodes was called in on Telford's advice, reporting in January 1834.[5] He set out the causes of indifferent navigation: lack of dredging and of bank protection, too small a lock at Naburn. Solutions, to include making York accessible for 200–250 ton steam and other vessels, would cost £33,354, of which £18,261 would be for a new lock, 140 ft × 36 ft, with 7 ft over the sill. The trustees, uneasily conscious of an annual income averaging about £1,320 p.a., decided to spend £10,000, which they borrowed from the Exchequer Bill Loan Commissioners. A new lock postponed, Rhodes spent the money mainly in dredging,† bank protection and towpath improvement, notably in removing the great 2 mile long shoal at Acaster Selby. By 1836 60 ton craft were free to reach York at all times, though the trustees had in fact spent £17,000 to achieve it.

By now, railway competition from the York & North Midland and Great North of England lines was threatened. The trustees therefore decided to raise tolls to pay off their debt quickly, and then lower them as soon as the railway threat became real, bringing with it rail-borne coal that was likely quickly to cut down the tonnages by river.

In May 1839 the York & North Midland was opened, and at once the toll yield fell: it fell still more when a rate cut was made. In 1841 the opening of the Great North of England added rail-borne coal from the north-east to that already coming from the south, so that for the year ending 1 June 1845 only 203 coal

† A steam dredger was built at Naburn lock in 1834.

vessels were unloaded at York, against 751 in 1838.[6] Income from tolls, £1,292 in 1832, was £4,546 in 1836 and £5,032 in 1838, years when takings must have been much inflated by the carriage of railway construction material as well as by higher rates of toll, but was down to £2,038 in 1845, at which level the trustees were only just balancing income against expenditure. Sadly, too, their dredger, hired to the contractors building locks for the new Severn Commission,[7] sank at sea. She was not replaced, the compensation money going to debt reduction. Some railway coal from the north-east was indeed transhipped at York to water for London and east coast ports, but this could only be a temporary alleviation. The trustees' position was difficult. Less so that of York business, who were secure against a railway monopoly so long as the city could maintain the waterway. (*To continue the history of the Ouse Navigation, turn to p. 438.*)

Howden Canal project

In 1796 a group of Howden inhabitants petitioned for leave to introduce a Bill for a canal to Howden Dyke, saying that 'the Town of Howden is almost a Mile distant from the Navigable River Ouze, and the Road . . . is very miry and bad'.[8] Nothing happened, though in 1825, after a local meeting, a committee was appointed to push the idea of a canal to Howden.[9]

Derwent Navigation

For a few years from 1792 schemes were promoted that might have linked the Derwent with the sea, by a canal to Scarborough or possibly to Whitby. A correspondent of Earl Fitzwilliam's, writing in 1791, raised a Scarborough extension with him, and later Henry Eastburn reported in 1794 that such a link would not be difficult to build.*

Probably earlier, certainly in 1799, small craft worked up to Yedingham: for that year an account exists 'of Coals Lime Etc sent from Malton and Norton up the Line of the Derwent to Yeddingham Bridge and that Neighbourhood by Land Carriage and small Boats up the River'.[10] In 1800, too, William Ellis of Norton (Malton) delivered lime in his vessels not only up the Derwent, but some distance, at any rate, up the Rye and the Costa.[11]

* For canal schemes to Scarborough and Whitby, see pp 325–8.

On 20 October 1799 Isaac Leatham of Barton near Malton issued a broadsheet once again proposing a drainage scheme for the Derwent and its tributary the Hertford, to include a navigation extension above Malton. As regards navigation, he hoped Earl Fitzwilliam could be encouraged to extend it

'from the Water-lane in Malton, to the End of Brompton Beck,† and I think to opposite Wykeham‡ . . . and erecting five Locks (viz) one between the Bridge and Waterlane-End, one to pass the New-Malton, and another Old-Malton Dam, and two small ones in the remaining part of the Space. This would bring the Navigation not only pretty near the Limestone, but also nearly come in contact with Mr Cockshut's Line of Canal,§ about eight Miles from Scarbrough; so that if Earl Fitzwilliam, and those interested in the Scarbro' End, should agree to continue it to that Town, near two-thirds of the Space between that and Malton would be made, and at a small Expence . . . and not in the least injurious to Earl Fitzwilliam's present Navigation, but on the contrary; for the Dues upon that would be increased, by a much larger Quantity of Coal being consumed, which must be brought thereon, and a considerable Return of Lime, and increase in that of Grain'.[12]

His drainage proposals were estimated at £21,000, with 14 miles of navigation for another £6,500. He added rough plans for also making the Rye navigable to its junction with the Costa Beck, and then along two branches, one up the Costa Beck towards Pickering, the other by the Holbeck to near Hovingham or along the Rye towards Helmsley.

A meeting followed in December which supported the drainage ideas and asked William Chapman, helped by Milbourn, to report. Clearly frightened of Earl Fitzwilliam, it shied away, however from 'any ideas of interfering with the rights of those who have a power of making the River navigable or with the property of those who possess mills upon it'.[13] Chapman reported early in 1800 suggesting what was in fact done, that the floodwaters of the Derwent should be diverted by Muston to the sea, but also estimating a possible navigation extension at £4,197, and warning the promoters that the Earl might 'avail himself of your Improvements of the River, and charge you Tolls into the Bargain'.[14] The Earl then let it be known that he would not oppose the drainage

† About 11½ miles above Yedingham.
‡ About 12 miles above Yedingham along the old river course.
§ The Scarborough Canal Scheme, see p. 325.

or the making navigable of the Derwent to Yedingham or, indeed, some miles up the Rye.[15] In order to prevent the natural opposition of Malton traders to an extension, the promoters then got a letter from Wentworth Fitzwilliam, the gist of which was included in a clause in the Muston Drainage Act of 1800.[16] This preserved Lord Fitzwilliam's right to extend the navigation above Malton under the powers of his original Act, and provided that should the drainage works create new river channels, he could use them and at his own expense adapt them for navigation. On the other hand, the drainage engineers must build their channels convenient for navigation.

Below Yedingham, however, drainage was hampered by the river's state: nor had anything been done on the navigation side when a newspaper reported at the end of 1803 that a petition was to be presented to Earl Fitzwilliam asking him to continue it to Yedingham,[17] though in 1804 Ralph Burton produced a plan of the river from the Rye junction to Yedingham bridge 'for an Intended Navigation',[18] and in September of the same year notice was given by a Malton solicitor of intention to seek an Act for a cut from Old Malton to the Rye, which was to be made navigable to Nunnington, with a branch from Little Habton to Normanby bridge; also a cut from the junction of the Derwent and Thornton beck to Thornton.[19] But about the end of 1809 George Leather senior was asked by the Earl's agent S. H. Copperthwaite, to prepare plans for making the Derwent navigable above Malton, and also for cutting a parallel drain as far as the Rye junction and then some way up that river. His son did the survey, sending his plans in June 1810. These provided for locks at New and Old Malton,* and Leather wrote: 'one or both of the Locks must be a gauge to Boat Builders that they may not be built too large to Navigate the Derwent above Rye mouth as they cannot exceed Twenty Tons'.[20] He reckoned that there would be no through trade to Yedingham, it being too small to support a merchant (Lewis in 1848 gives the population of the parish as 122),[21] and that all goods would be transhipped at Malton. He therefore at first planned a full-sized lock at New Malton, and one of 30 ft 6 in × 11 ft 9 in, to take craft 26 ft long at keel × 11 ft 6 in wide, at Old Malton. There were also to be some five miles of drain.

Earl Fitzwilliam then sent for Leather to discuss with him making the Rye navigable. He advised that the first 6½ miles

---

* New Malton is now called Malton. Old Malton is rather over a mile higher up the river.

Page 319 (above) The former lockhouse at lock 4 on the Tinsley flight of the Sheffield Canal about 1900. From a postcard; (below) craft in Elsecar basin, Dearne & Dove Canal, about 1900

Page 320   (*above*) A keelman on the Hull River gets free sails from Beecham's; (*below*) the keel *Venus* lies at Canal Head at Leven

could be dealt with by removing small shoals, a little widening, and making a towpath. Then a high-rise lock and ½ mile of deep cutting would be needed past the road and mill at Newsham bridge. Thence for 1¼ miles to Brawby the river was already navigable, he said, and only needed a towpath, which suggests that perhaps corn was sent to the mill and flour brought back by water. From Brawby to Nunnington he suggested a canal would be cheaper than trying to deal with the river course.

In November 1810 work began at Old Malton on a cut past the mill and a lock. Below Malton bridge a new quay was built, but it does not seem as if any lock was made there. Apart from building a towpath and making some improvements to the river channel, it seems no other navigation work was done, though a main drain of considerable depth and width was cut at a cost of nearly £10,000 round the whole parish of Old Malton, by-passing the mill dams at Old and New Malton and entering the river below New Malton mill tail. The extension to Yedingham, 13½ miles long, was probably opened from 1 January 1813, when tolls of 1s (5p) a chaldron on coal, 6d (2½p) on lime and 3d a quarter for corn was fixed: all other goods were one-third of the Derwent

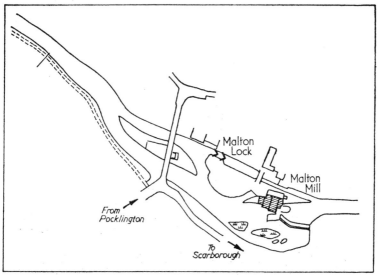

27. Plan for a lock at Malton as part of the Yedingham extension

E

tariff. It was said at this time that the lands to be drained above Yedingham would need much lime, and that coal would be wanted to burn it. Corn would be a back carriage.[22] Lower Derwent craft carrying perhaps 30 or so chaldrons would tranship their coal at Old Malton into small boats capable of carrying 6 chaldrons.[23]

In October 1814, referring to Chapman's report on the upper Derwent drainage, Leather said that above Yedingham the river was navigable to Foulbridge, and that two small locks would give enough water for it up to its junction with the river Hertford. I do not know for how long navigation above Malton continued; Duckham mentions coal to Yedingham in 1830,[24] and tolls to Yedingham, coal now 8d, lime still 6d and corn 3d a quarter, are still shown in a toll sheet of 1844. It had probably ended by 1846, when the Rye & Derwent Drainage Act empowered commissioners to buy and remove mills and dams obstructing the river at Malton and Old Malton.

For the fifty years from the mid-1790s the privately owned Derwent was a prosperous small business. The rent was raised from the previous £1,300 to £2,150 for 1794, £3,000 for 1799, and £3,048 for 1807 and 1808, the last letting years. Thereafter the Earl took the management into his own hands. Here are rounded-off average profit figures:[25]

Year ended 1 August	£	Year ended 1 August	£
1806–08	4,600	1824–26	4,500
1809–11	4,100	1827–29	3,000
1812–14	3,300	1830–32	3,600
1815–17	3,400	1833–35	3,900
1818–20	4,400	1836–38	3,900
1821–23	4,500	1839–41*	3,900

* 1839 and 1840 only.

The Earl seems to have run boats for his own estates, but not for common carrying. In 1807 35 craft other than those based at Malton itself were described as regularly trading on the Derwent, 17 others being listed as sometimes using it. Of the regulars, 8 were Knottingley boats probably in the lime trade, and about 8 more were based at or near Hull. A pamphlet of 1806[26] describes the Derwent as having:

'by slow degrees, extended a beneficial influence beyond its head, by making the Town of Malton, a Market for the surplus produce of the Country, towards Helmsley, and beyond

Pickering, in the direction of Scarborough, the Heslertons, and a small part of the Wolds'.

Private ownership had its disadvantages. The Earl regarded Malton as a borough that returned his two nominees to Parliament as a matter of course. When in 1807 the electors returned only one, the other being an independent, he was very annoyed indeed, and an unexpected election result was the immediate and selective raising of Derwent tolls—on coal from 1s 8d (8½p) to 3s (15p), on corn by a third—against those who had not supported the Fitz-william interest, whether or not they had anything to do with the election. Flour millers at Stamford Bridge, for instance, wrote sadly to the Earl that they, not being 'Freeholders in the County nor Freemen of the Borough of Malton as such was not able to vote'.[27] However, a House of Commons committee declared the independent's election to be invalid, the Earl's nominee replaced him, and the river tolls came down again.

Traffic was mainly coal upwards, some of it from the Fitzwilliam collieries on the Dearne & Dove Canal via the Barnsley and the Aire & Calder: and also lime and groceries to Malton. Corn was stored at Malton and then moved downwards, some to mills at Stamford Bridge and Sutton, some to the great corn market at Wakefield in barges which then brought coal back. In 1796, 56,065 quarters of corn, or some 10,000 tons, were shipped at Malton.[28] Lewis, writing in the 1830s, described the navigation more fully as carrying 'corn, butter, hams and other kinds of provision, which are . . . shipped for Hull, Leeds, Halifax, and other places; from the first-named, articles of grocery are brought back, and coal, woollen cloth, stuffs, &c., from Leeds'.[29] The craft were the usual keels and sloops, horse-towed when they could not be sailed, larger craft being excluded because the locks would not take boats bigger than 55 ft × 14 ft, some 10 ft shorter than most others in Yorkshire. On the other hand, the Derwent took craft drawing nearly 5 ft, more than the Selby Canal. Therefore the Earl was strongly in favour of compelling the Aire & Calder to improve the Selby line as part of the price for their 1820 Act. This con-siderable river trade greatly benefited the Fitzwilliam estates, as it did also the town of Malton and places along the navigation.

In an interesting letter to Lord Fitzwilliam, dated 29 April 1813, his agent S. H. Copperthwaite refers to competition with the Derwent in coal carrying from the Driffield and Foss Navigations, and fears that a rise in wool tolls will divert the wolds trade to Driffield. In 1807, indeed, possible competition from the Foss had

Take Notice, That from and after the First Day of July next, you are hereby required to deliver, or cause to be delivered, to the Lock Keeper, or Person appointed to receive and collect the Rates, Tolls and Duties, at Stamford Bridge, in the County of York, payable on the River Darwent, in the said County, a full, true, and particular Account, in Writing, of all the Coals, Corn, Goods, Wares, Merchandize, or Commodities, that shall be carried or conveyed up or down the said River, in any Boat, Barge or Vessel, belonging to you solely, or jointly with any other person or persons; and to pay to the said Lock Keeper or Collector at Stamford Bridge aforesaid, such sum of Money as shall be demanded, for every ton weight of Coals, Corn, Goods, Wares, Merchandize, or Commodities, that shall be carried or conveyed in any such Boat, Barge or Vessel, up the said River Darwent, from the River Ouze, to the Town of New Malton, or down the said River Darwent, from the said Town of New Malton to the River Ouze, not exceeding Eight Shillings, and so proportionably for a lesser weight, or for a less distance of place, to and from which any such Coals, Corn, Goods, Wares or Merchandizes, shall be carried or conveyed; and you are further required to take Notice, that no Boat, Barge or Vessel, belonging to you, will be permitted to pass the Lock at Stamford Bridge aforesaid, until such Rates or Prices shall be satisfied and paid. Dated this 16th Day of June, 1807.

Agent to EARL FITZWILLIAM,
Proprietor of the Navigation
of the said River Darwent.

Printed for Kerby, Stafford Street.

28. The Earl gets his own back on the electors

been a reason given to Fitzwilliam against keeping the post-election Derwent dues raised for too long.

In 1815 the Pocklington Canal was authorized, to leave the river at East Cottingwith. Opened in 1818, it brought a good deal of extra traffic to the lower river. Trade was predominantly coal upwards, plus some corn for milling; downwards, wheat, barley, oats, beans, malt and timber.

In the 1830s, Earl Fitzwilliam began to take a good deal of interest in railways, and in the next decade concerned himself notably with the South Yorkshire Railway which was to serve his collieries on the Dearne & Dove—he alternated with Lord Wharncliffe as its chairman. Realizing early that the Derwent would have to face railway competition, he had the river dredged in the 1830s, some of the work being done by a steam dredger hired from the Ouse Navigation. He also carried out improvements after advice from the engineer Thomas Rhodes, who surveyed the river in 1837. Depths were thereafter quite good: a notice of 1 January 1844 prohibits craft drawing over 5 ft 4 in passing in the winter, or 4 ft 10 in in the summer.

The competition came, first from the Hull & Selby line, opened in 1840, much more from the York & North Midland Railway's York & Scarborough railway, opened on 7 July 1845, which ran through Malton. Much of its construction material had indeed been carried on the river. The Earl's net profit, £4,145 in 1845, sank to £1,408 the following year. Tolls were immediately cut by the Earl, and the Aire & Calder gave a drawback on coal, but thenceforward the Derwent's story is one of commercial decline. (*To continue the history of the Derwent Navigation, turn to p. 440.*)

The Scarborough and Whitby Canal schemes

As we will remember, the original Derwent Act authorized the making navigable that river right up to Scarborough mills, though in 1793 works had not been built higher than Malton. In September of that year a group of promoters opened a subscription for a canal from Scarborough to Malton, with branches to Kirbymoorside and Pickering,[30] and decided on a survey and estimate. An engineer, Cockshutt,* then surveyed a line from Scarborough to Pickering and the Derwent. They met on 25 November to hear his first report. This proposed a canal 30 ft at surface, 23 miles long with 24 locks from a sea-lock and basin at

* Probably James Cockshutt.

Five Guineas Reward.

DERWENT NAVIGATION OFFICE, MALTON,

March 13, 1810.

WHEREAS some evil disposed Person or Persons have, of .ate, committed many Depredations and other mischievous Acts, on and about the Derwent Navigation, by drawing the Cloughs of the Locks, throwing in Stones, stealing Posts, damaging Bridges, Gates, &c. For the prevention of such Mischief in future, and detection of the Offender or Offenders,

Notice is hereby Given,

That the above Reward of Five Guineas will be paid on conviction of the Offender or Offenders, to any Person or Persons who shall give such information as shall be the means of bringing him or them to Justice.

Information to be given to Mr. SAMUEL HENRY COPPERTHWAITE, *Malton Lodge;* JOHN JACKSON, *Stamford Bridge;* or to SAMUEL GANT, *Barmby,* any of whom will pay the Reward on conviction of the Offender or Offenders.

GIBSON, Printer, Malton.

29. Vandalism: a notice of 1810

Scarborough to Pickering by way of the north side of the Derwent valley and the Costa Beck. From the beck a branch 3¼ miles long was proposed to the Derwent, whence Malton could be reached, and another 8⅛ miles long to How Keld Head mills near Kirbymoorside. This canal would be smaller than the Derwent below Malton, and transhipment would therefore have been necessary. His estimate was £71,087, of which £13,732 was for the mills branch. Cockshutt added another £8,420 should a canal direct to Malton be considered better than one to the nearest point of the Derwent. Various minor changes of line were discussed, and Cockshutt was then asked to do a final report.[31] In March 1794 an estimate was published that at 2d per ton mile (a considerable average toll) the revenue would provide a net profit of £6,028 p.a., enough to pay 7½ per cent.[32]

A meeting at Scarborough on 22 May 1794 to consider it was 'disorderly', and gave rise to a bitter newspaper controversy.[33] Some supporters reorganized the promoting committee, but could not reanimate it; others turned over to supporting Earl Fitzwilliam's plans for extending the Derwent navigation. After the meeting Isaac Leatham came forward with a broadsheet,[34] taking the view that Cockshutt's line would hinder rather than help drainage, as well as being unnecessarily expensive because entirely a still-water route. Instead, he pressed the extension of the Derwent upwards to Yedingham, a 12½ mile cut south of the river thence to a sea-lock at Scarborough, and the making navigable of the Rye and Costa Beck from the head of the latter, presumably on the Kirby Misperton–Pickering road. This, he thought, with 26 locks and necessary drains from Yedingham to near Muston, would cost £59,545, yield £6,500 p.a. more tolls than Cockshutt's line, and take 'vessels of the Burthen of those which come up to Malton', and so able to navigate all other local waterways. The canal scheme ended as a proposed canal branch of the Derwent to Pickering, with an extension by Middleton to Normanby bridge.[35]

Also towards the end of 1793 Whitby people began to interest themselves in a canal inland to Pickering to carry such commodities as lime, grain and timber.[36] Francis Gibson, collector of customs at Whitby, took a leading part, and it was he who negotiated for a survey by William Crosley. While he was at work, the Whitby people heard that those of Scarborough also had an inland canal in mind, and were being supported in Pickering itself.

Crosley proposed a narrow canal 25 miles long from Whitby to

Pickering, to cost £66,447, and yield a revenue of £5,017 and profit of £3,364, 'but on the Return of Peace it will of course be greatly increased'.[37] Gibson wrote to him:

'I think it best to go upon that Estimate at present, and if people enter into the Subscription with Spirit we may then be able to carry into execution that upon the broad Plan . . . the larger Estimate might startle them so much as cause the whole business to fall to the ground.'[38]

The line was to run up the Esk and Murk Esk valleys by Grosmont and Beck Hole, and then by Newton Dale to Pickering. Gibson asked Crosley to provide also for a branch towards the collieries at Danby, which would have run from Grosmont up the Esk valley, and for some estimates of income. But there was less impetus and hope of profit behind the scheme than behind that to Scarborough and the Derwent, and it quickly died.

Pocklington Canal

In 1801 the lawyer Thomas Plummer told Lord Egremont that about 1777 he was instructed to seek Lord Rockingham's consent to a canal from the Derwent to Pocklington, which was given.[39] Nothing had been done then, or earlier when Pocklington had been an objective of the first Market Weighton proposals (see p. 89). In 1801 the idea was revived at a public meeting at Pocklington, called to consider a canal to the Derwent.[40] Among those concerned were M. Constable Maxwell, Robert Denison, Henry Vavasour and George Bagley, surnames that were to recur later. Maxwell took the chair at that of 16 November, which unanimously agreed, 'That a Navigable Canal towards the Town of Pocklington would be of great Public Utility.' It had been suggested at the meeting that a line to Pocklington direct from the Ouse at Howden 'would be the most eligible Line as a great part of the Country would be thereby benefited which by a Cut from the Derwent would be excluded any Advantage'.[41] They may have thought a Howden proposal of 1796 (see p. 316) to build a canal from their town for about a mile to the Ouse might be revived to help them. Plummer had leaped in to say that such a line would deprive the Derwent of tolls and might deprive it of water, and would have Lord Egremont's opposition. This would also of course be true of Lord Fitzwilliam as the Derwent's owner. The point was taken, and it was decided to employ Eastburn to survey two possible routes from the Derwent.

The eventual report came, however, from William Chapman in August 1802. Chapman was an honest and competent engineer who, however, sometimes missed the finer nuances of a situation. Here, having surveyed two lines from the Derwent, 8 miles long from East Cottingwith or 9½ from Bubwith, he recommended instead one 13½ miles long from Howden which, he thought, would carry more and, because it was long, bring in more money. Chapman had said the wrong thing, and the idea quietly dropped. When it was revived, it was by Earl Fitzwilliam himself. The George Leathers, father and son, were in 1812 working for him on the upper Derwent navigation and drainage when George junior was asked by Earl Fitzwilliam's agent S. H. Copperthwaite to survey a line from above Sutton lock, presumably so that he could collect as much as possible in Derwent tolls. Leather reported this to be impracticable, and said the entrance should be at East Cottingwith, without a survey estimating a line to the Hull turnpike road with 8 locks at £43,630, and £8,257 if continued another ¾ mile with 2 locks into Pocklington itself, an extension that Chapman had earlier recommended if the most business were to be attracted. He also put the probable revenue, accurately enough, at £1,246·50 p.a.

Leather started his survey in August 1813, did part of it, and was taken ill. At this time he had in mind another Derwent lock at East Cottingwith 'below all the Shallows, to raise the water there about 4 feet, which is about the height that the Spring Tides rise'.[42] Even should the Pocklington scheme fizzle out, he thought this lock would be useful, for 'when I was down there I saw several Vessels laying on the Shoal for 7 or 8 Days'.[43] Leather was not able to finish his surveying until June 1814, when a meeting was called for 26 July to receive his proposals and estimate for a canal 'from the Turnpike Road near Pocklington into the River Derwent'.[44] It was followed by another of 25 August, with Robert Denison in the chair, which opened a subscription: 63 people at once came forward and put up £20,500, 39 of them, mostly small Pocklington people, in £100 units. The biggest contributors were Robert Denison with £3,000, Earl Fitzwilliam with £2,000 and M. Constable Maxwell with £1,600. Denison was a substantial Barnsley Canal shareholder, and was probably interested in getting a coal trade going. Some later increased these holdings.

George Bagley then wrote to Leather asking him to extend his survey over the turnpike road to Pocklington itself,[45] and a meeting on 22 September resolved 'that the Level from the Turnpike

Road up to the Town of Pocklington should be made upon the plan intended to be laid before Parliament'.[46] The wording suggests this was not a unanimous view, and differences over it may account for Leather writing in October that, according to Bagley, 'no further subscriptions have been received since last meeting, and tho' he seems rather to despair of its going on, he says he is not yet entirely without hope'.[47] Leather's extension, as shown on the deposited plan dated 25 September 1814,[48] shows the canal running to the edge of Pocklington itself, with five locks additional to the nine built. However, at another meeting on 20 October a compromise was reached over the Pocklington extension, that a clause authorizing it should be included in the Bill, but it should not be built unless a majority of shares by value should approve. Further subscriptions completed Leather's estimate of £32,032 to the turnpike road.

So the Bill went forward, and the Act,[49] giving power to raise £32,000 in £100 shares and £10,000 more if necessary, passed on 25 May 1815. Monopoly was avoided by a clause that votes per share held should be limited to a maximum of ten. The Act also enacted that Derwent tolls should be the same for traffic going up the river as for craft entering the canal. The Pocklington extension had by now been dropped, the line being authorized only to the turnpike road.

The shareholders met for the first time at the Feathers at Pocklington on 19 June 1815, with Sir Henry Vavasour in the chair. Unusually, they adopted the practice, kept up throughout the company's life, of electing a committee for three years instead of the normal one. By 7 July all the necessary money had been subscribed, and on 14 July Leather wrote to Earl Fitzwilliam's agent that he was about to start laying out the line, and wanted to know whether the Earl proposed to build a Derwent lock at East Cottingwith.[50] The answer must have been 'no'; thereafter Leather had to provide the canal with an entrance lock extra to the original eight. The committee now announced that on 7 August they 'will let by ticket the cutting of the canal from E. Cottingwith to Hagg bridge in such proportions and parts as the parties choose to engage for, having given sureties', and would also receive proposals for masons' and carpenters' work, and for supplying 50 wheelbarrows and materials.[51]

The canal was cut upwards from the Derwent, one stretch at a time, each seemingly the responsibility of one contractor. Money was called just as quickly as the Act allowed, and some debts incurred in anticipation of calls: indeed, the pace was too hot for some shareholders, who protested, but it kept down overheads and brought revenue in as quickly as possible. By about August 1816 the first section of canal to Hagg bridge was open for traffic, and by the spring of 1817 that to Walbut. Leather hoped to finish by the end of the year, but the weather was bad, and in fact the canal opened on 30 July 1818. Three weeks earlier Thomas Johnson of Pocklington had advertised space to be let on the south side of the basin adjoining the turnpike road, 'also a Substantial New-erected Granary, capable of Chambering 400 quarters of Corn'.[52]

The canal was 9½ miles long with nine locks having the larger than usual average rise of 11¼ ft, to take keels 58 ft × 14 ft 3 in. There were two short branches, to Melbourne and Bielby beck, the latter made on condition that local people built a road to it from Bielby, and a public wharf.* Its principal water supply came from the Pocklington beck at canal head. On opening the canal had cost £32,695, with £2,495 still needed—this had to be borrowed. Leather had in fact done the work for the estimate, the excess being due to additions not originally included in it, and was warmly thanked by the shareholders. However, the fact remained that the canal served no place of any size except Pocklington, and had only the slightest prospects of commercial success.

Before the opening, Mark Swann was appointed lock-keeper and toll collector at £50 p.a. and the house which was soon afterwards built for him. Just after it, the committee agreed with Johnson that he should build 'a Public Wharf Warehouse & Crane'[53] at canal head, charging for wharfage and warehousing the average of the dues at Driffield, Stamford Bridge and Market Weighton. However, such a private wharf proved inconvenient, and in 1819 Johnson agreed to the wharf being opened to all for £15 p.a., on condition goods were at once removed if they were not to pay wharfage. Optimistically, fixed handles were at first fitted to the lock paddle gear, but after some pounds had been emptied by the mischievous, they were replaced by portable ones given to the boat captains.

Takings began low, only £623 in tolls for 1820, partly because of road transport competition. Three land carriers were still working between Pocklington and Hull, though their charges had been cut from £1 to 15s (75p) a ton. Then in January 1822,

---

* In 1820 the canal company bought Bielby mill for £900, presumably to control the beck water.

'Several Tradesmen in Pockⁿ . . . joined in the purchase of a Packitt to convey Goods to and from Hull'.[54] Experimentally this would run weekly in alternate directions, taking five days, and carrying at 10s (50p) to encourage trade. This was the *Union Packet*, able to carry about 50 tons; nevertheless, road transport persisted, to Hull, Market Weighton and York. Traffic on the canal was of the usual kind for such a waterway: coal, lime, manure and merchandise upwards, corn, flour and timber downwards.[55]

To begin with, Derwent tolls were separately paid: of the 10s above, 2s 6d (12½p) was canal toll and 1s 6d (7½p) Derwent toll. But from April 1823 Earl Fitzwilliam agreed to commute Derwent tolls on Pocklington craft for £200 p.a., and thenceforward a single toll covered both navigations. In 1829 the Earl raised the payment to £250, and the canal company made a corresponding increase. Business was affected, and in 1831 it reverted to £200.

By the end of the 1820s the canal was free from debt, and the takings, though modest, allowed a dividend of 3 per cent to be paid in 1830. Here are averaged figures of the company's record:

Y.e. August	Toll receipts* £	Dividends§ per cent
1819–23	779	
1824–28	1,193	
1829–33	1,285	2·625†
1834–38	1,445	3·2
1839–43	1,432	3·0
1844–48	1,324	3·4‡

* All figures except for 1819–22 include Derwent tolls.
§ Originally there were 320 £100 shares: 15¼ were forfeited, so dividends were paid on 304¾ shares.
† 1830–33 only.
‡ Plus an additional winding up dividend of 3s 6d (17½p) in the last year, 1848.

The old committee, many of whom had served from the beginning, seem to have regarded the first dividend as a signal for younger men to take over. Of the fourteen who had been given a new three-year term in 1827, only six were re-elected in 1830.

In 1832 Robert Denison, son of the earlier promoter of the same name, became chairman, and thenceforward increasingly prominent in the little company's affairs. In 1834 and 1835 he leased land at canal head, and agreed to put up buildings there. He seems indeed to have taken the basin over, for in 1837 he offered to dredge it at his own expense.

In 1835 some frauds in cargo loadings must have been detected, for the company asked the Aire & Calder to allow their lock-keeper at Castleford to supply a monthly account of cargoes passing the lock for Pocklington, as a check.

And so to railways, when in August 1840 the committee were empowered 'to make such arrangements as they think respecting any Fly Boats or other conveyances thought necessary to be employed in connection with the Railway at Wressel',[56] Wressle being beside the lower Derwent, on the Hull & Selby Railway that had opened a month before.

During the railway mania year the company received a proposal from the projected York & Hull East & West Yorkshire Junction Railway, a line under the wing of the Hull & Selby Railway, of £18,000 (approximately £59 for each of the 304¾ shares) conditional upon obtaining their Act. This offer came before a special shareholders' meeting on 24 September 1845, with Robert Denison in the chair. He was himself associated with Hudson and the York & North Midland, and seems at the meeting to have immediately made an alternative offer of the same amount from that company, presumably because the Y. & N.M. had been leasing the Hull & Selby since July. At an adjourned meeting on 6 October he produced a letter from Hudson confirming the offer 'conditionally upon the said . . . Railway Company obtaining the Proposed Extension of their line from York into the East Riding',[57] the purchase to be completed upon the opening of the line. If the oddity of the canal company's chairman acting officially as agent for a railway company negotiating to buy his own concern struck anyone, it is not reflected in the minute book.

The company then proceeded to accept both offers in identical terms pending the necessary Acts. The Y. & N.M.R. got its Act in 1846 for a line from York through Pocklington and Market Weighton to Beverley. It was opened past Pocklington on 4 October 1847, in which year a further Act[58] authorized the purchase of the canal, along with the Market Weighton, Vavasour's, and the Leven. The railway paid for it by £13,393 of debentures for the larger shareholders, and £4,587 in cash to the smaller. Earl Fitzwilliam then held 36 shares, and the Denison family 47½. A final winding up dividend of 3s 6d (17½p) a share was paid, and the transfer took place on 18 November 1848.[59] The Act provided for the railway to keep the canal open and in good repair, and empowered the Railway Commissioners to intervene if necessary. (*To continue the history of the Pocklington Canal, turn to p. 445.*)

Wharfe River

The opening of the Selby Canal in 1778 probably soon ended the Leeds trade via Tadcaster, and reduced business on the Wharfe to traffic going to and from that town and its district. Certainly references are few: in 1797 there was a sloop owner there;[60] there are diary references to boat-loads of coal in 1793 and 1795, and Knottingley lime in 1792, so written as to sound exceptional,[61] in 1806 a news item records an accident in the Humber to a timber-laden sloop voyaging from Grimsby to Tadcaster;[62] and, though in 1822 Baines records no carrier by water to the town, in 1837 William Coates is listed by White as carrying 'every spring tide',[63] as he is in 1844 by Williams. In the 1846 Parliamentary session, the projected Leeds, York & Midland Junction Railway proposed to exchange traffic with the Wharfe at Tadcaster. The river trade was then small—rape seed, guano and bones from Hull—but the railway saw flax being imported there, brought by water to Tadcaster, and then taken on by rail to Knaresborough. Coal from Aberford would be a back carriage.[64] (*To continue the navigation history of the Wharfe, turn to p. 445.*)

Foss Navigation

The slow moving Foss[65] rises north-east of Easingwold, and runs curvingly to join the Ouse in the city of York. That corporation had itself thought of making the river navigable in 1725,[66] and Francis Drake the historian had revived the idea in 1736.[67] Between 1769 and 1773 also, there were proposals for the Kyle Navigation (see p. 112) from the Ouse at Newton upon Ouse to or near Easingwold, while in October 1770 a meeting of land-owners on the Foss between York and Sheriff Hutton considered removing Castle mills, on the river in York, and making a navigation 'up the said River'.[68]

When the project was revived, it arose out of a meeting held in July 1791 to consider the river's flooding problems.[69] The promoters, mainly interested in the drainage, originally decided to include in their scheme a navigation only as far as Sheriff Hutton 'at a moderate Expence', to carry coal and road materials. This was surveyed by William Jessop, who reported in November,[70] and estimated it at £16,274. Jessop regarded the scheme as mainly one for drainage. He proposed to drop the level of the Foss through York to 1 ft below the lowest land, by buying out Castle mills and then having an entrance lock with a 4 ft 4 in rise only. This would enable York to convert '60 or 70 acres of land immediately under its walls, which in summer is in a putrid state, into a rich and verdant mead'. In addition, drainage would be improved by widening the narrow and crooked river. These benefits alone, he thought, would make economic sense, but in addition a fair trade might be expected.

Then a group of landowners between Sheriff Hutton and Stillington, led by the two Stephen Crofts and Francis Cholmley, asked for its extension for another 4 miles to the York–Helmsley road at Stillington, itself about 4 miles from Easingwold. A general meeting on 6 January 1792 approved the extension, subscriptions were invited, and a plan deposited showing a navigation with eight locks following the river line to Sheriff Hutton, and then running with five more to Stillington.[71] In York a short branch from Foss Island to Tang Hall bridge on the York–Heslington road was included.[72] By February 1792 £25,400 had been subscribed,[73] and a Parliamentary petition was put in, but too late in the session for a Bill to be taken.

In 1793, with an amended survey now by Robert Gilson under William Jessop's supervision that proposed nine locks below Sheriff Hutton and the same five above, and with the Tang Hall bridge branch dropped, the promoters returned to Parliament for a broad waterway to take keels of about 58 ft × 14 ft 6 in, and a reservoir on Oulston Moor north-east of Easingwold, unusual on a river navigation.[74] The navigation estimate was £24,685.

The Act[75] of 30 April 1793 authorized a capital of £25,400 in £100 shares and £10,000 more if needed. As the Bill proceedings had cost £1,471, it was clear that it would be. In York, the company had to buy out the interests in Castle mills within two years. Separate commissioners with rating powers were to concern themselves with most of the drainage problems. Among the shareholders were two men prominent locally, and also connected with the Aire & Calder, Peregrine Wentworth and Sir William Mordaunt Milner, while the company's first clerk was Thomas Plummer, Lord Egremont's man of business. One of the two solicitors to the company and also a shareholder, John Lund, had been one of the original commissioners to build the Market Weighton Canal, and therefore understood the problems of reconciling drainage and navigation. Meetings were at first held at the Guildhall; then in November 1793 they moved to the York Tavern.

Jessop probably did the lay-out of the line; then, after specifying some reservoir fittings, his name disappears from the records. Presumably he was too busy with such bigger responsibilities as the Barnsley, the Grand Junction and the Ellesmere, all authorized in 1793, and all with him as engineer. Instead, unfortunately for the company at that canal mania time when good engineers were over-busy, John Moon[76] was unemployed. In August he answered an advertisement for a superintendent of works and was taken on. He was so self-confident that although the job required the navigation to be built 'according to a Section of the intended Canal by Mr. Jessop',[77] he proceeded radically to alter Jessop's line and proposals, seemingly to reduce the number of locks. This had two consequences; to increase the cutting and embankment necessary at each lock approach, and so construction cost, and to slow the river down through York and make drainage more difficult.* Therefore a proposal of Jessop's to drain the Foss Island area by building a 4 ft diameter tunnel turned out to be useless, the tunnel having to be blocked about 1813.

Work began late in 1793 at the York end, while the company negotiated to buy Castle mills, then worked under lease. They did so, and thereafter were continually occupied with the problems of their various lessees. Some tolls were being taken by November, though Castle mills lock was still being built. A year later, on 5 November 1794, the navigation was opened for $1\frac{1}{4}$ miles to Monk bridge:

> 'the first lock was opened, when a large vessel laden with coals belonging to Mr Mark Hesp coal and lime merchants in York passed through amidst the acclamations of a great concourse of spectators, and proceeded . . . to Monk Bridge to deliver her cargo. This . . . besides removing . . . a collection of putrid and stagnant water that was daily becoming more offensive, promises to be of great public utility'.[78]

Moon was told to 'treat the Workmen upon the Canal in such Manner as appears to him proper, not exceeding the Sum of Ten Pounds'.[79]

So far Moon had been considered good, having been given a rise in August 1794. But by mid-1795, with the line probably open to Haxby, staked out to Strensall and being staked to Sheriff Hutton, the committee got nervous at the way money was going, and called in John Rennie. His report of 30 November was severe,

---

* By 1810 the company were thinking of building an additional lock at the entrance to the Foss (as Jessop had proposed), to improve the levels through York, and enable the 10 ft Castle mill lock to be lowered.

Page 337 Sam Hodgson, with his crew, his mother, and coal men, unload a
keel at Tadcaster coal wharf, 1900

Page 338 (*above*) Craft near Newport, Market Weighton Canal, in the early 1900s; (*below*) a snuffbox of 1823 shows the proposed Newcastle & Maryport Canal

even though a few things for which he critized Moon were committee decisions. In sum: 'throughout the whole of the Work,
very little attention indeed has been paid to Mr. Jessop's original
design, by which not only many thousand Pounds have been
thrown away, but the Works rendered much less secure'.[80] If
Jessop's advice had been followed, Rennie said, the navigation
might by then have been open to above Sheriff Hutton; as it was,
there was not enough money to finish it to Strensall. Moon was at
once told to work to the works committee that Rennie had recommended, and six months later was dismissed. To get the
navigation finished and open to Strensall, and to pay off the most
clamorous creditors, voluntary loans totalling 20 per cent on
shares were raised from consenting shareholders, for 'in these
times money is not to be borrowed of strangers'.[81]

William Scruton, who replaced Moon, completed the two Oulston Moor reservoirs and the line to Strensall, originally intending
to build four locks in two staircase pairs, one above and one
below the village. In fact, two separate locks were built below
Strensall, and there for the time the navigation ended, having cost
over £25,000. Writing about now, John Tuke said that the main
upwards traffic was coal and lime; downwards, grain, butter and
bacon, and 'perhaps hereafter timber and stone for roads'. He
thought more business was likely on the river than had at first
been expected.[82] There now seemed 'scarcely any probability of
carrying on the Navigation to Stillington,'[83] though the company
thought the landowners in that direction might like to do it themselves in exchange for a 31-year lease of the tolls and then a conversion of their outlay to shares. So for a time work paused, the
shareholders unable to pay interest on the £5,000 or so they
owed, and refusing even to come to meetings. One can hardly
blame them: receipts for 1799 were £287, for 1800, £380.

In July 1800, enough having been gathered together, they decided to seek an Act to authorize compulsory excess calls on
shares, for 'the willing Horse has been rode to a stand still', to
repay loans, pay debts, and finish the line to Sheriff Hutton
bridge, which would be 'very beneficial and materially tend to
raise the value of the Shares'.[84] This Act[85] authorized them to
raise the £10,000 permitted under the 1793 Act by calls, and a
further £10,000 by borrowing, to pay off debts and build to
Sheriff Hutton bridge, but no further unless their balance
allowed it, or they had raised the money.

On 1 March 1802 the committee decided to start the extension.

F

Jessop had considered a cut necessary above Strensall, presumably because the river was too small, but his plan had followed the river line. Scruton seems to have suggested abandoning it and taking the cut from above Strensall straight to Sheriff Hutton bridge. William Pontey of Huddersfield, consulted, agreed and took charge, with Scruton under him. There was £4,000 in the bank. The cut, rising from the river by a staircase pair, then ran level to a basin near the bridge without rejoining the river, water being provided by a feeder. The extension was open by about end-June 1804, though some work remained to be done. A group of shareholders then lent enough money to build a small grain warehouse, stables, and a combined wharfinger's and beer house. The line was now 11½ miles long with 8 locks: it had cost about £35,000. The shareholders sadly calculated the profits would not pay 4 per cent, and in May 1805 raised tolls by two-thirds.

Potential traffic needed adequate roads to reach the waterway. Their Act provided that the company should pay half of certain road improvements: on other lines they applied now persuasion and now threats of indictment to persuade highway authorities to make improvements.

And then controversy began. In July 1808 a shareholders' meeting, strong in Stillington supporters, decided against paying a first dividend and in favour of abstinence until the navigation had been completed. The nervous then rallied, and six months later agreed by 124 votes to 92 'that it is inexpedient to carry on the Navigation to Stillington'.[86] Stephen Croft and Sir Charles Harland, prominent Stillingtonians, promptly filed a Bill against the company in the Court of Exchequer to compel them to continue. A year later the company gave way to Croft (Harland had died), agreeing to spend up to £10,000 on the extension. In July 1810 John Tuke was employed to do the survey, and the company felt confident enough to complain to the Ouse trustees about the state of Naburn lock and make a short wharfage branch, Wormalds cut, in York from a little above the first lock to what is now Navigation Lane—and then the Marquess of Hertford refused to sell essential land. Perhaps more relieved than otherwise, the shareholders turned to the contemplation of dividends on their shares* and practical problems of running their small concern, though for some years they went on pressing the Marquess to change his mind.

* Originally 258 shares were issued: some were forfeited, and one ceased to have a traceable owner. Dividends were paid on 253.

Trade improved in the first few years after the opening of the line to Sheriff Hutton, till toll revenue reached £1,385 in 1809, the highest figure achieved. Then it fell away, seemingly because of competition from the Ouse above York and the Derwent.[87] In 1823 tolls to Strensall and above were reduced. In 1814 the committee had decided to lease the tolls, hoping for £1,250 p.a. Rather to their surprise, however, inquiries did not lead to bids. It was not until 1831 that Christopher Hall, their tenant at Sheriff Hutton basin, took them at £900 p.a. for seven years, after the committee had paid him a substantial sum towards repairs. He at once restored the higher tolls to Strensall and above. Here are averaged toll receipts to 1829:

Years	£	Years	£
1800–02	472	1815–17	1,042
1803–05	757	1818–20	1,070
1806–08	1,324	1821–23	832
1809–11	1,240	1824–26	1,035
1812–14	1,200	1827–29	966

When the lease was re-let in 1838, to a man named Bower, the annual figure was £985. Business was very small-scale, as these figures of coal to Sheriff Hutton for three months of 1841 show:

Month	No. of craft	Tons of coal
May	4	219
June	9	303
July	6	241[88]

Dividends roughly reflect the fortunes of the navigation; here are averaged figures:

Years	Dividends per £115 share £	Years	Dividends per £115 share £
1809–11*	4·50	1833–35	2·66
1812–14	3·00	1836–38	3·33
1815–17	2·66	1839–41	3·16
1818–20	3·33	1842–44	3·00
1821–23	2·00	1845–47	1·66
1824–26	1·66	1848–50	0·33
1827–29	2·50	1851	0·50
1830–32	1·00		

* 1810 and 1811 only.

Business was good at the York end, though much was short-haul. By 1825 the masonry of Castle mills lock had moved to narrow the structure, and the company began to consider rebuilding it to its original dimensions. The work was done in 1829 at a cost of some £1,000.

After 21 June 1842 the managing committee did not meet for over six years, so it was a shareholders' meeting that on 1 January 1844 appointed a sub-committee to consider the demands for land of the York & North Midland Railway's prospective Scarborough branch, which a railway meeting had approved in the previous November.[89] They took the situation calmly. A year after the railway Act of July 1844, however, on 7 July 1845, the shareholders asked the sub-committee to consider terms for an offer of the navigation for sale or on long lease. It was an apposite day, that of the opening of the Scarborough line, the York end of which closely paralleled the Foss as far as Strensall. (*To continue the history of the Foss Navigation, turn to p. 446.*)

CHAPTER XV

North from York

++++++++++++++++++++++++++++++++++++◆++++++++++++++++++++++++++++++++++++

ABOVE York, navigation on the Ouse extended past Linton lock to Boroughbridge and Ripon. There was a scheme to extend it by a canal to Knaresborough and another to the Tees, but nothing came of either. Nothing, too, of other projects to carry Co. Durham coal to Stockton, to extend the navigation of the Wear to Durham, to link Wear and Tyne, or to enable Tyne craft to reach Hexham, Haydon Bridge, or pass the Pennines to Carlisle, Port Carlisle or Maryport.

After Rhodes's 1834 report, the trustees hoped that increased toll revenue would enable them 'in a little time' to improve the Ouse above York, for 'the raising and forming of a Towing Path, and the building of several necessary Bridges over the intersecting watercourses, along the whole length . . . terminating at or near the mouth of the River Nid, is very much wanted,'[1] for present users and to encourage more. The banks also needed to be 'sloped and sodded',[2] and some dredging and minor bank straightening done. In 1837 they dredged a 5 ft summer depth to the mouth of the Nidd, and arranged for it to be continued further to Milby lock on the Ure. Work on bank protection and the towpath followed.

For a time there was a sharp increase of traffic, probably helped by construction material for the Great North of England Railway, opened to York on 4 January 1841. In May 1840 the trustees' quarterly report noted that the 'very great increase of such part of the river traffic, as is carried on solely above York' made it imme-diately necessary to collect tolls on it efficiently, and a York col-lector was appointed. However, once the railway was opened, the upriver coal traffic from the Aire & Calder tended to be replaced by rail-borne coal from Durham, delivered along the line or sent back from York from the G.N.E.R. coal staith there.

Linton Lock Navigation

In 1795 the Linton lock commissioners petitioned Parliament that, interpreting their Act strictly, they could only collect tolls at the lock, which meant that the rest of their navigation was treated as if it were toll-free. Therefore 'the Produce of the . . . Rates, since the year 1778, hath not been sufficient (after defraying the Expences of supporting and maintaining the said Navigation) to pay the Creditors more than' 2 per cent interest, so that considerable arrears were now due. Should they be authorized to collect tolls more widely, they thought the tolls would be enough to pay interest without additions.[3] There was opposition from landowners below the lock, who saw themselves likely to be penalized,[4] and no Bill followed. Nevertheless, the navigation saw mild prosperity during the period, paying an average dividend of 6·1 per cent for 1816–20 and 5·3 per cent for 1821–5 on its £13,046 of subscription capital. In 1843 the figure was 5 per cent. Rhodes tells us that the main local trade was at Newton, where 'there is a great quantity of grain and coal shipped and unshipped, and considerable trade appears to be carried on at this point from various parts of the country'. But the river between Linton lock and York was often too shallow, boats having to be helped up to the lock by flashes which in turn were likely to inconvenience those above.[5] The towpath, too, had little to commend it.

In 1834 the Ouse trustees pointed out to the commissioners various deficiencies in their navigation that Rhodes's survey had revealed: as the two bodies shared the same clerk, such messages were easily passed. Three years later they were lent the Ouse's dredger to continue the 5 ft depth from the mouth of the Nidd to Linton lock, and later in conjunction with the Ure company on to Milby lock. (*To continue the history of the Linton Lock Navigation,* *turn to p.* 447.)

Swale Schemes

Some canal schemes of the 1790s included branches to Northallerton, Bedale and Thirsk (see p. 350), and later the making navigable of the Swale and Wiske past Northallerton to Great Smeaton, about eight miles from Darlington,[6] seems to have been briefly considered in connexion with the contemporary Stockton canal projects (see p. 352). Another scheme proposed a canal from the

Swale via Coxwold (north of Easingwold) and then to the junction of Holbeck with the river Ray, whence access was hoped for to Malton and the Derwent[7] (see p. 348); and in 1800 an advertisement called a meeting to consider reviving the Swale Act.[8] Meanwhile, there was some trade to Helperby. In April 1830 E. & T. Charnock jun wrote to Smithson & Co. of Wakefield that they had '350 Chaldrons of Coals at Helperby which is a famous stock to begin the summer with when we may expect low waters and no getting up there'.[9]

Ure Navigation and Ripon Canal

About the turn of the century the Ure had an established trade to Boroughbridge and Ripon. That to Boroughbridge included some to Knaresborough, this being sent on by road from the town or from above Swale Nab depending on the depth of water. That to Ripon included lead brought by road from the mines near Greenhow Hill west of Pateley Bridge to be shipped there.[10] It was then said, however, that, 'The Lead shipped at Ripon, is obliged to be unloaded at Boroughbridge, and re-shipped there for Hull,'[11] presumably because the canal was not deep enough for Humber sloops, though against that the tolls charged on the navigation were not high—1s (5p) for merchandise, including lead, against the authorized 3s (15p), the toll and freight combined from Boroughbridge to Hull being 11s (55p) a ton. Lead was a continuing trade, an advertisement of mine shares for sale in 1824 saying: 'the Lead may be conveniently conveyed by Water to any Part of the Kingdom' from Ripon.[12] Sloops then working to Boroughbridge were 50 to 52 ft long, 15 ft 6 in to 15 ft 10 in wide, and drew 6 ft to 6 ft 6 in loaded.[13] Disadvantages were the shoals at Ellenthorpe a little above Swale Nab, of which it was said in 1800: 'The Boroughbridge Vessels are sometimes obliged to unload part of their cargo here, there being a scarcity of water, particularly in summer.'[14]

At the beginning of 1796 William Morley, who was running three vessels between Hull and Ripon, took a lease of the tolls from the commissioners.[15]

Two connecting canal schemes were promoted at the turn of the century, the North Riding Canal from below Boroughbridge to the Tees (see p. 350), which offered a good supply of Durham coal, and in the opposite direction a canal to Knaresborough (see p. 347). The promoters of the second scheme hoped their line might attract Ripon's lead traffic, but neither came to anything. Perhaps in the 1810s Thomas Charnock built the ½-mile long Bishop Monkton private canal from the Ure about half a mile below Ox Close south to a small basin by the Bishop Monkton–Westwick road. The present Anchor House, formerly the Anchor Inn, marks its end. A coal yard was established there by 1821, and in 1830 Smithson & Co., the Wakefield colliery owners, who also had coalyards at Ripon and Boroughbridge, rented it at £31·50 p.a. for some three years. The Ure charged the same tolls to the canal as to Ripon. The cut probably ceased to be used during the 1840s.[16]

Up to 1820 the Ure was managed by commissioners. By then, arrears of interest of £11,450 had accumulated on the £16,400 of debt, and no one remained qualified to act as commissioner. Therefore the works, lacking maintenance and control, were in a bad state. Because 'the trade and carriage . . . hath of late years greatly increased . . . and it has become necessary to provide . . . additional wharfs, warehouses, landing places', etc,[17] in October 1819 some of the concern's creditors formed The Company of Proprietors of the River Ure Navigation to Ripon, subscribed an additional £3,033, and obtained an Act[18] in June 1820 to incorporate themselves. They were empowered to raise from their own number £34,000 in 200 £170 shares and £3,400 more if necessary. Of these shares, 164* were reserved for creditors, who could either accept them or keep their securities as they chose. The original tolls were reiterated, and finally the company were directed to spend £3,000 on repairs within five years, against an estimate of £2,730 which included enlargements to the warehouses at Milby and Ripon.[19]

It was said that in 1822 only craft carrying 30 tons could get up the navigation,[20] but the improvements now made, and others about 1838,[21] must have succeeded. In 1837 White's *Directory* tells us that a weekly boat ran from Boroughbridge to York and Hull, while at Ripon, Keddy & Co's, William Scatchard's and the 'Ripon Fly Boats' all worked to that port. By the end of the 1840s vessels carrying 70 tons and drawing 4 ft 6 in were reaching Ripon.[22] In 1834 the company, encouraged by the Ouse trustees' efforts, had suggested setting up a £3,000 company to run a regular passenger and goods steamer between York and Boroughbridge, to connect with a daily fly-boat thence to Ripon.[23] The

* That is, the debt of £16,400 was divided into 164 £100 shares, to which £70 each was added to cover the interest arrears.

steamer seems to have been too ambitious a proposal, but fly-boats did run, as we have seen.

The coal traffic to Boroughbridge and Ripon was seriously affected soon after the Great North of England Railway from Darlington to York via Northallerton and Thirsk was opened on 4 January 1841, for it brought coal from the northern fields to compete down to York with that from the Aire & Calder and the Barnsley Canal, as the North Riding Canal had been planned to do forty years before. However, for 1841–4 the Aire & Calder sent on average 26,931 tons of their coal a year to the Ure.[24] For May–July 1841, coal traffic was as follows:

	No of vessels	Coal tonnage
To Boroughbridge	29	1,717½
To Ripon	43	2,626 [25]

In October 1843 competition was intensified when the railway arranged with 'the Durham Coal Masters . . . to convey Coal to York for . . . one farthing per Ton per Mile'.[26] The Aire & Calder's drawback on coal from their own navigation up the Ouse —they refused to give one on that from the Barnsley Canal— could not meet the case, and in July 1846 it was said by the Barnsley's manager that since the railway had opened the 'united efforts of the Coal Masters and Railway Company have so reduced the price of the Silkstone Coal . . . as almost entirely to destroy that Trade'[27] on the Ouse above Selby, compelling the Silkstone owners to look for new markets south of the Humber. In the same year it was said that the average Ure and Ripon tolls for the ten preceding years had been £2,013, and expenses £1,127, giving a net average profit of £886.[28] (*To continue the history of the Ure Navigation & Ripon Canal, turn to p. 450.*)

Knaresborough Canal Schemes

The river Nidd, entering the Ouse 8 miles above York and 2¼ below Linton lock, has always been unnavigable for trading craft. By the end of the eighteenth century the well-established flax-spinning industry of Knaresborough, which had just turned over from hand to power spinning, using water power, was over-crowding the steep river valley sides near the town, and was therefore tending to disperse. To keep it, cheap coal was needed, so that steam could be substituted for water power. But apart from one small low-grade mine, coal had to be brought 18 miles by road transport from the Garforth area east of Leeds, and more than doubled its pit head price in doing so.[29]

This was the strongest motive of the Knaresborough men who, at a meeting in February 1800, appointed a committee to get a plan and estimate for a canal to the Ouse or Ure, though they looked also for the carriage of lime for the land, and hoped to attract lead traffic from Greenhow Hill west of Pateley Bridge, higher up the Nidd, which was then taken by road to Ripon and the canal there. The committee commissioned William Chapman to do the survey and Ralph Burton to take the levels. They reported in July,[30] offering two alternatives. The committee recommended that from the Ure below Ellenthorpe shoals as the 'most eligible'. This line was to run between Boroughbridge and Aldborough, then east of Minskip and Staveley to ample springs at Keld, a point between Farnham and Scriven and some 1½ miles from Knaresborough. Such a canal, able to take Humber sloops, 8 miles long and with 12 locks would, Chapman estimated, cost £22,908. As it would leave the Ure just below Swale Nab, no tolls would be payable to the Ure Navigation. A cheaper and shorter line, 6 miles long with 9 locks, to take smaller craft 54 ft × 9 ft could, he said, be built to Keld from a point a mile above Boroughbridge for £13,189. This would have involved paying Ure tolls, and for this reason and because it would not take sloops was not recommended, though it was clearly favoured by Chapman. It was not possible to get nearer Knaresborough without 60 ft more lockage, but the committee suggested a railroad might bridge the distance.

The committee saw a saving of 3s 6d (17½p) a ton on 18s (90p) in merchandise from Hull, and 3s 6d (17½p) on coal, presumably from the Aire & Calder. For coal they looked more hopefully to the proposed North Riding Canal (see p. 350) from Boroughbridge to the Tees to supply them with Durham coal, as well as building stone; even more hopefully to the benefits of the suggested canal from the Swale by Coxwold to the junction of Holbeck with the river Rye and so by another vague scheme to the Derwent at Malton, which would connect also with the North Riding Canal.

However, their estimate of tolls from traffic to Knaresborough itself (not the neighbourhood) was only £1,075 p.a. Given the estimate, it was not attractive financially, while without access to Durham coal the saving in price was not very great.

It therefore fell. The end of the war in 1815, however, brought home to Knaresborough men that their town must have cheap coal or fail to develop, and in March 1818 a group of linen manufacturers and others met to appoint another promotion committee. These asked Telford to make a survey. He reported on 19 May, and produced two schemes on lines different from Chapman, one to the Ouse a mile below Linton lock, the other to the Wharfe a mile above Tadcaster. After investigation, however, these were withdrawn in favour of two other plans, one for a canal from Acaster Selby on the Ouse below Naburn lock and just above the Wharfe entrance past Tadcaster (with a branch to it) and Wetherby to near Little Ribston near the Nidd. Thence a double-track railroad would run to Knaresborough, crossing the Nidd on the way, and be continued by single-track to Pateley Bridge for the lead and stone traffic. The estimate was £92,864 for the canal and double-track railway, and £39,000 more for the single-track extension. Alternatively, a double-track railway could be built all the way from the Ouse to Knaresborough for £60,000.

Rather naturally the committee chose the railroad, but because it was found that additional tolls, including 2s (10p) on flax, were payable above the mouth of the Wharfe, the terminus was switched to near Bolton Percy on the lower part of the Wharfe itself. In this form, and with the possibility of using locomotives in mind ('locomotive engines might . . . do the work at less expense than horses') they put the proposition to the public in 1820. Though it promised a reduction in coal prices from 25s (£1·25) to 16s (80p) a chaldron* it probably seemed too great a sum to put at risk, and did not attract investors. This meant that Knaresborough failed to develop, a population of 6,656 in 1821 remaining at under 7,000 throughout the century.[31]

Tees Canal Schemes

In 1796, not content with promoting his Tyne and Wear schemes, Ralph Dodd was busy surveying along the shallow and winding Tees. At this time, we must remember, Stockton and Yarm, the only two places of any size on the lower Tees, had a combined population of about 6,000, Darlington of some 5,000. Middlesbrough was a hamlet. High Worsall was the limit of navigation, though craft usually worked to Yarm, 3¼ miles below. This small port, formerly with some trade in corn and Swaledale lead, was now declining before Stockton's competition. In 1812,

* About 25½ cwt.

however, the Yarm & Cleveland Shipping Co. was established with four schooners intended for the London trade, and some coastal business survived there until 1870.[32] Dodd's scheme[33] was for a canal roughly on Whitworth's and Brindley's old line (see p. 114) from Stockton by Darlington and Staindrop to Winston, but connected now by branches with the Wear near Durham, and with the Ure at Boroughbridge by way of Northallerton and Thirsk, thus providing a southern outlet for coal from the Staindrop area, and through inland navigation from the Aire & Calder to the Wear and maybe the Tyne.

He was an optimist, but the idea was picked up three years later, when George Atkinson, on the instructions of a meeting held in April 1800, surveyed for a narrow-boat North Riding Canal from the Ure near Boroughbridge past Northallerton and Cowton to Piercebridge on the Tees 5 miles west of Darlington, 42½ miles long, to cost £61,650, with branches in one direction to Bedale and Richmond, in the other to High Worsall, these branches, 27 miles long, being estimated at £45,703 more. For part of its course it made use of the Swale, and on the Bedale branch of Leeming lock, 'which will require some repairs', and the beck above it. Atkinson placed his junction with the Tees 'a little below the Warehouses formerly used for depositing goods brought from the port of Stockton for the purpose of being taken to the west country, by land carriage'. Traffic on the canal, he thought, would be mainly lime, coal, lead and stone, and he estimated an annual revenue of £14,558. County Durham coal, he reckoned, would by it supply Boroughbridge, Knaresborough and York, especially if George Dixon's tub-boat canal were built from the coalfield to the north bank of the Tees, whence a waggonway over the river would transfer the coal to the new canal. Atkinson suggested that the Worsall branch would 'prove a substitute for the canal so much wished for by the gentlemen of the counties of Durham and York about the year 1768'.[34] All that came of it was the Thirsk & Yarm Road Act of 1803.

These over-ambitious schemes fell away, but the need to provide better transport for the coalfield between Staindrop and Bishop Auckland remained.

In 1808 an Act[35] incorporated the Tees Navigation Company to improve the Tees below Stockton, and in 1810 the first major improvement was made when the 154 yd long Mandale cut was built by William Chapman to save 2½ miles of river passage. At the dinner held in September to celebrate it, the Recorder of Stockton

30. Map to illustrate waterway schemes in the North East

successfully moved a resolution that a committee should 'inquire into the practicability and advantage of a railway or canal from Stockton, by Darlington and Winston, for the easy and expeditious carriage of coals, lead, etc'. They reported favourably, and early in 1812 Rennie was asked to come and advise. When he could spare the time, he came, and favoured a canal, to cost £179,578 from Stockton to Winston, and £26,040 more for branches to Yarm, Croft Bridge near Darlington, and Piercebridge. The line was much the same as Whitworth's old one, but the cost was thought too high at a time of depression and high prices.

After peace had come, Rennie's report was again looked at, but by now the idea of a railway, or of a part-canal, part-rail line was taking hold. In 1816 Rennie estimated for a canal from Stockton to Darlington, and a railway thence to Winston, at £141,460, a good deal less than for a canal throughout. Prospects of Durham coal in turn led in early 1818 to vague proposals for a navigation from the Ure north by the Swale and Wiske to Great Smeaton not far from the Tees.[36] Then an alternative line was suggested, from Stockton to the river Gaunless near West Auckland, and George Leather was employed by Christopher Tennant of Stockton to survey it. He produced a line for this Stockton & Auckland Canal from the Tees at Portrack below Stockton by way of Whitton, Mordon and Bradbury to Shildon and the Gaunless at Evenwood, 29½ miles long, a broad canal with 50 locks, to cost £205,283, subsequently raised to £225,283.[37] Later a branch, 9¾ miles, to cost £35,812 more, was surveyed from Bradbury to near Durham. Tomlinson, in his history of the North Eastern Railway, has told the detailed story of the rivalry of the two lines, their gradual conversion from canal to railway projects, and their eventual building as the Stockton & Darlington and the Clarence Railways.[38]

In 1825 a plan of H. H. Price's was deposited, for a ship canal some 4¼ miles long from the lower end of the 1810 cut to a basin at Cargo Fleet, with entrance locks at either end. A modified scheme for a river cut without locks, authorized in 1828, was made unnecessary by railway development,[39] but the 725 yd Portrack cut was begun in 1829 and finished in 1831.

Middlesbrough–Redcar Ship Canal Project

In 1832 the port of Middlesbrough was finding it difficult to compete successfully with Sunderland and Hartlepool. In that year W. A. Brooks, engineer of the Tees Navigation Co., projected a new harbour at Redcar, connected to Middlesbrough by a ship canal.[40] After meetings in London had supported the scheme, in October 1834 subscriptions were invited. But the opposition was too great, and it was thrown out.[41]

River Wear: Durham Canal

The idea of a canal from the Tyne near Gateshead to the head of the navigable portion of the Wear leading to Sunderland and an extension upwards to Durham, was revived during the canal mania as a means of relieving pressure on the numerous tramroads as the output of the Durham collieries increased. William Chapman, mainly concerned with Newcastle–Carlisle–Maryport schemes, mentioned it as possible. J. Thompson, another contemporary canal pamphleteer, thought, however, that the need for it had passed: 'most of the collieries, near Chester,* are now working and vended on the river Wear. The port of Sunderland is in an improving state, and the carriage from thence to Durham not expensive; add to all this, the duty of one shilling per chalder on all coals shipped on the Tyne, payable to the Duke of Richmond.'[42]

However, the idea was picked up by a group of promoters at Durham, who employed the ever-hopeful Ralph Dodd. He reported in September 1796 to 'the subscribers for the Durham Canal Survey'. He proposed to make the Wear navigable from just above Durham down to Picktree below Chester-le-Street at the head of the navigable part, with 11 locks; a 7¼ mile canal thence by way of the Team valley to the Tyne, with 10 rising and 10 falling locks, and from this a branch 2⅞ miles long with 15 rising locks to Beamish. These navigations were all to take Humber keels. At Beamish there was to be a 395 ft inclined plane, and then a tub-boat canal for another 2⅞ miles on the level to the collieries at West Kyo near Stanley, this to take 7-ton boats carrying two tramroad waggons each. These would be transferred to the plane before being emptied into river craft at Beamish basin. His estimate was £77,586, of which £25,338 was for the Wear section, £29,604 for the Wear–Tyne Canal, and £22,644 for the West Kyo branch. Revenue he put at no less than £25,058 p.a., most of it from coal.[43]

The committee then employed Robert Whitworth to re-survey Dodd's lines. He reported[44] in January 1797, and accepted Dodd's

* Chester-le-Street.

plans with few alterations, the principal ones being to drop the summit level of the Wear–Tyne Canal to save two locks, bring the branch in at the summit to enable its water to be used in both directions, and use somewhat larger craft on the Kyo-inclined plane section to carry more waggons each. Dodd tended to produce serious under-estimates, but in this case Whitworth's figures were little different; £21,281 for the Wear (ending a little lower than Dodd's at Durham), £33,497 for the main canal, and £24,280 for the branch, totalling £79,058.

Phillips[45] says that probable dividends were calculated at over 20 per cent, but nevertheless the war situation deterred the promoters, and nothing was done. Eventually a tramroad was built about 1809 from Beamish South Moor to Fatfield on the Wear below Picktree.

In the autumn of 1802 Parliamentary notice was given of a Bill for the Durham Canal by a Durham solicitor, this to amend the Wear Act of 1759 and authorize a canal from Picktree to the Tyne, and a branch to West Kyo.[46] A year later a Gateshead solicitor gave notice of another Bill, this time only for a canal 'from the Rivulet of Team, near Beamish Iron Works . . . to the River Tyne, near Gateshead'.[47] In 1825 a Mr Dodd (perhaps B. R. Dodd), a surveyor, was called in by a Durham group to plan a canal thence to Sunderland,[48] but without result.

Tyne and Trans-Pennine Canal Schemes

In 1794, Ralph Dodd, that enthusiastic but rather unpractical engineer, had been surveying for the improvement of the river Wear when he was asked by a group of promoters to make a quick survey for a sea to sea canal from the Tyne to the Solway Firth.[49] He did a rapid reconnaissance of the country through which it might pass, and addressed meetings at Newcastle and Carlisle, at the former of which he said:

'The present local trade from hence to Carlisle, though very considerable, might be still improved; and when to that we add the immense Lead Trade, the vast quantity of Limestone, Coal, Iron, Iron-Ore, Stone, Timber, Hemp, Flax, Slate, Glass, &c. that will employ this Navigation, the ingenuous mind, charmed with national improvement, dwells upon the picture before it with astonishment and delight, and seems to wonder that a scheme so pregnant with blessings to society should never before have been carried into execution.'[50]

However, the meeting seems to have asked, not Dodd, but William Chapman[51] in association with William Jessop to survey and report in detail on a possible line, and Chapman had got his preliminary result ready before Dodd, working on his own and with little money to spend, had completed the first part of his. Dodd's pamphlet of June 1795[52] proposes a Stella–Hexham canal on the south side of the river, where, he said, most of the collieries were. It was to be only 27 ft wide at surface, though able to take keels 19½ ft wide, and therefore single-track, with three passing places in each mile. Water resistance would have been high, one feels, and traffic jams frequent. His estimate for 18 miles with 12 locks was £35,709, with a revenue of £9,926 p.a. mainly from coal, lead, limestone, lime and timber. He seems to have advocated ending the whole line at the Solway Firth beyond Carlisle, and sensibly enough proposed that the two ends of the sea to sea canal should be built before the centre section was attempted.

On 5 January 1795 William Chapman made a preliminary report[53] upon a canal to join the two seas for 'the Gentlemen delegated from the Committees of Northumberland and Cumberland', and between 26 June and 10 August followed with a more detailed study, issued in three parts. He saw the canal as starting in Newcastle on the north side of the Tyne, 205 ft above sea level (the lockage down to the river at the Ouseburn could be left, he thought, until the end), and running level to Hexham and Haydon Bridge, and so up the south Tyne and down the Irthling valleys to near Carlisle (where he disliked possible junctions with the Solway Firth), and on to sea level at Maryport. It would be a barge canal 93½ miles long, rising 240 ft from the 205 ft starting point at Newcastle to the summit which, he pointed out, would be 50 ft lower than that of the Leeds & Liverpool Canal, and then fall 445 ft. If necessary, a practicable branch could be built to Penrith.

He only incidentally referred to Dodd's plan, but thought the size of craft he proposed far too big for the waterway, his line difficult to build, and the angle of his banks impossibly steep. He defended his northern line against a possible alternative on the south side, but did envisage a local, coal-carrying part-river, part-canal line 9¼ miles long from Eltringham down to the mouth of the Derwent, where it would join the tideway, as practicable, though special narrow-beam keels would have to be built to use it.[54]

On 26 October 1795 William Jessop, to whom Chapman's report on the various schemes had been referred, reported. He agreed with Chapman that 'the line laid down by him on a high

G

level on the north side of Tyne, is, upon the whole, much preferable to any' on the south, and that one further north (such as
Jonathan Thompson had suggested[55] from North Shields by the
valley of the Pont to Hexham) was impracticable. He thought the
estimate not high at about £3,737 a mile, and that 'in a country
like this, abounding with heavy natural products, and capable of
great improvement in its agriculture and commercial advantages;
it is highly probable that it will be productive of sufficient emolu-
ment to those who may be adventurers in it'. He recommended a
broad canal usable by craft similar to those on the Yorkshire
navigations, about 65 ft × 14 ft, which could use the tideway, and
against a narrow canal, which did not save a great deal of money,
and whose boats, 'though convenient for the conveyance of
heavy articles, are not so for mercantile goods'.

He and Chapman jointly signed the estimates, which provided
for:

	£
205 ft of lockage at or a little above Newcastle	21,080
30¾ miles on the level past Hexham to Haydon Bridge	108,414
32 miles of canal to Carlisle, rising 240 ft and falling 374 ft	145,509
1,430 yd level branch from summit towards the Coal Fell	1,404
740 yd level branch into Carlisle	2,734
30¾ miles of canal from Carlisle to Maryport, fall 48 ft	75,926
95 miles	£355,067

They also gave an estimate for a canal from the Tyne at Stella,
5½ miles above Newcastle, to Hexham, 17⅛ miles long, with 10
locks rising 107 ft, at £69,081.[56]

In February 1796 an anonymous pamphlet,[57] seemingly written
by Chapman, set out estimates of traffic and suggested a revenue
of at least £30,659 p.a. There must have been criticism that the
trade between the continent, the west coast and Ireland could not
bear double transhipment costs, for the author said that smaller
seagoing vessels would be able to use the canal. In early April the
promotion committee had not been able to raise enough money
for the whole project to go forward, but had nearly enough for
the Newcastle–Haydon Bridge section, which they thought could
well be built first and would be viable by itself.[58] A Bill for this
canal, 31 miles long, which was described as communicating at
Haydon Bridge with a turnpike road through Haltwhistle to

Carlisle, was introduced in December 1796. Though supported by Newcastle and North Shields, it attracted a number of adverse petitions from landowners and others and got no further than second reading.[59]

Dodd's Stella–Hexham line had meanwhile been referred to the forcible and far from tactful Yorkshire engineer John Sutcliffe by the separate committee which had been formed to promote a line south of the Tyne. He tersely rejected Dodd's proposal: 'I cannot recommend you to pursue that plan as at all eligible.' He goes on to say that Dodd's ideas have prejudiced a south-side canal, and that, 'Mr Chapman and his friends have availed themselves of this imprudent survey, by representing this line as impracticable; and with a great deal of art and cunning have endeavoured to persuade the public that a good and useful line of canal cannot be made on the south of the Tyne.' He himself proposed a different Stella–Hexham line 44 ft at surface and 6 ft deep, to take 50–60 ton craft, but not existing keels, 17 miles long, with 18 locks, at a cost of almost £90,000. His estimate of revenue was £23,460 and net yield £17,595.[60] He followed this up with a report on such a canal's extension to Haydon Bridge 'and from thence to the West Sea, whenever circumstances shall render it expedient', in which he proposed a canal some 29 miles long with 64 ft of lockage at a cost of some £72,000, or about £162,000 through from Stella to Haydon Bridge. He also reported with a detailed estimate upon the north side line, and threw in personal attacks on Dodd, Chapman and Jessop, especially the last named.[61]

Finally, in spite of the new unfavourable financial climate, Robert Whitworth was called in to look over Sutcliffe's proposals. He agreed early in 1797 that they were practicable, though the line:

'is a rugged one; I never before saw a good line like it; yet so far as I can discover, I believe it is the best the country affords: It is certainly practicable, and I have no doubt but that a good and useful canal may be made (with some variation) upon it; but it will be exceedingly expensive: I am, however, told the trade that will come upon this canal will fully answer that expence, even were it twice as much.'

He agreed that Sutcliffe's estimating was good, and that his line only needed minor changes, though he thought the canal should be carried below Stella to the mouth of the Derwent to get a better river navigation. Asked later whether he preferred the south or north lines, he replied: 'the line upon the south side has certainly very much the advantage, both in point of tonnage, and expence and safety in the execution'.[62] About this time, the committee of the north line seem to have decided to connect the head of their canal at Newcastle with the Tyne by a counter-balanced inclined plane having a 200 ft fall, a decision Whitworth approved, though on balance he favoured the south line.

But by now money had become too tight, and costs were rising too fast, for men to feel encouraged to speculate; all such projects were laid aside. The Haydon Bridge scheme was briefly revived in 1802, and Chapman also had his anonymous pamphlet of 1796 reprinted with a new introduction, in which he repeated the commercial advantages of a sea to sea canal, raised the former estimate to £400,000, pressed the military advantages of having the canal by which to send troops and stores either way across England in case of a French attack on Ireland or on the east coast, suggested the army might help to build it, and that a government grant might be obtained, as had been done for the Forth & Clyde.[63] In 1810 again, a prospectus appeared for the Newcastle & Hexham Canal[64] 'designed to be farther extended by way of the City of Carlisle to the West Sea'. It had been surveyed by Barrodall Robert Dodd, perhaps Ralph Dodd's son.[65] A south-side canal 17¼ miles long from a little above Gateshead to Hexham was proposed to take specially built small keels 70 ft × 15 ft, at a cost of £105,800. The revenue estimate was £22,267 p.a. It created little interest. Neither did a plan of the following year to build a horse railway along the south side of the Tyne to serve the mining country, with a possible extension to Carlisle.

The rest of the story is part of the history of the Carlisle Canal.[66]

PART THREE—1845-1972

CHAPTER XVI

To Bartholomew and Beyond

DURING the railway mania four schemes were proposed for railways to Goole. After a battle with Hudson, one was authorized in 1845, the Wakefield, Pontefract & Goole, half the capital being subscribed by the Manchester & Leeds, with whom the company amalgamated in 1847 to become the Lancashire & Yorkshire Railway. General traffic to Goole began on 1 April 1848,[1] coal shipments in August. The canal passenger service probably ended with the railway's opening, though the *Eagle* packet, running between Goole and Hull, was not taken off until 1857.

Following the policy decided upon in 1844, the Aire & Calder worked amicably with the railway on the basis of agreements made while the Bill was in Parliament. These provided for the Aire & Calder to build lines, with station, dock, wharves and sheds, within the dock estate, and for the Wakefield, Pontefract & Goole to pay 7 per cent on the outlay. By 1849 the navigation company had spent £77,732 on railway works at Goole, including the new Railway dock (1848), and had also improved and cheapened their tugging service to the sea. A long-standing dispute about the agreement's terms was settled in 1855, when the Lancashire & Yorkshire Railway agreed to pay £1,300 p.a. rent and take liability for repairs and renewals of railway works. By 1857, however, the Aire & Calder's original idea of providing all railway facilities against payment of interest on capital expended had proved unworkable, and was replaced by a straight 1,000 year lease; thenceforward both waterborne and railborne traffic contributed to the development of the port.

In 1846 the Aire & Calder wisely made a traffic agreement with the Manchester & Leeds Railway, followed by others (now with the Lancashire & Yorkshire Railway) in 1848, 1850 and 1853. In spite of their realistic attitude, the immediate consequence of the Lancashire & Yorkshire Railway's coming to Goole was to knock one-third off waterway toll receipts: the £103,734 of 1850–1* had become £66,115 by 1856, after which various counter moves restored the figure to £79,287 in 1862. Dividends, £60,000 in 1850, were £40,500 in 1862. The railway gained much profitable merchandise business, and slowly eroded the staple trades of corn and coal: not so much by winning existing tonnages as by taking natural increases and by keeping tolls low. At that time the basic business of the navigation was corn from Lincolnshire and the east coast to the great corn markets of Wakefield and Leeds, and coal as back carriage: 'the prosperity of the Navigation is dependent on these two staple articles'.[2] In fact, the grain trade was to slip away, partly for causes then unforeseen, but that in coal was to grow enormously. Here are comparative figures for the Goole Canal section:

	Coal tons	Stone & Lime† tons	Corn tons	Merchandise tons	Total tons
1845	313,449	129,675	126,357	131,294	700,775
1855	286,202	169,647	88,778	66,854	611,481

† And 'other minerals'.

Other traffic agreements‡ followed with the York & North Midland, soon to be part of the North Eastern Railway.

In 1851 Joseph Priestley retired, being succeeded by John Hall. The Wakefield office was closed and the company's headquarters transferred to Leeds. Two years later their engineer T. H. Bartholomew, brother of Charles of the Don Navigation and the South Yorkshire Railway, died, to be succeeded by his son William Hamond, whose office moved from Lake lock, now to be closed, to Leeds also. The younger Bartholomew, born in January 1831, was then twenty-two. A traffic manager, John Hargreaves, was also appointed to watch business, especially relations with other companies.

He was needed, for in 1855, after long negotiations with the Lancashire & Yorkshire and North Eastern Railways for traffic agreement revisions, the Aire & Calder chose independence, 'adopting such a system of moderately low rates, as will give to all kinds of traffic access to the water', though this might lead to 'a severe struggle with the Railways'.[3] It did, though they were to some extent protected by a traffic agreement with the Calder &

---

* The Aire & Calder's financial year began on 1 July of the year quoted.

‡ Such agreements usually allocated traffic between the parties. Should one carry more than its allocation, a payment was made on an agreed scale to the other.

Hebble, and their lease of the Barnsley Canal from 1 December 1854, which secured that line's coal trade, and with it, they hoped, the back carriage trade in corn.

In September 1855 heavy cuts had to be made in tolls and carrying rates—the bale goods rate was halved—to meet North Eastern Railway competition. Price-cutting against each other by such powerful companies was not sensible; it reduced Aire & Calder toll revenue for 1856 to £66,115, against £108,854 ten years before. Later in the year a new agreement was reached with the North Eastern Railway, tolls and freight rates then being raised.

The Aire & Calder was a leader of opposition to railways obtaining advantages canals did not have. Out of their objections to the 1844 amalgamation Bill of the York & North Midland and the Hull & Selby Railways, which contained powers to vary tolls on different parts of the line, came meetings of canal company representatives, called at Aire & Calder invitation. In 1844 these introduced, and in 1845 got through, a general Bill to enable canals to vary tolls, together with the Canal Carriers' Act, which cleared up doubts whether canal companies could legally carry. In 1855 the company again called a meeting to watch public and private Bills, 'and also to consider any measures for the promotion of the Canal interest'.[4] It resulted in Col. J. G. Smyth of the Aire & Calder becoming chairman of the United Body of Canal Proprietors, out of which the Canal Association was born on 18 June 1855, with Smyth as chairman and Thomas Wilson, auditor of the Aire & Calder, as secretary. Later, W. T. Spencer Stanhope of the Aire & Calder was to become chairman of the Association, so maintaining the navigation's close link with it.

In 1855, faced with the lease of the Rochdale Canal by four railway companies,[5] and the raising of the bale goods toll from 1d to 4d maximum, so killing the traffic, the Aire & Calder joined the Bridgewater trustees in seeking counsel's opinion upon its legality. It was unhelpful, for the railways had found a loophole in the law. Under the Canal Carriers' Act, canal companies were allowed to lease others, and each of the railways concerned had become the owner of a canal company before preventive legislation had been passed: these companies were the legal lessors. However, after a deputation headed by the Aire & Calder had seen the Board of Trade, the practice was temporarily stopped by a clause in the Cheap Trains Act of 1858,[6] pending the permanent legislation that followed.

Meanwhile the Aire & Calder tried to get a carrying trade to Manchester re-established by way of the narrow-boat Huddersfield Canal. Thoughtfully, they had had a maximum toll of 1d on bale goods included in the 1847 Act which had transferred the canal to London & North Western Railway control. They leased a warehouse at Manchester, and appointed an agent; 14 more narrow boats and horses were bought, and a man engaged to superintend transhipment at Huddersfield. But the experiment did not last long. Seriously hindered by the closing of Standedge tunnel in February 1857 for some weeks for what the Aire & Calder thought were unnecessary repairs, the boats were taken off, and the Manchester office closed in October. Thereafter the Calder carrying trade did not extend beyond Halifax and Huddersfield.

The Aire & Calder had also been developing its own waterway system. In 1847 they had considered a lease of the Calder & Hebble, in 1852 they and the Leeds & Liverpool company had agreed to make a yearly allowance to the Bradford Canal[7] lessees in exchange for a 7 year restriction on toll increases and other concessions, and in 1854 the Aire & Calder had leased the Barnsley Canal. Now they themselves were to receive a railway offer. Early in 1856 H. S. Thompson, chairman of the North Eastern Railway, suggested a lease of the Aire & Calder for 21 years to the North Eastern and Lancashire & Yorkshire Railways jointly, for £45,000 p.a. (the current dividend), and 4 per cent interest on the £420,000 of debt, with an undertaking to apply after a period of years for an amalgamation Act. The Aire & Calder were willing to negotiate, subject to their obligation to other companies, and meanwhile made a useful temporary traffic agreement that considerably helped their corn and merchandise receipts. Talks lasted until early 1858, when, after agreement had been reached on most points, the two railways differed with one another, the Lancashire & Yorkshire then withdrawing. The North Eastern were willing to take a lease alone, but now Aire & Calder shareholders began to object, and negotiations ended. They left the navigation company in a better trading position.

Goole was now competing not only with Hull but with several other ports, some railway-developed, like Hartlepool and Grimbsy, some older, like Newcastle. To hold its own, the Aire & Calder thought, Goole must have foreign as well as coasting trade. In 1835–9 the company-backed Goole Steam Navigation Company had failed to get a Hamburg service started.[8] Then in 1854 two Clyde-built steamers were put into service, to be withdrawn almost at once as unsuccessful and transferred to the government for Crimean War use. That year, the Aire & Calder's board approved the setting up of the Goole Steam Shipping Co to build ships for the continental trade. Eleven directors subscribed £21,500, the company the rest. Two steamers were built, but again the venture collapsed, the ships being sold in 1856. The Aire & Calder then limited themselves to giving financial support by way of loans or subsidy to independent concerns who were trying to maintain a service, though as part of this support they in 1862 authorized the lengthening of the Steamship (Ouse) lock from 210 ft to 263 ft, and its conversion to hydraulic working. At the end of 1865, however, the position was so precarious that they reformed the Goole Shipping Co, which with their support and later that of the Lancashire & Yorkshire Railway thereafter continued in being alongside other services from the port,[9] competing with 'the Steam Ships of the Manchester Sheffield and Lincolnshire Railway Co,* and with the Liverpool and Continental Traders'.[10]

The Aire & Calder board considered the Calder & Hebble's management to be supine. In August 1861 they ordered a report on the coal, corn and stone trades preparatory to a meeting, but having learned from it some flaws in their own practice, they first made some changes, such as equalizing the tolls on coal from the Barnsley Canal to a flat rate of 1s 4d (6½p) per ton to Goole whatever the distance from the colliery. Pits on the Barnsley line were thus put on a near equality with those on the Aire & Calder itself. In June 1863 they then wrote to criticize the Calder & Hebble's condition, and nine months later sent a deputation to urge how inadvisable was the Calder & Hebble's current proposal to raise coal tolls (lowered six months earlier) from ½d to ¾d a ton-mile, in view of the current low railway rates. The meeting took place later in the year, and after the Aire & Calder had urged reductions in coal and corn tolls, the Calder & Hebble replied that this would cause them serious loss 'as a separate and independent concern'; they then suggested 'an union of the two interests would be desirable',[11] and proposed a lease. The Aire & Calder, considering it important to control traffic west of Wakefield and prevent it falling into railway hands, offered 6½ per cent, but eventually agreed to the Calder & Hebble's demand for a 21 year lease at a sum equivalent to an 8 per cent dividend, this to be raised to 8½ per cent should the lease be made perpetual.[12]

* From Grimsby.

Their leases of the Calder & Hebble and the Barnsley both cost the Aire & Calder money. The justification was, however, the maintenance of their own tolls by preserving the traffic of the weaker companies. As the 1865 report said, the Aire & Calder tolls on Calder & Hebble traffic yielded over £20,000, and on Barnsley traffic over £7,000, together nearly a third of the whole. Later, as competition stabilized and rates understandings with the railways came normally to govern charges, this argument became less important, and, as we shall see, the Calder & Hebble lease was relinquished.

The Bradford Canal was unpopular locally for health reasons, unprofitable, and in danger of railway purchase. In July 1865 a deputation arrived to ask for help in getting a court order to abate pollution reversed, and in obtaining a future supply of water. Nevertheless, the canal had to close in 1867, but it reopened in 1873. The Aire & Calder then had their own wharf on it. In 1877 the Leeds & Liverpool and Aire & Calder companies thought the canal important enough to be jointly bought and managed, the transfer Act being passed in the following year.

In 1865 Bartholomew proposed what he called the Leeds Extension Canal, to carry the navigation above Leeds bridge to Armley mills. This had been put forward in 1837 by an independent Leeds & Armley Navigation Company, but the scheme had come to nothing. Later, we may remember, the Leeds & Liverpool company had built a branch from their canal through Arches lock to the river above Leeds bridge, this stretch being thereafter used for about half a mile.[13]

Steam tugs had been used on the Aire & Calder since 1831, and by 1855 two-thirds of the company's own carrying mileage was steam-hauled. In 1852 the board at Bartholomew's suggestion authorized a fly-boat to be experimentally fitted with an engine and propeller to convert her to a cargo-carrying tug which, if successful, might 'lead to a cheaper mode of Haling, not unattended with greater speed'.[14] The experiment was considered successful in both its aspects: further cargo-carrying tugs were authorized mainly for merchandise traffic, and in 1856 a minerals tug. In 1857 two public tugs were put on the Wakefield–Goole run to haul bye-traders' boats on a daily trip each way. Bartholomew reported to the annual meeting that year that though a good deal of prejudice had to be overcome, in-coming heavily-laden corn vessels especially had used the tugging service, which had moderated the horse towers' demands, 'whose charges previously in cases of a large influx of vessels into Goole, were most exorbitantly advanced, very Commonly as much as 100 Per Cent'. Indeed, two years earlier Ann Asquith had asked for a rent reduction 'in consequence of her employment as a Haler being superseded by the use of the Screw Tug'.[15] The cost of haulage per boat per mile, 6·64d in 1854, had by 1858 been reduced to 2·56d. The result of moderate charges and regular delivery, the company a little prematurely announced in 1857, the 'confession of the Railway Co, that it had entirely abandoned the Goods traffic between Leeds and Hull'.[16]

Steam tugging, both of company's and bye-traders' craft, was of proved value. Then, in the 1859 report, shareholders were told that Pollington, the only main line single lock below Castleford, was to be extended to three times its length, with intermediate gates. The object, said the report, was not just to speed up traffic:

'the full benefits and economy of Steam Traffic can only be realized by enabling a larger class of Vessels to proceed with their Cargoes as far as possible up the navigation and by means of increased facilities for the passage of trains of Boats drawn by a Tug. By the enlargement of one more Lock, that at Whitley, Vessels capable of carrying from 150 to 250 Tons, propelled by Steam, would be able to reach the Newton Collieries, and by another lock being lengthened they would be able to pass up the Navigation for 27 miles and load at the Collieries of Kippax, Allerton, Popplehole and Whitwood—thus securing increased economy of transit and avoiding the injurious breakage which attends the transhipment of Coal'

at Goole or Hull. Such locks, it was estimated, would save a tugged train of six vessels one to two hours at each.

Pollington lock, now 206 ft long, the extension being 22 ft wide, reopened in October 1860. The lengthening of Whitley followed in 1861, then Bulholme; then Ferrybridge flood lock in 1864. Castleford flood lock followed in 1867, so completing lock extensions from Goole to Castleford. This work done, the lengths of tugged trains was increased from six or seven to nine or ten, and on one occasion to thirteen or more craft. To help efficient working, hydraulic cranes were installed at Leeds to speed up fly-boat handling, and in 1861 an agreement was made with a a telegraph company for free transmission of company messages in return for permission to erect wires along the navigation.

At the board meeting on 20 December 1861 we get a historic proposal, born out of steam haulage of keel trains and lock lengthening, and immediately out of representations reported to the board that the Steamship lock at Goole was too small and slow in working for the steamer trade, and the costs of carrying coal on the navigation too high to continue to compete with that hauled by rail. Bartholomew therefore proposed an expenditure of £13,302, to include lengthening the ship lock and fitting it for hydraulic-powered operation, but also:

	£
'For building 3 sets of Iron Boats in compartments, each carrying 25 tons	3,300
For erecting a Hoist capable of raising and discharging one of these compartments	2,500
For further Hydraulic Machinery to work the Hoist generally	1,720'

His plans were referred to a sub-committee, who on 14 January 1862 authorized Bartholomew to extend and rebuild the Steamship (Ouse) lock, and to contract with Sir William Armstrong & Co for hydraulic power for the gates, with provision for extending this later to work a hoist for coal transhipment. Finally, he could contract with the newly-established firm of Hudswell & Clarke for one train of iron boats at a cost not exceeding £1,200. Three weeks later, on 7 February 1862, he was granted his patent No 330.

His description in the patent is of a compound articulated vessel made up of separate compartment boats close-coupled, yet able to change direction, with a bow compartment in front and a steering compartment at the rear. The

'steering of the compound vessel is . . . to a great extent effected by chains or other connections, which pass along each side of the compound vessel from stem to stern; they are each attached at one end to one of the terminal barges, and at the other they are passed round a capstan or windlass at the other extremity of the compound vessel, and the chains or connections are passed through suitable guides on each of the intermediate barges. By turning the capstan or windlass, the chain on one side of the compound vessel is wound up, and the chain on the other side is slacked out to a corresponding extent, and thus the compound vessel is drawn into a curved form, each barge pivoting about its projecting cutwater.'

He ended: 'The barge (by preference one of the terminal ones) may, if desired, be fitted with propelling apparatus.' Bartholomew's accompanying drawing shows a train of six compartment boats, headed by a bow-shaped boat much bigger than the false bow later used, and at the rear a round-bowed steam tug fitted with a windlass and a rudder.

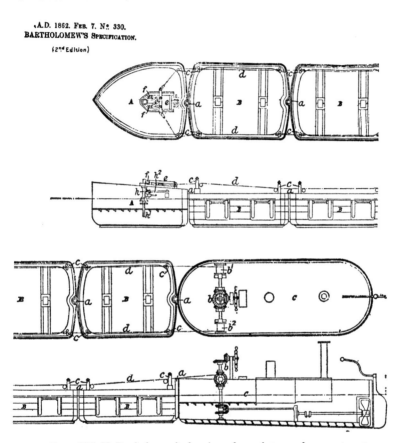

31. Part of W. H. Bartholomew's drawing of a push-tug and compartment boat train, accompanying his patent of 1862

What Bartholomew thought basic to his invention was, therefore, the idea of an articulated vessel made up of smaller, 20 ft × 15 ft, units, which could be steered from the front, back or centre, by tightening up wire ropes along one side and loosening them along the other, as well as by a rudder. He himself called it a steam train, and the company described compartment boats as 'a combination of Vessel and Railway Waggon'.[17] We may notice that in the specification Bartholomew provided his compartment boats with watertight doors in the side or bottom for discharging their cargoes (that is, he provided for the craft being tipped should it prove impossible to invert them in the hoist).

Compartment boats* were a development of tub-boats, then commonly operated in trains on such canals as the Shropshire.[18] Primitive forms of tipping boats, for instance at Coalisland basin at the end of the Tyrone Canal,[19] were also known. Steering by hauling on or slackening cables running the length of the train was probably quite new: push-towing, or propelling a barge-train from the back, was known at the time in America, but seemingly not in Europe. Bartholomew soon dropped both, but push-towing has in our own day returned again to Bartholomew's Aire & Calder where it was born.

On 1 August 1864 the annual shareholders' meeting was told that, 'The Experimental Train Boat propelled by Steam, constructed in Compartments . . . and the Hydraulic Hoist at Goole . . . are both completed and promise to answer effectively.' Commercial working began in 1865, the boats carrying and transhipping 1,144 tons in the first quarter and 2,625 in the second. During the year Bartholomew reported that a 7-boat train carrying 168 tons could do 5 m.p.h. on the river and 3 on the canal. Capacity was now increased from 25 to 30 tons; by 1866, 35-tonners were being run and, later, 40-tonners; regular orders for boats followed. In 1867 a second tug was working. Self-acting cylinders controlling the wire ropes were now provided on the push-tug to give power steering.

In 1871 the company awarded Bartholomew £1,000 plus £220 for his expenditure on models. In exchange they were to have these, and the right to use his patent, though he might use it elsewhere for any purpose not prejudicial to them. From the beginning of 1876, Thomas Wilson having retired, he became general manager as well as engineer, at £1,500 p.a.

I do not know when push-towing ended. W. H. Bailey in 1890[20] describes it as if it were the only system then in use, and says up to 12 boats were pushed. Bartholomew himself in his evidence to the Royal Commission in 1906, describes it as still used in flood times.[21] Probably some years before 1890, Bartholomew had

* Compartment boats are often called 'pans' at and near Goole, and 'Tom Puddings' higher up the navigation.

H

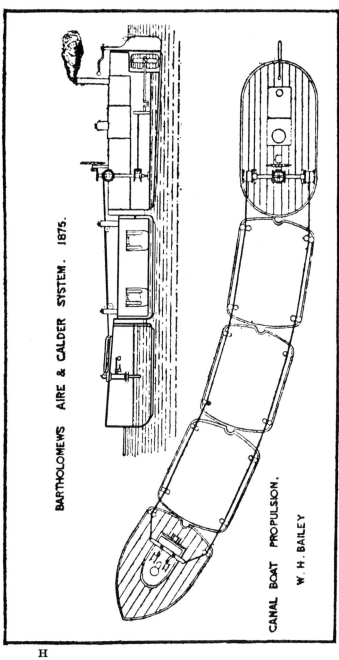

BARTHOLOMEWS AIRE & CALDER SYSTEM. 1875.

CANAL BOAT PROPULSION.

W. H. BAILEY

THE BARTHOLOMEW SYSTEM, AIRE AND CALDER CANAL.

32. The Bartholomew system at work (*above*) side view; (*below*) taking a corner

realized that he could lengthen his train of boats by putting a tug at the head, a false bow behind it and ahead of the first boat, and fitting each craft with spring-loaded buffers at one end. A train could then be towed so that it would curve round a bend and then straighten without the need for steering. The smaller false bow now used was so lashed that it tilted upwards, easing the tug's propeller stream beneath the leading boats. These were more lightly loaded than the rest of the train, and so lashed that they were slightly raised in the water with the same purpose as the false bow. When the train ran light, the false bow was pushed in front of the tug; if behind, it would have ridden deeper than the empty compartments. Trains of up to 30, occasionally as many as 40, boats were now run.

Bartholomew's innovations proved themselves. At first, tonnage carried by the steam trains rose only slowly; the 9,145 tons of 1865 were 15,913 in 1868 and still only 38,832 tons in 1871, though from 1869 onwards small quantities of sacked grain and merchandise were carried as return cargo. Here are a few figures of compartment boat growth:

Year	Coal tons	Other tons	Total tons	Number of boats
1877	53,422	9,422	62,844	125
1888	273,717	18,352	292,069	270
1897	473,061	18,256	491,317	401

The compartment boat experiment had also been highly profitable; in 1879 Bartholomew reported that, after interest on capital and depreciation, it was yielding $10\frac{3}{4}$ per cent.

Other ideas to improve navigation had meanwhile been approved. An Aire & Calder request to Trinity House, Hull, in 1861 obtained the lighting of Whitton Sand in the Humber. In 1862 Bartholomew got board consent to the deepening of Goole reach of the Ouse by 3 ft to take bigger steamers. This ran into opposition from the Ouse trustees at York, who thought their authority was being questioned, but Bartholomew and his board got their approval in 1863 to a scheme jointly prepared by himself and Thomas Page, the trustees' engineer. The work was done in 1864, and enabled the tonnage of foreign-going vessels using Goole to rise from 62,244 in 1864 to 90,981 in 1866, in addition to a steady 100,000 tons or so of coastwise traffic less affected by river depth.

Lock lengthening between Goole and Castleford having been

finished in 1867, Woodnook lower lock on the Wakefield line was then lengthened and the upper eliminated by raising the banks of Woodnook cut. By about 1869 lock extensions had been completed to Wakefield,* by 1873 to Leeds.† Finally, the locks on the Selby line—Bank Dole, Beal, Haddlesey Flood and Selby, were rebuilt between 1885 and 1886 to take craft 78 ft 6 in × 16 ft 6 in and drawing 6 ft.

In 1868 the company decided that Goole should be supplemented by a permanent stake in Hull. They therefore talked to their old enemies the Hull Dock Company, agreeing in December to subscribe for £10,000 worth of shares. In 1871 the Aire & Calder bought premises in Hull for their carrying trade. At the end of the sixties Bartholomew discussed improvements to the Humber below Hull with the engineers of the dock company and the Manchester, Sheffield & Lincolnshire Railway. Their proposals were then sent to the Humber Conservancy Commissioners, who had been set up in 1852. In 1871 these obtained powers to improve the estuary and levy tolls, and at once imposed 1d a ton toll on shipping using the river to finance improvements. Three years later the Aire & Calder started to build the wooden Blacktoft jetty,‡ near the Humber and Ouse confluence, where vessels could moor while waiting for the tide.

The North Eastern Railway had in 1863 promoted the Hull & Doncaster line from the Hull–Selby line via Goole to Thorne to join the South Yorkshire Railway. It was opened in 1869, and gave the Manchester, Sheffield & Lincolnshire Railway, who had taken over the South Yorkshire, direct access both to Goole and Hull. Coal rates from the South Yorkshire field were reduced, and so pressure came on the Aire & Calder's. However, thanks to Bartholomew, coal traffic was increasing, helped by the company's policy of building colliery loading basins against guarantees of annual tonnages, improving facilities at Stanley basin, and increasing the Barnsley Canal's water resources. From 1870 we notice the M.S. & L.R.'s expanding Grimsby being used as an import port for the Aire & Calder, when a timber rate thence to Rochdale and Manchester was agreed.

Let us now quickly look at changes in traffic during the twenty or so years before 1870. In 1852, 1,119,650 quarters of grain

* This had involved buying Wakefield mills for £27,000 in 1868.
† Above Castleford to Leeds, Kippax, Leamonroyd, Woodlesford, Fishpond, Knostrop Fall and Leeds; to Wakefield, Woodnook, Kings Road, Birkwood and Broad Reach Flood.
‡ Work on rebuilding the jetty in reinforced concrete began in 1954.

(roughly, 5 quarters to the ton) had been carried on the Aire & Calder. It had come from almost every east coast port: from London, Maldon and Colchester, Woodbridge, Ipswich and Lowestoft, Yarmouth and King's Lynn, Wisbech, Boston and Louth; from the navigations of the Hull River and the Ancholme: the Trent, Fossdyke and Witham, the Derwent and the Yorkshire Ouse, and included nearly 277,000 quarters of unattributed grain probably from the continent. By 1870 only 538,732 quarters entered. The growth of overseas, mostly American, imports caused the change. These mainly came into Liverpool, to be distributed eastwards by the Pennine waterways and railways.

Coal shipped from collieries on the Calder & Hebble, Barnsley and Aire & Calder, and passing Castleford, more than doubled between 1851 and 1870:

	1851 tons	1860 tons	1870 tons
Calder & Hebble	81,648	69,116	66,606
Barnsley Canal	97,346	130,367	179,220
Calder below Wakefield	303,745	377,580	460,505
Aire	111,969	420,814	496,245
	594,708*	997,877*	1,202,576*

* The figures apparently only include coal passing Castleford going downstream until in 1860 upstream traffic is added. There are other small discrepancies, and the figures should be treated as guides rather than accurate totals.

Coal distribution figures show, as we might expect, much more coal being sent to Goole and Hull; much more also used on the Aire & Calder itself, or sent to neighbouring waterways, the Leeds & Liverpool, Calder & Hebble, Ouse above Selby, and those off the Humber. Less, however, went up the Derwent and the Trent, much less down the east coast. This traffic was falling away in face of railway attack, in absolute figures and even more in relation to the total trade.

Of the two other main classifications, that of minerals other than coal stayed steady: 256,290 tons in 1852 had become 308,511 tons in 1870. But the other, merchandise and imported timber, showed a large increase, from 104,409 tons in 1852 to 156,103 in 1860 and 192,890 in 1870. The Aire & Calder was in fact gaining merchandise traffic from its competitors.

As the seventies began, the company was still the leader among British canal concerns, especially against renewed railway efforts at control, notably the sale of the Bridgewater canals.[22] They pressed a policy of:

'securing to the Public the advantages of free competition between Railways and Canals, either by making the Companies independent of Railway influence or by securing to the Public the free use of all Canals connected with Railways at low rates of Toll with all necessary facilities for the interchange of Traffic and by prohibiting the making of all Traffic Arrangements between Railways and Canals without the sanction of a Public Department'.[23]

Considering the series of traffic agreements with railway companies the Aire & Calder had themselves sought and operated during the previous twenty-four years, we may take the last sentiment with a pinch of salt. Perhaps this thirst for competition did not look as hopeful to smaller concerns as it did in Yorkshire, for the Aire & Calder 'failed in their attempts to continue the whole of the Independent Canals in common action'[24] in giving evidence before the Joint Committee on Railway & Canal Amalgamations, though the committee accepted some of their argument, which was embodied in the Railway & Canal Traffic Act 1873, with its machinery for fixing through tolls.

Ironically, in 1873 Sir Edward Watkin, on behalf of the railway-influenced Bridgewater Navigation Company, proposed a joint purchase of the Rochdale Canal by the B.N.C. and the A. & C., with an agreement for through rates and traffic interchange. The two companies talked, but nothing came of it.[25]

While compartment boats were developing, the rest of the carrying trade continued steadily. It worked at an average loss of some £5,000 p.a., which was of course much more than balanced by the tolls received. Craft operated remained around 100, and the tonnage carried at about 250,000. The company also gave some financial support to independent carriers, for instance £1,800 in 1875 to William Jackson & Sons to buy the fleet of the Rochdale Canal railway lessees, and continue the trade. The seventies saw expansion: more boats built for the growing Hull and Leeds traffic, hydraulic cranes put in at Leeds and Goole, wharf accommodation taken at Huddersfield and Bradford, and in 1878 the old Dewsbury cut on the Calder & Hebble finally bought and the Savile Town depot developed (see p. 392) 'to improve their connection with the town and trade of Dewsbury'.[26]

The fifties had been critical for Goole, but by the early sixties overseas trade was expanding well, and by the seventies coastal also. So was the town itself. At first, the company had done or controlled everything important. Then they shared authority with an elected Board of Guardians, until in 1875 a Local Board was set up, which in 1894 was replaced by an Urban District Council. Goole had grown up. The population, 2,321 in 1831, had by 1871 reached 8,200. It was to be 11,187 in 1881 and 15,617 in 1901.[27] In 1933 Goole became a municipal borough.

In 1880 Bartholomew became chairman of the Goole Steam Shipping Co, whose fortunes had so improved in the seventies that by 1874 it had declared a dividend of 23¾ per cent, before running into difficult competition in the short sea trades. He re-built the company, which in 1882 was advertising services to Rotterdam, Antwerp, Ghent and Dunkirk with 9 ships. These connected at Goole with the Lancashire & Yorkshire Railway and the Aire & Calder, 'whose Trains and Fly Boats run alongside the Steamers, from which the merchandise can be transhipped direct'.[28]

Bartholomew's responsibilities at Goole—once called 'Bartholomew's Vineyard' by a Parliamentary lawyer wit—including the building of the Aldam* dock and the Victoria entrance lock, 500 ft × 47 ft, opened respectively in 1881 and 1888. The impetus thus given to the port's trade led in time to the completion of the Railway Extension dock† in 1891 and the widening of its entrance. In 1884 a major improvement was authorized by the Ouse (Lower) Improvement Act,[29] whereby the Aire & Calder company, who had already spent £22,500 on improving the Lower Ouse and building Blacktoft jetty without power to levy tolls, replaced York corporation as conservators of the 9½ mile stretch of the river between the railway bridge just above Goole and Trent Falls, and were empowered to improve it, by dredging, building training walls and realigning the bends, charge Ouse tolls, except upon craft to or from the Dutch River or Stainforth & Keadby Canal, and provide and license tugs. Also to create £950,000 debenture stock, partly to replace existing debts. The Ouse lower improvement cost £250,000, and enabled bigger ships to reach Goole. In 1907 the Humber Conservancy Board replaced the older commissioners and were given greater control over the river below Trent Falls.

In the late seventies, as a result of inter-railway price cutting to Hull between the North Eastern and the Manchester, Sheffield &

---

* William Aldam (1813–90) had been from 1853 until his death chairman of the company. He was succeeded by Sir Walter Spencer Stanhope (1827–1912).
† Called the Stanhope dock from 1906.

Lincolnshire Railways, the Aire & Calder too had to reduce rates on Barnsley coal. In 1885, too, the opening of the Hull & Barnsley Railway and of the Alexandra dock at Hull caused another outbreak of rate cutting until 1893. In 1886 grain and merchandise tolls from west coast ports had also to be cut against railway competition.

In 1881 Bartholomew went to America to inspect 'the Canal system there and . . . Machinery and other Appliances applicable to the uses of the Navigation'.[30] Two years later he led Goole's successful opposition to a railway bridge over the Humber, promoted by Hull interests, which, he thought, if built would almost extinguish Goole. Another Humber bridge Bill failed in 1932, and only now is it likely to become a reality. In 1884 and 1885 Pollington lock was widened and lengthened; the work cost nearly £10,000, and was followed by further extensions to Bulholme, Whitley, Ferrybridge, and others. However, the lock enlargement programme the company had been carrying out on the Calder & Hebble was stopped and the lease allowed to expire at the end of 1885. In 1887, Bartholomew said, the Aire & Calder took craft up to 187 tons, carriers doing only one-tenth of the carrying.[31] William France Ltd, steamship owners of Goole, in 1889 gave notice to give up their 'Carting Establishment for the collection and delivery of their London Traffic'[32] at Leeds, whereupon the Aire & Calder took it over.

In 1891 the Aire & Calder was empowered to build the New Junction Canal from Kirk Bramwith on the Don to Sykehouse on the Goole Canal, 5½ miles long with one lock at Sykehouse, 215 ft × 22 ft. Half the cost was to be recovered from the Sheffield & South Yorkshire Navigation (see Chapter XVIII). Work did not begin until 1896. Intended for compartment boats and small sea-going craft, 10 ft deep, built by direct labour under Bartholomew's supervision at a total cost of some £300,000 and opened on 2 January 1905, it was the last important canal to be built in Britain.

Bartholomew formally retired in 1895, but he continued his work on the New Junction and was active as consultant director until shortly before his death in November 1919, aged 88. Thomas Marston, who had come from the Calder & Hebble to be his assistant from 1888, succeeded him as manager in 1895 with reduced powers. Gerald FitzGibbon was appointed engineer in 1899, Henry Pickard in 1907; both must have had a difficult time with this elderly but energetic and perhaps now eccentric colleague, who as late as 1914 accompanied Pickard to a conference

33. *The Goole Times* masthead for 1893 shows a panorama of the port

at York 'where the question of the necessary steps to be taken in the event of an invasion of the East Riding . . . had been explained by the Commanding Officer'.[33]

The eighties and after were prosperous times: in 1881 the Aire & Calder's dividend rose from £40,500 to £45,000, in 1888 to £50,000, in 1890 to £55,000 and the following year to £60,000. There it stayed to 1905, after which it climbed again to its pre-war maximum of £83,700 in 1909 and remained there to 1914.

In 1892 the company found the preliminary schedules of proposed tolls under the Railway & Canal Traffic Act, 1888 'highly unsatisfactory',[34] and with little success argued against them before the appeal tribunal. The final schedule came into force at the beginning of 1895, its effect being forecast as likely to be 'very serious'.[35] In practice, it made no difference to toll receipts or the dividend.

In 1896 the North Eastern Railway cut coal rates to Hull, causing the Aire & Calder to lower theirs. Working with Hull steamship owners, the railway also cut so seriously into the Goole Steam Shipping Co's continental trade that a year later the Lancashire & Yorkshire Railway and the Aire & Calder were helping to bear the company's losses. In the autumn of 1897 the North Eastern Railway ended the price cutting, but shipping competition continued, and in 1904 it seemed sensible that the Lancashire & Yorkshire Railway should take the Goole Company over.

Frost still meant hardship and unemployment on the waterways. Here is a minute of 1893:

'with a prospect of the disappearance of the Frost, and of the Traffic being resumed, it was considered unnecessary to give any instructions in regard to the Boatmen: the Notices to whom were about to expire: or in respect of other members of the permanent Staff. And it was ordered that in the case of the return of Frost, Half Wages be paid to the Boatmen. And that one man remain on board of each Boat.'[36]

The frost had lasted through most of December, and was to continue through January. It cost the company £5,000 in lost receipts, and was the beginning of a bad year, for a 6-week dock strike and 3½-months miners' strike followed. A worse frost occurred in January and February 1895, which cost the company another £6,600.

In 1895 an Act[37] modernized the structure of the company. The undertakers' capital, the Act said, 'had never been defined and the shares or interests of the individual Undertakers can at present only be indicated by the proportion of dividends to which they severally are entitled'. As it was calculated that in the past some £1,860,000 had been spent by the undertakers, this figure was taken as the company's share capital, and new fully-paid stock was authorized to that amount, this to be personal and not real estate. The issued loan capital at this time was given as £728,700. A further Act of 1899[38] perpetuated the ancient system of vesting the undertakers' property in trustees. The company new look deserved new offices: those at 1 Dock Street, Leeds, were completed early in 1906.

In 1902, after hearing a report that the railways were about to introduce larger coal wagons and bigger locomotives to cut the cost of working coal trains, the board started to lengthen, widen and deepen locks from Goole to Woodnook on the Calder and Kippax on the Aire to about 215 ft × 22 ft × 9 ft standard, as well as to enlarge the waterway's cross-sectional area. Compartment boats could then work through at one locking. These craft were still proving a huge success. In 1891, an interesting development took place, when Locke & Co of St John's colliery, Normanton, put in an inclined plane at Stanley Ferry new basin. By using a locomotive, empty compartment boats could be hauled out on bogie railway wagons, taken for 1½ miles to the colliery and be loaded, brought back, and lowered again into the water. The system worked well, and Locke's increased their shipments so quickly that the basin had to be enlarged in 1898.* Compartments were the salvation of the Aire & Calder, the stock growing to 1,100, and the tonnage conveyed from 527,404 tons in 1901 to 1,050,672 in 1906 and 1,297,226 in 1910. In that year, tolls on coal

* It closed about 1941.

and the profits of carrying it made up 57¾ per cent of the navigation's revenues. Goole's peak year for coal was 1913, when 2¾
million tons were shipped, 1,563,789 tons having arrived in
compartment boats.

In 1889 a second boat hoist was provided in the Aldam dock,
and by 1910, when the South dock was built by enlarging a part
of the canal, two more had been built, one of them floating. The
railways had also put in two truck hoists of their own. Some coal
brought to Goole was not hoisted, but transhipped to seagoing
lighters and sailing craft for the short distance trades. This had
formerly been loaded by hand into skips and then transferred by
crane, but in 1907 the company ordered a grab for the job.

Considerable traffic changes took place between 1870 and the
end of the century: coal tonnages, 1,202,576 in 1870, were
1,694,452 in 1899: other minerals had fallen from 308,511 to
255,225; merchandise and foreign timber more than doubled
from 192,890 to 412,461, corn increased from 538,732 quarters
(about 110,000 tons) to 154,548 tons. Total tonnage had risen
from 1,811,722 to 2,516,686. It was to reach 3,597,921 in 1913.

In 1912 the West dock was built, giving Goole 38 acres of
docks. Two years later the Lancashire & Yorkshire Railway had
25 steamers working from the port. The last year of peace saw the
Aire & Calder well placed: paying a dividend of 4½ per cent,
costing £83,700, it was more prosperous than the average railway.

The war dealt the navigation severe blows: an air raid in August
1915 damaged warehouses and property at Goole: toll revenue,
£119,415 in 1913, came down to £33,567 in 1919, and compartment boat tonnage to 203,626 out of a total of 1,563,504, though
thanks to government subsidy the dividend, 4½ per cent in 1913,
did not fall below 3¼ per cent. Five of the Lancashire & Yorkshire
Railway's steamers had been sunk, and many Aire & Calder craft
transferred elsewhere. However, the company quickly recovered,
and were one of the very few canal concerns to maintain a carrying
fleet after 1922. They were helped by the railway grouping of
1921. This created a group of east coast ports, Hull, Grimsby and
Immingham, controlled by the London & North Eastern Railway.
The London, Midland & Scottish shipped through Goole alone,
so providing the A. & C. with a considerable revenue from rents,
dock dues and Ouse Improvement tolls. Given Goole's special
usefulness for coal exports because of the shorter haul from the
collieries, the coal trade flourished, as did a good merchandise
traffic. There were now ten coal hoists, five for boats, five for rail

wagons. Goole was, however, too far inland for perishables such as fish or fruit. Though tolls had only recovered to £71,146 by 1925, total revenue was enough for a dividend of 5 per cent plus a 1 per cent bonus, costing £111,400. The Bradford Canal, still owned jointly with the Leeds & Liverpool company, could not survive, however, and in spite of much money spent on it, had to be abandoned in 1922.

At the end of the twenties a new Ocean lock was planned. The mouth of the Dutch River having been first altered in 1928–32, and further Ouse improvement works completed in 1935, the new lock, 375 ft × 80 ft, was then built and opened in 1938 by Sir Josiah Stamp, chairman of the London, Midland & Scottish Railway. In spite of the new lock, the port suffered from the condition of the upper Humber, controlled by the Humber Conservancy Board, on which Goole was in a minority when faced with the block of L.N.E.R. ports. As long ago as 1909 the Lancashire & Yorkshire Railway had commissioned Sir William Matthews to study the Humber. Though, after his critical report, the Board had obtained an estimate of £367,000 for the necessary work, the war intervened and when peace returned, still nothing was done.

In 1939, just before World War II, and perhaps the last year of the old days, the company had practically recovered their 1913 position. Net revenue for 1937 had been some £193,000, and 1,768,908 tons of coal (950,000 tons in compartment boats) and over ¾ million tons of other goods, including oil, had been carried. Apart from Goole shipments, there were growing coal movements to waterside electricity generating stations. The navigation's ordinary stock stood at 96: much higher than the L.N.E.R.'s. The main line took craft 120 ft × 17 ft 6 in × 7 ft 6 in. Compartment boats carrying up to 40 tons were loaded by chutes or from railway wagons, and discharged to ship mainly by the Goole hoists, where the first anti-breakage device had been fitted in 1933. The locks from Castleford to Goole could take a 19-boat train. Goole then had 46½ acres of wet-dock and 3 miles of quay, and had had a turnover of 3,088 vessels in 1937. The docks and the new Ocean entrance lock would take 4,000 ton ships, though the Humber approach made them difficult to reach for craft over 3,000 tons.

The railway lines on the dock estate, together with some warehouses and other facilities, were assigned to the London, Midland & Scottish Railway under various leases, some going back to that of 22 September 1845 to the Wakefield, Pontefract & Goole Rail-

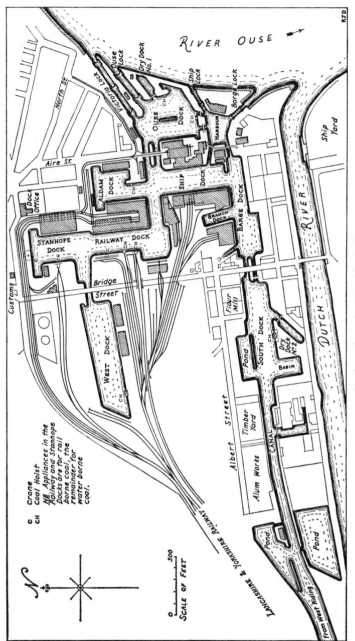

RJD

RIVER OUSE

Ship Yard

RIVER

DUTCH

CANAL

From West Riding

LANCASHIRE & YORKSHIRE RAILWAY

Customs

North St.

Aire St.

Dock Office

STANHOPE Dock

RAILWAY DOCK

Bridge Street

WEST DOCK

Albert Street

Alum Works

Timber Yard

Pond

Pond

SOUTH DOCK

Dry Dock No 2

BASIN

Flour Mill

BRANCH DOCK

BARGE DOCK

Pond

ALDAM DOCK

SHIP DOCK

OUSE DOCK

Victoria Lock

Ouse Lock

Dry Dock No. 1

Ship Lock

Barge Lock

HARBOUR

c   Crane
CH   Coal Hoist
NB Appliances in the
Railway and Stanhope
Docks are for rail
borne coal; the
remainder for water
borne coal.

N

0   300
SCALE OF FEET

34. Goole at the end of World War I

way, others as recent as the 1930 lease of land on the north side of West dock for a quay and rail-connected shed. Other equipment was railway-owned, leased from the navigation, or owned jointly. The old Goole Steam Shipping Co's fleet, bought in 1904 by the Lancashire & Yorkshire Railway, had become the London, Midland & Scottish Railway's East Coast continental fleet of 13 ships based on Goole, part of Associated Humber Lines.* Craft sailed at least weekly to Dunkirk, Antwerp, Ghent, Rotterdam, Amsterdam, Hamburg and Copenhagen. The war meant scarcity of shipping and of foreign trade, loss of craft and men to man them. Among its casualties was the old fly-boat service from Leeds to Goole and Hull.

In May 1947 the Aire & Calder applied for the Barnsley Canal's abandonment. Seven months later the old company came to an end, the Aire & Calder becoming part of the British Transport Commission under the Docks & Inland Waterways Executive. The last shareholders' meeting was on 10 September 1948, when a final dividend of 5·09 per cent was paid. In 1953, the Docks & Inland Waterways Executive was broken up, which resulted in the administrative separation of Goole docks from the waterway, the former going to what became the British Transport Docks Board, which also became the authority for the Ouse Lower Improvement, the latter to British Transport Waterways and at the end of 1962, on the break-up of the Commission, to the British Waterways Board.

The post-war period has been one of transition. In 1953, the changes were becoming apparent. The last horse-drawn boat had gone two years before, but a few family craft were left, and one was independently owned. The old wharf at Dock Street, Leeds, with its fly-boat dock, was still in use, and past it barges worked up the Leeds & Liverpool with coal and sometimes wool as far as Bingley and Skipton. Coal shipments had again recovered to the 1913 level, and compartment boats were commonly seen, working as a 19-craft train below Castleford, and above in 17-pan trains in two lockings, 10 pans in one and the tug and 7 in the other. Commonly seen also were John Harker's 250-ton oil tankers. These and other large craft worked on the Aire & Calder itself; smaller barges went on to the Leeds & Liverpool: the smallest to the West Country, the Calder & Hebble beyond Wakefield. Lock mechanization had begun, but the Barnsley Canal had gone—it

* Associated Humber Lines closed down in 1971.

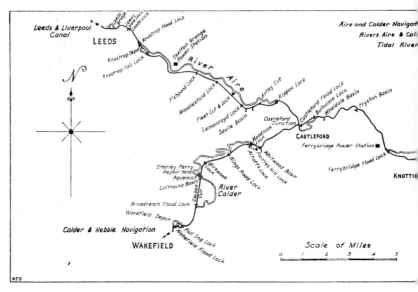

35. The Aire

was abandoned in 1953. Total tonnage in the following year was 2,581,150.

Thenceforward the picture began to change. Coal shipments from Goole fell away as alternative sources of power developed and canalside collieries closed, and though some successful efforts were made to develop new kinds of short-haul carrying, notably in 1968–9 by Cawoods-Hargreaves to Ferrybridge 'C' power station using large compartment boats and pusher tugs* in conjunction with a large boat tippler, the general tendency of the coal trade was one of decline. By 1962 the compartment boat fleet had fallen to 696, by 1971 to 416. Tonnage carried by small compartments, 680,000 tons in 1955, was 489,067 in 1962, and 193,698 in 1971.

The emphasis turned towards developing merchandise traffic. In 1956 the British Transport Commission authorized almost £1 million of capital expenditure. Under it a new large depot was opened at Leeds in 1958, which enabled the old one at Leeds

---

* Each boat is 56 ft × 17 ft 3 in × 9 ft 6 in, and will carry 150–65 tons, three being usually worked in a train 195 ft long with its tug. Steering of the tugs is by changing the direction of propeller thrust.

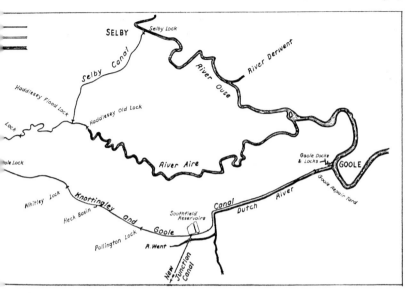

er today

bridge, with its storied warehouses, fixed cranes and cramped spaces, to be let off to others. Extended road services also replaced the depots at Dewsbury, Cooper Bridge, Ravensthorpe and Huddersfield on the Calder & Hebble and Ramsden's. The Commission's programme also included bank protection, straightening work, the mechanization of 8 locks between Knostrop Fall and Pollington, new workshops at Goole, dredging equipment, and improving the carrying fleet. In 1962, traffic was up to 3,198,249 tons, including coal, 2,265,089, liquids in bulk, 569,131; general merchandise 364,029 tons. Toll revenue was £357,725.

In the late 1960s, as a result of an oil contract signed in 1967, the British Waterways Board agreed to enlarge the Goole–Leeds line and ease some bends to take 500-ton craft 180 ft × 18 ft 6 in, by providing 10 ft depth and 100 ft top width. Another improvement was the removal of the old Thwaite locks and island to give a clear run to Knostrop Fall lock.

New craft, tankers and general merchandise (some adapted for containers) have appeared, the latest, here as on the Sheffield & South Yorkshire, the push-tugs and large compartment boats (similar to those used at Ferrybridge 'C') that the Board have provided to work with the planned B.A.C.A.T. (Barge Aboard Catamaran) barge-carrying ship. Tonnage in 1971 was 2,082,672, toll revenue £146,392.

John Hadley, John Gott, William Jessop, George Leather and W. H. Bartholomew would have approved of their successors' work.

CHAPTER XVII

The Calder & Hebble
and the Barnsley

++++++++++++++++++++++++++++++++++◆+++++++++++++++++++++++++++++++++

The Calder & Hebble Navigation

THE Calder & Hebble had lost their railway lease, the Rochdale the promised railway purchase. Both needed new umbrellas.

In the summer of 1847 the Aire & Calder approached the Calder & Hebble 'for re-establishing a system of co-operation between the various Water Interests'[1] by low rates and uniform management. The latter, unwilling to reduce tolls without gaining security, countered by offering the Aire & Calder a lease. So did the Rochdale. But the Calder & Hebble asked more than the bigger company was prepared to pay, and negotiations failed. So, consequently, did those with the Rochdale company.

This company then took the initiative late in 1847 in approaching the other two 'to consider the propriety of a Union of Interests in working their several Canals'.[2] The Calder & Hebble stuck on toll reductions. However, by March 1849 they had changed their minds, helped by falling receipts as traffic left their waterway, and agreed to what the Rochdale had proposed the previous year, a standard rate of $1\frac{1}{2}$d a ton-mile on all traffic, with cuts also in coal and stone: '25 to 100 per cent below their former Rates'.[3]

The Calder & Hebble now joined the other two companies in an ambitious effort to get the railways to agree that water should carry grain, minerals and imported timber, rail everything else, in quantities sufficient to bring in a standard income. They, the Lancashire & Yorkshire Railway* and the London & North Western then met, and broadly agreed along these lines. And then it all seemed too difficult, legally and practically; instead the Rochdale and Calder & Hebble decided to back out and rely on toll

* As the Manchester & Leeds had become from 9 July 1847.

cuts instead. Most through traffic now came down to 1d, and was soon to fall further. Whereupon the Aire & Calder made a traffic agreement of their own with the Lancashire & Yorkshire Railway which discriminated against the Calder & Hebble. And so it went on. In 1850 Charles Norris the clerk, who had been prominent in the railway lease, was removed from office against his will, being replaced by Matthew Oates.

During the endless negotiations, certain practical things could be done. Certain traffics were encouraged: potatoes from the Trent to Manchester, Lincolnshire flour and malt going west, salt going east. Establishments at Brighouse, Salterhebble, Elland and Horbury were closed, and property sold. Halifax was expanded, the wharf and premises there being enlarged in the early 1850s, especially for coal, stone and timber, though the company tried also to discourage manure and nightsoil traffic from the town by charging maximum tolls. Short distance coal traffic was now charged extra, as on the Rochdale, for it was just as expensive in water as that going further, but paid less. And in 1850 the committee's private craft, the *Savile*, which dated from 1801, was put up for sale.

On 1 January 1852 the Sowerby–Halifax section of the Lancashire & Yorkshire Railway line from Sowerby Bridge on to Bradford and Leeds began work. This opened the corn trade, hitherto fed by Lincolnshire, to imports at Liverpool. In 1854 we find the first reference in the Calder & Hebble records to corn from the west. By 1861 it could be said: 'When the chief supply of Corn to this district is via Liverpool very little of it reaches the Calder & Hebble Navigation, and that only for a few miles.'[4] The competing railways also passed through the stone country, so that wagons could be loaded in sidings at the quarries, whereas riverborne stone had to be carried by carts to the water.

In 1850, the Rochdale company had thought of starting their own carrying business; the idea developed into two. One, which collapsed in 1853, was an attempt by the Rochdale and Calder & Hebble canal companies, the South Yorkshire & River Dun and the Great Northern Railway to establish a regular trade between Manchester and London, by canal to Swinton and then rail to London, with Sheffield goods as back carriage. The other was for a single carrying concern supported by the water companies to run a service between Liverpool and Hull. A meeting took place in April 1852 in the office of Fereday Smith, agent of the Bridgewater concern, and in 1853 Jackson's the carriers, who hoped to be the favoured firm, asked the Calder & Hebble whether they intended to lengthen their locks, before they invested money in new boats. Our company replied that they were not at present in a position to entertain the question. Then in April 1855, by which time little Hull–Manchester traffic remained on the water, the chairman of the Aire & Calder wrote to suggest that 'a greater degree of cordiality of Intercommunication between the Calder & Hebble Navigation, the Rochdale Canal, and the Aire & Calder Navigation would tend to the General Interest & the benefit of each'.[5] He went on to say that the Aire & Calder now proposed to act independently of railways as far as possible (see p. 362), and would be glad of an arrangement to carry Manchester trade by canal, preferably by the wide Sowerby Bridge route rather than the narrow Huddersfield. His idea was a single carrying service, operated jointly or by one on behalf of all. He thought the Rochdale would be favourable to negotiations; were the Calder & Hebble? Finally, he emphasized that talks must be confidential, or the railway might cut off a link from the chain—he meant the Rochdale—and leave only the Huddersfield route.

The two companies met on 7 May 1855 at Halifax. After a good deal of further discussion, the Calder & Hebble on 6 August signed a 21 year traffic agreement with the Aire & Calder. But meanwhile their competitors had acted. On 23 July four railway-owned canal companies leased the Rochdale Canal[6] for 21 years. Though the Aire & Calder tried to get the government to intervene, the lease was legal. A quick result was the raising of the Rochdale's toll on bale goods from 1d to 4d, and therefore the traffic's transference to rail.

Though the agreement came too late for the Sowerby Bridge route, it allowed Aire & Calder craft to pass along the Calder & Hebble at very favourable rates to establish a carrying trade in bale goods and merchandise via the Huddersfield Canal. It did not last long (see p. 364).

In the middle of the following year the Calder & Hebble were told that a railway consortium were offering to lease the Aire & Calder itself. The latter company had, however, safeguarded the former's position, and now asked them whether they wanted to come in on the arrangement. The committee, hurriedly summoned, and conscious of the damage done by rate-cutting and railway control of the Rochdale, were in no doubt that 'an Arrangement with the associated Railways in conjunction with the Aire & Calder Company is highly desirable if it can be effected on terms satisfactory to the Proprietors';[7] they hopefully suggested a perpetual annuity of $12\frac{1}{2}$ per cent against their 1855 dividend of 9 per cent. They were offered 8 per cent, reiterated $12\frac{1}{2}$—and then the Aire & Calder ended negotiations (see p. 364).

The Calder & Hebble were in an increasingly awkward position, with much of their through bale and merchandise traffic via the Rochdale and Huddersfield Canals gone; leaving them heavily dependent on corn upwards, coal and stone downwards. Early in 1862 a deputation arrived from the Aire & Calder to discuss the preservation of the coal and corn trades. Rejecting toll cuts, our company saw amalgamation as the only hope of maintaining dividends. Next year they did cut coal to $\frac{1}{2}$d, but in March 1864, having found that the increased tonnage did not compensate for the reduced takings, restored it to $\frac{3}{4}$d.

This probably lost trade again, and proved the last straw to the bigger company. In August the Aire & Calder's shareholders were told that interchange traffic with the Calder & Hebble, especially in coal, had greatly fallen:

'partly owing no doubt to the rates of Toll on that Navigation, but in a much greater degree to the small size of the Locks, and the . . . neglect of dredging'.[8]

The Calder & Hebble committee had been unco-operative about:

'measures to restore the Traffic, and finding that it was in vain to expect any improvement so long as the Navigation remained in their Hands and considering it of the utmost importance to have the control of the Traffic Westward of Wakefield as well

as to guard against its falling into the power of the Railways', the Aire & Calder offered to lease the navigation.

The Calder & Hebble wanted a perpetual lease; the bigger concern offered one of 21 years to give a $6\frac{1}{2}$ per cent dividend. The former accepted the period, but asked for 8 per cent. This the Aire & Calder agreed to pay: it amounted to £12,771 p.a. from 1 January 1865. They also took over the navigation's tiny debt of £1,000. Thanks to the policy of financing capital improvements (some £189,000 since 1801) out of revenue or by calls on shares, the company had never had a large debt. They had the option until the end of 1875 of seeking an Act to buy at a perpetual rent-charge equal to $8\frac{1}{2}$ per cent. Average dividends had been:

	Dividends
Years	*per cent*
1845–49	15
1850–54	9·3
1855–59	7·6
1860–64	6·7*

* 4 per cent plus 1 per cent bonus in the last independent year.

As the waterway brought traffic worth £20,000 p.a. to the Aire & Calder, with prospects of increase when tolls had been reduced, dredging done, and the navigation 'rendered capable of being used by the Vessels that now traverse the Aire & Calder and Rochdale Canals',[9] the bigger company thought their move justified. The Rochdale company now minuted that 'it was likely the Locks on the (Calder & Hebble) Navigation would be lengthened'.[10]

By February 1865 the new owners were actively at work. Within a few months J. D. Oates, the manager, and three agents had been given notice, and toll-collecting concentrated at Wakefield, Sowerby Bridge and Cooper Bridge. A new dredger was bought, Greenwood lock enlarged to Rochdale dimensions, and a warehouse and premises at Huddersfield leased for the Calder carrying trade. This was now to be separately organized: in 1868 the Aire & Calder were building three fly-boats, two of them iron, specially for it. For the lease's first year of 1865, the Aire & Calder spent £19,502, including the rent, and received £17,915.

Reform continued for the next two or three years, Battye lock (one down from Cooper Bridge) and Ledgard Bridge floodgates being altered to Rochdale standards, and hydraulic hoists being provided at Halifax and Fall Ing for the carrying trade. In April 1867 the coal toll to Sowerby Bridge was reduced to ½d a ton-mile, and in 1869 to ¼d for Barnsley Canal and Aire & Calder coal going upwards. And then lock rebuilding to Rochdale dimensions stopped.

Back in 1855 the Calder & Hebble had protested to Halifax corporation against the 'increased nuisances of the Main Sewerage being turned into the Halifax Brook',[11] from which water was pumped back into Halifax canal basin. In 1868 the corporation promoted a Waterworks Bill, against which the navigation company petitioned. It was agreed in 1870 that a culvert should be built to the Calder so that in case of necessity pumping could be from the river instead of the Brook. In spite of the Waterworks

Act, however, the corporation in 1873 were complaining of foul water at Salterhebble, and the Aire & Calder were trying to find the source of pollution.

In 1861 the Calder & Hebble company sold the derelict Dewsbury old cut, running from the Thornhill cut to the Calder in the town, to Lord Savile's trustees for £250. Later these developed the land on either side for housing and commercial use, bridged the cut to give access to the town, blocked off the Dewsbury end, and reopened the rest. Then in 1878, while the Aire & Calder still held the Calder & Hebble lease, the former acquired the cut for themselves, on a 99 year lease, built the Savile Town basin and warehouses, costing some £6,300, and charged their own tolls on the cut. The Calder & Hebble company, though indignant, found they had no legal remedy, and the cut remained in Aire & Calder hands to nationalization.[12]

In connexion with the new railway works at Halifax of the Halifax & Ovenden Junction Railway in the early seventies, the Lancashire & Yorkshire paid £15,000 compensation to the Calder & Hebble for closing Navigation Road and replacing it with a new one. The company decided to invest £12,000 and spend the rest:

'in pulling down and in restoring the Buildings at the head of the Wharf, rendered necessary for connecting the latter with the new Road, and also upon the construction of a number of Coal Hoppers to meet the necessities of the Coal traffic, which traffic is now very small by water to Halifax and further in putting down Hydraulic Machinery for working Coal out of Vessels into such Hoppers, with a view also of applying such power to the working of Goods Hoists and Cranes in the Warehouse'.[13]

Coal from the Calder & Hebble passing on the Aire & Calder fell from 81,648 tons in 1851 to 60,077 tons the following year, and then kept steady for some twenty years: 69,116 tons in 1860 and 66,606 in 1870. Of these figures, the following tonnages went to York, Hull and Goole:

Year	York tons	Hull tons	Goole tons
1851	196	31,740	2,742
1852	204	24,237	2,306
1860	805	28,778	447
1870	1,701	30,748	803

There was also a considerable reverse trade in coal from the Aire & Calder to the Calder & Hebble:

Year	Tons
1861	29,206
1865	36,678
1870	41,351

On 1 January 1876 the Aire & Calder's option to purchase was to expire. A relevant factor in helping them to decide policy was the date for the end of the joint railway lease of the Rochdale Canal on 31 August 1876, and so a likely reopening of that route to through traffic.* In 1875 the Aire & Calder asked for talks on purchase, but the Calder & Hebble, presumably thinking they could get better terms by waiting until the Rochdale was free, procrastinated. Then in 1878 the bigger company proposed a new 21 year lease on the current terms until the original lease expired, and then at £9,578 p.a. (6 per cent) minimum, plus a half-share of profits above a base-line, on condition that they could enlarge all locks to Rochdale standard and convert flood-gates to flood-locks. The Calder & Hebble replied pressing for the current rent as the basis of a new lease, and hopefully offering amalgamation, which would have increased their shareholders' security as much as it would have diminished that of the Aire & Calder's. The Aire & Calder refused. Whereupon the Calder & Hebble suggested that negotiations should be laid aside, and a start made on enlarging the locks, presumably thinking that the results would increase their navigation's value to the Aire & Calder.

In May 1882 the Calder & Hebble company offered £20,000, and if necessary up to £40,000, to improve and enlarge their locks and navigation, 'in such a manner and on such conditions as the Directors of the Aire & Calder Navigation and their Engineer may judge most desirable',[15] subject to reasonable approval; the sum offered included what was to come from the Lancashire & Yorkshire for the Halifax works. Under W. H. Bartholomew's supervision, work then started on the 21¾ mile long navigation, with its 28 locks, four flood-locks and four sets of flood-gates, the plan being to enlarge up to and including the Shepley locks as a first instalment, thus giving an improved navigation past Horbury and Dewsbury to Mirfield, as well as doing urgent minor improvements elsewhere.

* In fact, the lease was continued as an arrangement by mutual consent until the end of 1890.[14]

By mid-1883, the two Fall Ing locks had been converted to a single lock some 130 ft × 22 ft, and one of the two side by side at Thornes was being similarly lengthened, the extension being widened to 22 ft also. As well, Cooper Bridge canal bridge had been raised and Ledgard flood-gates converted to a flood-lock. At this point the Calder & Hebble lost heart, asking Bartholomew what locks 'he considers at present expedient to widen . . . and whether looking at the changes in respect to Canals that may probably take place in a short time he thinks it necessary that such alterations should take place at the present time'.[16] The shareholders also wanted Bartholomew's opinion upon whether the L.N.W.R. should be asked to enlarge the Ramsden's Canal locks. However, Broad Cut Lower lock was similarly extended, and Shepley locks were not, as intended, converted to one enlarged lock. There work ended, for though Broad Cut Upper was authorized, the work was not done.* Craft carrying 90 tons could now work through the enlarged locks, 60 tons in the remainder.

By now the lease was running out, and the shareholders were getting anxious. They could continue their link with the Aire & Calder, 'which all would desire', or join some other navigation, or work the canal independently. If they did so, they reflected that on the one hand the Rochdale Canal was still under railway influence, but on the other that the likely building of the Manchester Ship Canal suggested greater Pennine trade, which they would be able to carry because their water supply had been improved by Waterworks Acts such as those for Halifax and Wakefield, which 'by obliging the maintenance of compensation Reservoirs afford protection against floods and secures a constant and permanent supply of water to the Canal'.[17] They had spent £20,000, but might go on to complete the lock enlargement programme and promote through traffic.

In the end they settled for a short extension of the existing lease as the best solution, but were refused it. They then offered one in perpetuity at 8½ per cent, only to find the Aire & Calder making no offer at all, but letting the lease run out. Somewhat taken aback, they advertised for a general manager, getting Thomas Marston, Manchester manager of the Bridgewater Canal,† and started out at the beginning of 1886 to run a business again. But it took them a year and the threat of legal proceedings to get £5,700 from the

---

* I do not know when it was widened to 18 ft.

† In 1888 he became assistant general manager of the Aire & Calder, being replaced by H. P. Swindells, who served until his death in 1918.

Aire & Calder for dilapidations. Bartholomew, they said, was 'treating the Company very cavalierly'.[18] In the last year of the lease, 1855, the navigation had carried 509,325 tons and taken £11,911 in tolls, the Aire & Calder having lost £4,470 on the year. Averaged over the 21 years, the situation showed a slow worsening:

Years	Tonnages tons	Tolls £	Loss £
1865–67	545,080	15,196	2,124
1868–70	527,939	12,755	4,112
1871–73	535,979	12,327	4,477
1874–76	547,489	13,106	3,659
1877–79	521,268	12,418	4,417
1880–82	515,877	12,092	4,754
1883–85	507,727	11,722	4,997

Independence proved possible, but only on the basis of a 5 per cent dividend instead of the 8½ the shareholders had asked from the Aire & Calder, and of close co-operation with the bigger company on such matters as toll collection and common mileage rates.

In 1888, inspired by the lock lengthening programme the Aire & Calder had some years before carried out on the Barnsley Canal, the company considered enlargement of locks to take 84 ft craft with a minimum draft of 5 ft 4 in, carrying 100 tons.[19] They got an estimate for enlarging Broad Cut Upper lock, and a year later were pressed to continue their programme by a deputation from Halifax Chamber of Commerce and Elland and Brighouse Local Boards. But, though they agreed to raise up to £40,000, they did no more than begin on a considerable programme of replacing old bridges with steel ones. Perhaps one reason was that water was not now so plentiful, because of various abstractions and their own water sales.

In 1894 the Rochdale company, now again independent, proposed that they and the Calder & Hebble should jointly work boats on the two canals: otherwise they threatened the ending of trade on the eastern end of their canal. The Calder & Hebble refused, on the grounds of the upset caused by the new toll structures then being worked out under the Railway & Canal Traffic Act, 1888. By 1895, however, through tolls had been negotiated between the Rochdale, Calder & Hebble and Aire & Calder companies; the following year they were extended to the Bridgewater Canal.

The Calder & Hebble did, however, give William Jackson & Sons a special arrangement. This firm, formerly a Bridgewater carrying subsidiary, had been bought by the Rochdale in 1891. Some of the business was in 1894 taken over by Albert Wood, who carried between the Liverpool–Manchester area and Hull via Sowerby Bridge until 1923. Later, early in the 1900s, H. P. Swindells the then manager started a subsidiary concern, the Calder Carrying Co. It had four boats in 1905.

In 1901, when electric traction was in the wind,[20] they discussed its possibilities with the promoters of two new electric power companies, but otherwise they quietly followed the dangerous path of issuing debentures or selling property to finance capital improvements so that their precarious 5 per cent dividend could be maintained. Apart from bridge building, their main new activity dates from 1906, when they started to provide coal storage bunkers and steam cranes on a rental basis to encourage coal merchants, for instance at Brookfoot and Brighouse. Pollution was now becoming a problem, against which they combined protest with, in one case, successful legal action. So was subsidence, for the company preferred not to buy support, but rather to suffer the consequences, which they sometimes did.

Traffic had come down somewhat in the twenty years since the end of the Aire & Calder lease: in 1905 it was 465,285 tons, three-quarters of which was exchanged with the Aire & Calder. One-sixth of the total only passed a mile on the Calder & Hebble, one-third less than five miles. On the Halifax branch the tonnage was 56,983.

The First World War, as to others, brought financial strain followed by government control. Afterwards the company got the dividend back to 4 per cent, which was held until 1931. Modernization was minor: an electric crane for Halifax woolshed in 1924, a £120 loan to a single boat carrier in 1926, membership of the Institute of Transport for their manager in 1927. Against which was set the removal of the Cooperative Wholesale Society from the Sowerby Bridge warehouse in 1927, 'the Society for the present intending to abandon transit of Goods by Canal'.[21] In 1928 the manager, A. W. Horsfall, was trying to get petrol traffic, and in 1929 he pressed for Broad Cut Upper lock to be enlarged to give bigger craft access to Horbury. But the company failed to spend the necessary £3,600. In 1930 the C.W.S. seem to have come back to the water on terms more favourable to themselves, and in 1931 the company obtained an Act empowering them to raise tolls.

The dividend fell to 3 per cent and then in 1934 to 2 per cent. In 1933 the Rochdale company withdrew from the carrying trade, and in the same year Brighouse gasworks ceased to use canal-borne coal, 'owing to less rates for Conveyance by Motors'.[22] Horsfall's successor, Jackson, tried to restart Rochdale trade. He did get a little, though the bad state of the Rochdale's eastern section prevented its development. He also canvassed energetically for traffic (at this time the company were represented at Hull, York and London, and had agents at Hamburg), bought a motor lorry and a mechanical horse and trailer, and got the committee to order six gross 'Pencils bearing the name of the Navigation for distribution among Customers and the like'.[23] But the lucrative petrol traffic still eluded the company—their locks were too small for suitable craft. It seems a little odd that as late as 1936 the company were for the first time since the 1790s building stables for bye-traders' horses.

Thus, in decline but still trying, the Calder & Hebble reached the Second World War. The Halifax branch, long unprofitable, was abandoned as unnecessary from 1 July 1942 by a warrant of 2 June. Then, after an agreement of 29 March 1944 between the Calder & Hebble and the London, Midland & Scottish Railway, the former were authorized to buy the lower two pounds of the Huddersfield Canal and the whole of Ramsden's under the London, Midland & Scottish Railway (Canals) Act of 1944, which authorized the abandonment of the rest of the Huddersfield Canal. The transfer was effective from 1 January 1945, the purchase price being £4,000. The London, Midland & Scottish Railway agreed also to supply sufficient water from the closed section of the Huddersfield Canal.

On 1 January 1948 the Calder & Hebble was nationalized. Three months later, Hargreaves took over the Calder Carrying Co, which then had over twenty craft able to carry a 60–75 ton pay-load. They had been carrying general cargo from Hull, but Hargreaves put them on to carrying coal to power stations and similar work.[24]

In 1952 the Rochdale Canal from Manchester to Sowerby Bridge was abandoned, thus ending the Calder & Hebble's 150 year old place in a through east–west route, though the last cargo to pass from the Rochdale had been in the Calder Carrying Co's *Thomas* from Manchester docks to Dewsbury on 13 September 1937. In 1939 the *May Queen* passed through light, the last to do so. The last commercial craft up to Sowerby were Hargreaves'

Frugality and *Sowerby Bridge* on 6 September 1955 with wood pulp. The last coal cargo, for Sowerby Bridge gasworks, had come up the previous August in *Cissie*.[25] After that, there was little traffic higher than Brookfoot, and by 1958, little above Thornhill, Dewsbury. The power station here is supplied, along with down canal trade, from colliery staithes above Broad Cut Upper lock. The section above Dewsbury was scheduled as a cruiseway in the 1968 Transport Act.

In 1963 a short length of the Huddersfield Canal back to Aspley was abandoned, but Ramsden's and the Calder & Hebble itself remained open.

Sir John Ramsden's Canal

The history of Ramsden's is largely that of the Huddersfield Canal with which it connected. The year after it was absorbed by the London & North Western Railway in 1847,[26] Ramsden's carried 120,207 tons.[27] Thenceforward through traffic declined. A brief revival about 1856, when the Aire & Calder tried to re-build a carrying trade to Manchester via the Huddersfield after a railway consortium had leased the Rochdale, broke against obstacles the railway company conveniently found in Standedge tunnel. Local traffic on Ramsden's, however, held up well till past the turn of the century.

In 1863, 18 to 25 boats a day were passing it. In 1872 W. H. Bartholomew of the Aire & Calder was told to arrange with Sir John Ramsden for land adjoining the existing Huddersfield wharf so that enlarged carrying trade premises could be built. He did so, in 1873 leasing the existing wharf and a stretch of adjoining land, round which quay walls were built the following year. In 1875 hydraulic hoists were installed, but the railway company gave up canal carrying. At about the same date the London & North Western Railway began to sell canal water, the *Huddersfield Chronicle* of 15 May of that year reporting the sale of about 200,000 gallons a day.

In the 1890s about 75,000 tons a year were being exchanged with the Calder & Hebble, three-quarters of which was to and from Huddersfield itself. By 1905 the figures were 53,580 with the town, and 11,020 with the narrow canal beyond it. Ramsden's was then rather shallower than the Calder & Hebble, so that craft carrying 70 tons had to lighten to 50.

On 1 January 1945, by agreement with the London, Midland &

Scottish Railway, the Calder & Hebble company bought Ramsden's and a short length of the Huddersfield Canal for £4,000, the rest of the narrow canal being abandoned. At this time some 80 barges a month were using it, carrying power station coal. Ramsden's was nationalized on 1 January 1948. In October 1953 the coal trade ceased and commercial traffic then ended. Ramsden's was listed as a cruiseway under the 1968 Transport Act, and Aspley basin now has a marina.

Barnsley Canal

Independent still, their negotiations with the Don and the Aire & Calder having both come to nothing, in March 1846 the company decided to petition against the Bill for a threatening Barnsley branch of the Sheffield, Ashton-under-Lyne and Manchester Railway to join the Midland Railway (as the North Midland had become). Then, in April, they petitioned against a potentially worse threat, the Hull & Barnsley Junction Railway, and the possibility of losing their Humber trade.

The trade in coal from Silkstone had been by this time seriously hit—the market up the Ouse from York had virtually gone, and the colliery masters' efforts to find another south of the Humber was being 'met by the Northern Coal competition by Sea. This competition has been very severely felt since the regulation of the Vend of Coal from the different Collieries in the North was done away with.'[28] Added to which the Aire & Calder, perhaps in revenge for their flirtation with the Don, were refusing to extend to coal from the Barnsley the drawback they granted to their own. Also, when the Don took over the Dearne & Dove on 1 January 1846, they cut coal tolls by more than half, and this had also taken trade off the Barnsley. Moreover, the first steam railway to come within working distance of Silkstone, the Sheffield, Ashton-under-Lyne & Manchester, was completed at the end of 1845, and from 1846 Clarke's sent coal to Oxspring on this line to be despatched west. When the first section of the Barnsley branch from this line was opened to Dodworth near Silkstone, rail despatch became more convenient still. Lime and limestone carried in coal boats had fallen sympathetically, and there was little satisfaction to be got from an increase in sundries traffic, because most of it was materials for railway construction. However, the company had bought land for another reservoir at Haw Park adjoining the existing reservoir.

Negotiations with the Aire & Calder being in abeyance, the Manchester & Leeds Railway stepped in to ask the canal company for their terms. The canal was offered them at £200 per share on 720 shares (£144,000) or on a 21 year lease at £10 per share (£7,200 p.a.), with an engagement to purchase during the period. This offer promptly brought the Aire & Calder back. They were offered the Barnsley at £11 per share (£7,920 p.a.) on a 14 year lease, but rejected it. So back the Barnsley's committee went to the Manchester & Leeds. Meanwhile, they agreed to oppose a Manchester, Sheffield & Lincolnshire Railway line to join the Midland by way of branches, and the revised South Yorkshire Bill, especially because of its proposed branch from Barnsley to Penistone. Opposition to the South Yorkshire led to an agreement; in exchange for South Yorkshire willingness not to enforce their water rights in the Dearne, the Barnsley company agreed to equalize the rates on coal put on canal above Barugh locks, whether it was going to the Calder or to the Dearne & Dove.

In May 1847 the Barnsley company again offered themselves to the Aire & Calder, this time on a 21 year lease at £10 a share or £7,200 p.a. The latter, considering that the Act for the South Yorkshire Railway, which had now passed, and the likelihood of another for the Barnsley Junction, had greatly altered the position, offered 'such reduced terms as the altered circumstances and diminished prospects of their Navigation* rendered it prudent to offer',[29] namely a 7 year lease at £8 per share (£5,760), with an option to renew for another 14 years. This the Barnsley refused, and for a time went its own way. One cannot help being surprised. The Barnsley's toll revenue in 1846 had been £9,367, against £16,663 in 1840: in such a case a quick choice of partner would seem preferable to long flirtations.

In December 1847 the Manchester, Sheffield & Lincolnshire were negotiating to acquire the Silkstone tramroad to form part of their proposed link with the Midland—the former Barnsley Junction Railway. The Barnsley company decided first to inquire whether the South Yorkshire company were willing to make an offer, and in any case to get the tramroad valued. The South Yorkshire did show interest, and agreed that, should the railway's Bill for a branch to Penistone be authorized in the current session, they should be offered the tramroad for £8,000, the railway company not to charge more on the branch that would replace it than on their main line, and to provide a link between it and Barnby

* The Barnsley proprietors'.

basin. In February 1848 the railway company offered £6,000, but by then the canal company seem to have preferred a sale to the Manchester, Sheffield & Lincolnshire at the same price and approached them. In the end the matter dropped.

By now, railway competition was seriously affecting the canal's coal trade: coal tonnages, 204,000 in 1844, were down to 118,000 in 1846. Seemingly also, the Aire & Calder were not hurrying to help the collieries on the Barnsley line to compete with those on their own, for they persistently refused to grant toll reductions on Barnsley coal to York and above, though they were doing so for coal from collieries on their own line. In December 1847, rather desperately, the Barnsley company offered a drawback of one-third of tolls on coal to Goole if the Aire & Calder would make the same allowance on Barnsley coal to Selby and upwards on the Ouse as they already made for coal from their own line. It seems to have been agreed. The years 1848, 1849 and 1850 saw heavy reductions, by drawback or otherwise, in coal and other tolls, the Aire & Calder now co-operating, and in 1850 an economy drive. The dividend, £11 for 1845, fell to £4.

A tonnage account for the second half of 1850[30] shows the coal traffic almost equally split between the 52,949 tons taking the Dearne & Dove line, and the 50,818 going to the Aire & Calder. The tolls yielded were £527 on the Dearne & Dove traffic, £1,610 on that to Heath, and £4 probably for local traffic at Barugh. The lime trade, 1,077½ tons yielding £19, was all on the Barnsley's own line, that in limestone split 5,834 tons (£276) on their line, and 2,570 tons (£15) through the junction lock. Of the corn trade, 9,005 quarters (£71) came up the Barnsley, and 6,815 quarters (£16) through junction lock. Finally, the sundries trade yielded the Barnsley's own line 4,032 tons (£222), while 929 tons (£17) came from the Dearne & Dove.

In 1851 yet another negotiation began with a railway company for a junction with the Silkstone tramroad—this time with the Sheffield, Rotherham, Barnsley, Wakefield, Huddersfield & Goole, but without result. By this time, however, there was railway access to the Silkstone pits for the South Yorkshire & River Dun and therefore for the Great Northern Railway via the former's Worsbrough branch, a serious blow to the Barnsley's and Aire & Calder's coal traffic.

In 1853 Hall, the company's engineer, was told to survey and estimate for a railway from the canal near Barugh locks to a proposed colliery near Mapplewell, north-east of Barugh. This led to an approach a year later to both the Aire & Calder and the South Yorkshire Railway & River Dun company to ask whether either would join the Barnsley in building 'a Railway from the Barnsley Canal for the purpose of developing the Coal field on the Eastern side of the Canal in the event of such measure appearing desirable'.[31] This led to an offer from the South Yorkshire to take a long lease of the Barnsley, with subsequent purchase. The company replied that they had no power to lease for more than 21 years, but would meet a deputation. At once the Aire & Calder stepped in, claiming a right of first offer 'in consequence of prior negotiations and recent arrangements for traffic'.[32] The argument was doubtful, but all the same the Barnsley agreed to negotiate first with the Aire & Calder.

The latter's trade was closely tied up with the Barnsley, for craft carrying corn upriver to Wakefield were then accustomed to go up the Barnsley to collect coal to take back, often via the Dearne & Dove. But coal supplies from the Barnsley Canal had fallen from 204,000 tons in 1844 to 84,000 tons in 1853 owing to 'its diversion to the line of the River Don by a lower rate of Dues',[33] and total tolls from £13,216 to £4,736. Because to 'restore the trade to its original channel would have required a larger reduction in Dues than it was the interest of the Barnsley Canal, as an independent body, to make',[34] the Aire & Calder agreed to lease the canal from 1 December 1854 for 21 years at £2,880 p.a.* They also assumed Barnsley liabilities of £1,933, and agreed to pay the company's principal officers five years' salary whether the Aire & Calder employed them or not.

The much lower terms offered and accepted reflected the great deterioration of the Barnsley company's position. All the same, the Aire & Calder regarded them as very favourable to the Barnsley, pointing out to their own shareholders that these would also be benefited 'by securing . . . at the most favourable point for vessels employed in the Wakefield Corn trade, a large supply both of the best House Coal and the best Coal for Steam Navigation'.[35] In 1856 a Bill was introduced to authorize the transfer and give the Aire & Calder enlarged powers over the canal. The Barnsley company remained in existence to receive the rent and for certain formal business.

Here are toll figures to the end of independence:

* It was a double lease, £1,440 p.a. being to lease the tolls, and £1,440 the canal itself and other property.

Page 403   Compartment boats on the Aire & Calder: (*above*), a steam tug and train of loaded boats in Pollington lock, 1954; (*below*) a push-tug and 160 ton large boats on their way to Ferrybridge 'C' power station, 1970

Page 404 Goole: (*above*) the Railway dock about 1886. Except for the paddle-driven river boat on the extreme right, only sailing craft are to be seen. The wooden structure on the left is a railway wagon coal hoist: it was demolished after World War I; (*below*) the basin, Ouse dock, coal hoists and compartment boats in 1920

Years	Canal tolls £	Tramroad tolls £	Total tolls £
1845–47	9,266	931	10,197
1848–50	6,578	752	7,330
1851–53	4,607	632	5,239
1854–56	4,643	219	4,862
1857	4,502	241	4,743

Taking 1853 as representative of the early fifties, Barnsley coal went mainly to places on the Aire & Calder (21,892 tons), Goole (16,807 tons), Louth (9,748 tons), and points upwards from Goole on the Yorkshire Ouse (17,371 tons). These out of a total of 84,203 tons passing on to the Aire & Calder at Heath.[36] But total tonnages of coal passing on to the Aire & Calder from collieries on the Barnsley Canal were increasing, and nearly doubled between 1851 and 1870:

Year	Coal: tons
1851	97,346
1855	109,687
1860	130,367
1865	170,272
1870	179,220

The few years following 1851, however, saw a serious falling away in Barnsley Canal coal carried to York: 19,840 tons in 1851 were only 6,794 tons in 1856. At about this level they remained until 1863, and then fell again to 958 in 1870. Of these totals, Clarke's Silkstone coal were 8,397 tons in 1851, 3,075 in 1856, 2,569 in 1863 and 164 tons in 1870. On the other hand, the trade to Hull greatly increased: only 579 tons in 1851, but 23,610 in 1856, 49,825 in 1863, and 46,424 in 1870. In the same period that to Goole rose also, but fluctuatingly: 15,123 tons in 1851, 10,210 in 1856, 34,208 in 1863, and 24,950 in 1870.

In 1860 the Aire & Calder altered Barnsley tolls. None now were to exceed 1½d per ton-mile: coal and timber ran out at about ¾d, stone and iron at ½d, and limestone at ¼d. At this time nine firms were shipping coal from ten collieries above the Dearne & Dove junction.

Immediately after the lease, a new reservoir adjoining the old one at Cold Hiendley had been built for £1,000 to hold 3,000 lockfulls. Some years later, in July 1861, the Barnsley was 'much in want of cleaning as large accumulations of weed and refuse are

K

in many parts of the Canal', and the Barugh locks were 'in a very dilapidated state',[37] although the Aire & Calder had already spent £7,000 on improvements. The following month, on 6 August, the canal burst at Royston, depositing a loaded sloop and her crew in a field 400 yd from the canal. It took nearly three weeks to reopen the line, by which time a hundred boats were waiting to pass.[38] Four years later, the canal was reported in 'an efficient state of repair, at least as far as Barugh'.[39]

In 1861, the Barnsley Coal Railway was authorized. A protégé of the South Yorkshire company, it had been promoted from Ardsley nearly to Wakefield, but cut back in Parliament to near Royston. Taken over in 1863 by the South Yorkshire, it drew coal traffic from the canal.

Toll cuts had increased the canal's coal trade from 179,295 tons in 1855, the first year of the lease, to 291,313 tons in 1863: the tolls paid by the Barnsley trade on the Aire & Calder had also risen from £5,316 to £9,200. Nevertheless, the Aire & Calder were making a loss on operating the Barnsley, to set off against the gain to their own receipts. Because the bigger seagoing craft could not get up the canal, in August 1861 the Aire & Calder ordered 'an engine and apparatus' to be erected at Heath lock to tranship coal to them, the floor being lowered 10 in to take the large vessels. A few months later Craik's of East Gawber colliery (on the Barnsley–Barnby bridge section) asked to build a railway over the canal to the Lancashire & Yorkshire Railway. The Aire & Calder briskly refused. Eventually, by calling out the commissioners appointed under the Barnsley Canal Acts, Craik's got their way. The Aire & Calder seem to have accepted the position, but the Barnsley's clerk gave notice that his company reserved the right to contest the decision when the lease ended. In 1864 the Aire & Calder did not object when the Silkstone Furnace colliery wanted to connect itself to the Barnsley Coal Railway.

The Aire & Calder did well with the Barnsley Canal in the early part of the lease, working its coal tonnages up to 272,180 in 1865, when the ton mileage figure was 2,519,842. Toll receipts were now £4,395, and the loss on working £736. Then, slowly but inexorably, the figures fell, until by 1874 the tonnages were 203,197, with ton-miles more heavily down at 1,580,607, toll receipts £3,326, and the loss £2,214. At the same time, subsidence costs, or money paid out to buy support, were a yearly drain on finance. For instance, in 1866 the Barnsley's committee went to look at the aqueduct, and reported 'considerable damage caused by the sinking of the land . . . Great caution will be required in preventing both the fissures in the rock and the cracks in the arches of the aqueduct becoming larger'.[40]

For the years 1867 to 1870, the traffic divided as follows:

Date	To and from the Aire & Calder tons	To and from the Dearne & Dove tons	Division unknown tons	Total tons
1867	157,797½	68,023½	1,345	227,166
1868	143,095	49,480	1,088	194,473
1869	185,990½	52,712½	1,352	240,055
1870	204,249	43,049	800	248,098

From above Barugh, there was now little traffic: 15,785 tons in 1867, 4,815 in 1870.[41]

In 1862 the Aire & Calder had bought Barugh mill for £1,125, the better to control the Dearne water, and at the end of 1864 Bartholomew was authorized to increase the capacity of Cold Hiendley reservoir by 1,000 lockfulls. The Barnsley's main supply of water came from the Dearne's catchment area, supplies being taken from Silkstone Beck and at Barugh mill. The situation was not a legal one, though understood between the Aire & Calder and the former River Dun Company. However, Barnsley corporation, having taken over the local waterworks, decided they needed more water to flush sewage down the Dearne. Therefore in May 1870 they ordered the Barnsley company to stop taking Dearne water, giving them the alternatives of pumping from the Calder, or seeking an Act to legalize the Dearne abstractions.

Consultations on the possibly expensive implications then took place between the Aire & Calder and Barnsley companies. After agreement that the canal above Barugh might be converted to a tramway, the Aire & Calder consented to continue to rent the concern until 30 November 1875, and then to buy it at £65 a share, or £46,800. The arrangement was authorized by the Barnsley Canal Transfer Act of 1871. Dividends ended with a distribution of 17s (85p) from the balance in hand, and the canal was transferred on 17 August 1871. The Act also safeguarded water supply from the Dearne at Barugh mill, and authorized, if desired, an inclined plane from near the southern end of the third Walton lock to the northern end of the lowest, so by-passing ten of the twelve locks, and a steam engine there. We may remember that the Blackhill plane on the Monkland Canal, opened in 1850, was working at this time.[42]

Here is the company's dividend record, much of it, of course, during the lease period:

Years	Dividends per £160 share					Dividends per cent
	£	s	d			
1844–46	9					5·625
1847–49	6	6	8	(£6·33½)		3·96
1850–52	2	10	0	(£2·50)		1·56
1853–55	3	10	0	(£3·50)		2·19
1856–58	4					2·5
1859–61	4					2·5
1862–64	4					2·5
1865–67	4					2·5
1868–70	4					2·5
1871–73	4					2·5
1874–75	4	1	10	(£4·09)		2·56

In 1874 55 acres were bought to increase reservoir capacity, and another pumping engine ordered for Cold Hiendley.* The top part of the canal above Barugh was now virtually disused. No tramway was built, and by an Aire & Calder Act of 1893 the five locks and 1 mile 23 chains above Barugh wharf were abandoned after a new feeder had been put in. Between 1879 and 1881, however, the Aire & Calder lengthened all the Barnsley's other locks from their original 66 ft to 84 ft, the width being 15 ft and the depth on the sills 6 ft 6 in, to take craft 79 ft by 14 ft 9 in drawing 6 ft. Powers to build the Walton inclined plane were renewed in 1889.

In 1905 the New Sharlston Colliery Co wanted to ship coal from their Walton colliery by compartment boat; the Aire & Calder then noted that in principle they favoured widening certain locks and bridges to enable this to be done, if they got a proper guarantee of future traffic by water.[43]

On 20 November 1911 the wing walls of the Barnsley aqueduct and part of the embankment gave way, due to subsidence. The canal had to be closed, and was not reopened until 10 July 1912. Ten years later, in 1922, drought closed the line from 1 September to the end of the year.

Traffic held up well. Here are averaged figures from 1880 to the beginning of the First World War:

* This beam engine by Harvey's of Hayle worked until about 1946.

Years	Coal tons	Total tons	Net toll revenue £
1880–84	164,781	195,486	2,957
1885–89	197,308	229,842	3,561
1890–94	183,068	217,378	3,006
1895–99	195,744	257,798	
1900–04	183,807	224,045	
1905–09	172,574	207,675	
1910–14	159,237	192,406	

After the war, and into the next, traffic slowly fell as canalside collieries were worked out, though as late as 1943, 856 craft had passed the electrically-powered lift bridge at Royston which the county authorities had built in 1934.

On 13 June 1945 a large leak near Barnsley aqueduct flooded Mottram Wood colliery, £2,375 having to be paid in compensation. In November the general manager reported more trouble at the aqueduct, 'and that we were likely to have continuous trouble on this section owing to subsiding ground causing the canal to stand more and more above the solid ground, as the sides are continuously built up'. The board then asked for a report on the consequences of abandonment up from the aqueduct.

A year later, on 22 November 1946, the canal burst its bank at Littleworth about a mile from the Dearne & Dove junction, allowing 53 million gallons of water to escape into the countryside and a neighbouring housing estate. The resulting gap was large— 43 ft wide and 11 ft deep: compensation cost the company £3,500. The accident caused the Aire & Calder to review recent history— losses on the canal since 1942, accentuated by extra expenditure to counteract subsidence. Soon afterwards, with the Transport Bill to nationalize the Aire & Calder in Parliament, Ministry of Transport officials met the board in January 1947. The board unanimously recommended abandonment of the whole canal. In March the Ministry agreed to abandon from Cronkhill to Barugh. However, after the board had explained the technical and legal difficulties of doing this, the Ministry consented to total abandonment, the company then applying in May under s.45 of the Railway & Canal Traffic Act of 1888.

On 7 December 1950 the last boat passed Royston bridge, and on 10 June 1952 the last craft used Heath lock,[44] though the abandonment warrant was not granted until 1953. The Barnsley aqueduct was then demolished as potentially unsafe.

CHAPTER XVIII

The Sheffield and South Yorkshire

━━━━━━━━━━━━━━━━━━━━━━◆━━━━━━━━━━━━━━━━━━━━━━━

THE South Yorkshire, Doncaster & Goole Railway's Act received the royal assent on 22 July 1847, but the company could not proceed to their agreed amalgamation with the Don until half the railway's capital had been raised and expended. So for the moment the navigation concern, which also controlled the Sheffield and Dearne & Dove canals, went its own way. One piece of unfinished business was quickly settled, for after a brisk tussle with the Stainforth & Keadby company, they were absorbed from 1 January 1849. However, revenue accrued to the railway company from the Don under the agreement, and therefore they could, unusually, pay 5 and 6 per cent dividends from the date of their Act with warrants cashable one month after amalgamation. The rates were better than most paid later.

The railway company[1] had been authorized to build a line from Doncaster to near Barnsley, with branches to Elsecar and Worsbrough—in other words, to supplement the Dearne & Dove as a coal carrier. Charles Bartholomew, already engineer of the Don, and brother of Thomas Hamond Bartholomew of the Aire & Calder, was appointed engineer also to the railway from the beginning of 1848. The line was opened from Doncaster to Swinton, where it joined the North Midland Railway, on 10 November 1849, the Elsecar mineral branch on 1 February 1850,* and to Worsbrough in mid-June.

The engineers wanted as soon as possible to eliminate coal transhipment, and in February 1850 told the shareholders:

'Although we have been enabled to use the Canals to bring Coals from the more distant Collieries to the nearest accessible

---

* The canal basin was moved back about 200 yd to make room for the railway.

points of the Rails, yet it has been thought desirable to push on with the further extension of the Line to the Worsbro' Collieries, and up the Dodworth Valley to the Silkstone Pits.'[2]
The line reached Moor End for Silkstone in April 1852. Before that, on 1 July 1851, the main line had been opened to Barnsley for an end-on junction with the Lancashire & Yorkshire Railway. Though the line's opening tended to reduce Dearne & Dove traffic, it probably increased that on the Don and the Stainforth & Keadby.

On 19 April 1850, the conditions having been fulfilled, the railway and navigation companies amalgamated, an Act of the same year renaming the combined concern the South Yorkshire Railway & River Dun Company. The navigation part was valued at £928,188, as follows:

	£
Don shares	450,000
Dearne & Dove shares	210,000
Stainforth & Keadby shares	34,350
Loan debt	233,838
	928,188

Each Don shareholder was entitled under the agreement to 150 shares in the amalgamated company for each share he held. At the 1850 shareholders' meeting it was farsightedly proposed, and subsequently agreed, that instead of depending upon the earnings of the combined company for their dividends, they should have a perpetual 4 per cent. Most chose to do so. New maximum tolls now replaced those under the four old navigation companies' Acts. Lower than any previously, at 1½d for merchandise, 1d for iron and ½d for coal per ton per mile, they nevertheless did not involve any actual reductions, for such rates had been charged for some time. The waterway side of the amalgamation consisted of the Don itself, 26¼ miles long from Tinsley to Stainforth junction, with 2¾ miles also from Stainforth to Fishlake old ferry; the 3⅞ miles of the Sheffield Canal, the 12¾ miles of the Stainforth & Keadby, and the 13⅞ miles of the Dearne & Dove.

The shareholders' meeting of August 1850 was told that during the previous few years the Don itself had been greatly improved, and arrangements had been made for water to be pumped from it to the Sheffield and Dearne & Dove canals. Therefore 'it is hoped that little or nothing will be required for the further improvement of the Canals and Navigations above Doncaster'.[3]

As their rails did not extend below Doncaster, a rail branch was opened to the river there on 1 July 1851, and a coal chute built, as evidence of the company's intention to develop the navigation thence to Keadby as a coal-exporting rival to the Aire & Calder. All bridges below the town had already been made to open,* thereby allowing bigger craft to navigate, and the company now went ahead with raising banks by some 3 ft to give an 8 ft 6 in waterway through to Keadby. In August 1851 it was reported that the Customs now 'permitted foreign-bound vessels to load Coal at the point where the Railway and Navigation met at Doncaster, and also at Keadby'.[5]

In February 1852 the South Yorkshire were suggesting an extension of their rails from Doncaster to the mouth of the Trent, and a new port there. This came to nothing, but emerged again in 1855 as a proposal by Charles Bartholomew for a single line on the banks of the Dutch River from Thorne to Newbridge and then beside the canal to Goole, this to be made jointly by the two concerns.[6]

In 1852 the company came to a provisional agreement with the Great Northern Railway for a working arrangement, to end in amalgamation, which would have provided the South Yorkshire with an assured market in and around London for their coal. The necessary Act was passed that year, but the Great Northern then backed out, the agreement ending in 1854. Unfortunately, it had caused the South Yorkshire company to adopt 'arrangements diverting Trade from their Navigations which cannot now be recalled'; that is, towards London and away from the Don.[7]

In 1854 a rail line had been opened from Aldam junction near Barnsley to Blackburn junction, which enabled trains to run through from Barnsley to Sheffield. This was followed by the abandonment of the old policy of transhipment at Doncaster and the opening of a tortuous rail line without an Act alongside the waterway from Doncaster past Barnby Dun, Bramwith and Stainforth to Thorne lock, on 11 December 1855, whence coal began to be shipped via Keadby to Hull.[8] The shareholders were told in 1856 that the extension would 'obviate, for the future, the severe loss which the company sustains, in times of scarcity of water, from drought'.[9] Indeed, the previous year had been a bad one, for low water and for frost. At this time the South Yorkshire

---

* The present Stainforth bridge is almost certainly not more than about thirty years old and was preceded by a sliding drawbridge: other modern bridges over lock cuts etc are high level.[4]

company had about 16 coal carrying craft of their own. Dow tells us also that in August 1856 Bartholomew was authorized to buy a steamer for a packet service from Thorne to Keadby, whence passengers and parcels could be transferred to Trent packets for Hull or Gainsborough. Between 1858 and September 1859, however, the Thorne line was extended, again without an Act, alongside the canal to Keadby, where arrangements were made to tranship coal by chute to seagoing craft. The waterways were still important: in 1857 the railway carried 878,816 tons of coal, the waterways 431,204 tons. Two years later, the combined Don and canal receipts for 1859 were £54,731, against £51,554 for 1858. In 1860 they were £59,855.

In 1855 a coal distribution agreement was come to with the Great Northern, which enabled the South Yorkshire company for a time to sell Barnsley coal in London, and distribute it widely in the east and south of England. In this year also the South Yorkshire joined the Manchester, Sheffield & Lincolnshire Railway and a French group in forming the Anglo-French Steamship Company to export south Yorkshire coal from Grimsby.* This naturally pulled the company towards that port, and in 1856 the shareholders were told that the export trade through Grimsby was considerable. In 1861, too, they and the M.S. & L.R. jointly promoted the Trent, Ancholme & Grimsby Railway from the South Yorkshire at Keadby across the Trent to the new ironstone deposits near Scunthorpe and to Grimsby. This, the Barnsley Coal Railway, the Hull & Doncaster, to give them a line to Hull, and a shortened route for their own line into Sheffield to make use of their own wharf and warehouse at Sheffield Canal basin,† were all being considered or promoted when in the summer of 1861 a working agreement was reached with the M.S. & L.R. It was followed in June 1864 by a Transfer Act which authorized a 999 years lease.

After the agreement, the Manchester, Sheffield & Lincolnshire wanted to build a rail line from Mexborough to Sheffield using the upper part of the Rotherham cut, so that it could pass under the Midland branch from Masborough into Rotherham (Westgate). Therefore a new navigation channel was made from the cut below Rotherham past a lock into the river there. The navigation then used the river for a short distance before entering another new cut

* They sold their share at a loss early in 1861.
† In September 1854 the ½-mile long Park goods branch had been opened from the M.S. & L.R. to the canal basin at Sheffield.

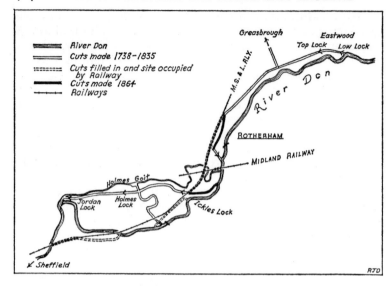

36. Changes in the upper Don

leading to Ickles lock and the 1836 canal line to Tinsley. The Rotherham section of the railway using this new line opened on 1 August 1868, the continuation to Mexborough in 1871.

The Don waterway system now ceased to be an important partner in a small concern using both rail and water transport, and became an appendage of little importance to a rapidly growing and ambitious railway company. Ten years later the South Yorkshire company was dissolved and power given by an Act of 1874 to vest its constituents in the Manchester, Sheffield & Lincolnshire Railway. The Act also laid down revised maximum waterway tolls.

Although a railway from Doncaster through Goole to Hull had been proposed as far back as 1855, and again in 1860, not until 1869 did the North Eastern Railway open it. The river trade was of course affected.

Under the M.S. & L. the waterways held their own, with tonnages of 982,000 in 1878 and 927,254 in 1888, but lack of modernization was beginning to tell. Some fifty years after steam craft had been introduced on the Aire & Calder, they were still prohibited on the Don and the canals. In 1882 575,000 tons of south Yorkshire coal were carried by water, in 1892 544,000 tons, in a period when rail carryings from the coalfield had more than doubled. The railway company seemingly tried to divert traffic by reducing rail while maintaining water rates, the latter running higher than the admittedly very cheap Aire & Calder. Nevertheless, before the Royal Commission of 1906, the Great Central (as the M.S. & L.R. had become) claimed that up to 1894 waterway earnings had been enough to pay 3·28 per cent on the £1,150,829 of purchase price.

The Don itself still had 16 ordinary and 2 flood-locks. Most traffic was long distance, that in coal being mostly for Hull. Very little went to Goole. On the Dearne & Dove about 25 yd of the Worsbrough branch collapsed on the morning of 15 June 1884 because of colliery working beneath, flooding the railway. Repairs cost nearly £19,000, and traffic was not resumed for six months.[10] The Sheffield Canal was beginning to be a problem. In 1892 90 per cent of traffic was long-distance upwards, with hardly anything back, so that craft ran empty. Yet the cost of pumping the canal's only water supply (except for some bought from Nunnery colliery) up 69 ft from the Don was 5s 10d (29p) a lockful, or 11s 8d (58½p) for a single loaded journey when returning empty. The Greenland arm was sold off at some time during M.S. & L.R. ownership.

Dissatisfaction with comparatively high waterway rates, failure to allow steam haulage, and lack of an effective competitor to railways led traders to seek an alternative, and on 20 August 1888, a year when the Manchester Ship Canal was being built, big canals were being projected from the Mersey or from the Severn to Birmingham, and the Royal Society of Arts in May had held a two-day symposium on canals. G. F. Lockwood, President of the Sheffield Chamber of Commerce, invited Charles Hawksley the engineer and B. P. Broomhead, a prominent local solicitor, to be present at a meeting of the Council of the Chamber on 16 August, at which he spoke of investigations he had made into Sheffield's waterway to the sea. As a result, an influential committee was appointed, met four days later at the Royal Victoria Hotel, and came to the radical conclusion:

'That the construction of an independent new Canal for the purpose of placing Sheffield, Rotherham, Doncaster, the South Yorkshire Coalfields and the Don Valley in more direct communication with the Sea is of the utmost importance for the preservation of the heavy trades carried on in those places and districts and the future development thereof and for the profitable working of the said Coalfields.'[11]

A committee was appointed to organize action, and subscriptions were invited.

The committee, soon enlarged to include the mayor of Sheffield and the Master Cutler, quickly commissioned T. & C. Hawksley (to whom James Abernethy was added) to report:

> 'whether a navigable Canal to accommodate Seagoing Vessels of moderate size can be constructed between Sheffield and the Ouse, Trent or Humber and if so the best route and probable cost'.[12]

The engineers came back late in October to say that:

> 'the existing waterway from Sheffield to Keadby was an excellent one but was spoilt by the fact that the locks were altogether inadequate and that the Engineers so far as they had gone considered that if new Locks were made side by side with the existing Locks without interfering with the traffic . . . that the waterway would then be available for Vessels of from 300 to 500 Tons capacity'.*[13]

A week later they estimated the cost of these new locks, and also of a new canal from Tinsley to Sheffield and basin there, at £1 million apart from the cost of buying the waterways from the M.S. & L. After having considered a report on the financial aspects and probable traffic, the committee decided to form the Sheffield & South Yorkshire Canal† Company Ltd, with a capital of £30,000 in £5 shares 'to promote and procure the passing of an Act . . . for the incorporation of a company' to build the new waterway. It was registered on 15 November 1888.

Sheffield Corporation gave cautious support, the veteran Charles Bartholomew was appointed a director, the Duke of Norfolk promised £5,000 and Earl Fitzwilliam £3,000, both offering also to take payment for lands needed in shares, some £28,000 was borrowed from the bank for the deposit to accompany the Bill, a prospectus was issued, and shares in the preliminary company allotted. The Bill had its first reading on 28 February 1889, public meetings in support were held, and a number of opposing petitions appeared, some outright, like that of the M.S. & L.R., some to establish a position for negotiation. Hull shipowners, for instance, as the price of their support, forced the company to drop powers they were seeking to run vessels abroad or coastwise. On

---

* Cory & Co then had 200–300 ton barges running on the Aire & Calder and on the Trent to Keadby. It was thought that these might also work to collieries on the Don.

† Originally they had called it the Sheffield Canal.

26 August the Act passed,[14] setting up an operating company, the Sheffield & South Yorkshire Navigation Co, with a capital of £1,500,000. It empowered them to acquire all four south Yorkshire canals by agreement or, after nine months, compulsorily, improve them or make new canals, and be inland carriers. They had to deposit £20,000 within six months as an earnest of serious negotiation. All this time the tonnage on the system was about 900,000, of which 400,000 was local, and 500,000 to and from the Trent at Keadby. The prospectus compared this total to the 2 million tons of the Aire & Calder.

The promoters were encouraged at having got their Act at the first attempt, and that the chairman of the Commons Committee had said: 'The Committee find that the Preamble of this Bill is proved, and they desire to state that they have arrived at their conclusion on the grounds of public policy.'[15] The promotion company, with the same board of directors as that set up under the Act, remained in existence until 1895, by which time terms had been negotiated with the railway company. They had spent some £25,000 in preliminary expenses, and received fully paid shares in the navigation concern in exchange for those of the canal company.

At the time of the Act, it seems that the promoters were proposing to rebuild the Don and the Keadby Canal to a 300 or 400 ton standard, but to enable both it and the Dearne & Dove to take compartment boat trains, for while the Bill was still in Parliament the board said that the Dearne & Dove:

'would be dredged and made available for Compartment Boats for the Carriage of Coal which could be shipped into larger Vessels either at the junction of that Canal with the River Dun Navigation or at Keadby and that it was anticipated that the Compartment system would be preferred for the Carriage of Coal from the Collieries to Keadby for Shipment there into larger Vessels instead of Shipping the Coal at the Collieries into Vessels capable of carrying only 300 to 400 tons and that if this were found to be the case the Manvers Main Colliery and the other Collieries on the Dearne & Dove Canal would derive the same benefit from the improved navigation as the Collieries on the Main Canal'.[16]

This also implies that they intended then to develop Keadby as a coal-shipping port along the lines of Goole.

The board was now an impressive one: it included the managing director of Newton Chambers, the chairman and managing director of John Brown, the chairman of Denaby Main colliery, a director of Wombwell Main colliery, Joseph Mitchell of Mitchell's Main colliery, agents of the Duke of Norfolk and Earl Fitz-william, and representatives of local authorities. They raised and deposited the £20,000, and then tried to start negotiations with the M.S. & L. The railway company made their attitude imme-diately clear: 'My company must not be taken as willing sellers of their Navigations, this they shewed by their opposition to the Bill.'[17] They therefore delayed until the nine months had passed: then, a notice requiring them to sell having been served, they started a long campaign of obstruction by beginning an action against the navigation company to restrain them from taking proceedings until the whole of their capital had been subscribed. Simultaneously, the S. & S.Y. applied to the Court of the Railway & Canal Commission. The M.S. & L. lost their action, the navi-gation company gained theirs, and went on to ask for plans and particulars of the railway company's property in the waterways. By the time these were first produced it was early 1891.

Meanwhile the company's thinking about the use of compart-ment boats had led to discussions with the Aire & Calder, with the idea that the S. & S.Y. would use Goole also, so making it unnecessary to develop a second similar port at Keadby. Agree-ment was reached in August 1890 on building the New Junction Canal from Bramwith on the S. & S.Y. for $5\frac{1}{2}$ miles to the Aire & Calder about seven miles from Goole, with one lock, Sykehouse, capable of taking compartment boat trains. A Bill was then pro-moted by the Aire & Calder to authorize such a canal and enable the S. & S.Y. to become joint subscribers and owners, and was passed on 28 July 1891.[18] Sheffield & South Yorkshire participa-tion had, however, to wait until they had actually acquired their waterways from the M.S. & L.R., and this was far off.

By early 1893 the properties to be bought had finally been de-fined and agreed, and financial bargaining began, this in turn hampered by the railway's coyness in allowing their accounts to be examined. After an appeal to the Railway & Canal Commission, terms were finally agreed in 1894, and incorporated in a S. & S.Y. Act of 31 July.[19] The agreed figure for the navigations, together with certain lands, mineral rights, plant and machinery, and compensation for severance, was £1,140,000, £600,000 of which was to be paid in cash. The balance the railway were willing to take in ordinary shares, giving an option to the S. & S.Y. to buy them at par upon six months notice. Meanwhile, as long as they held ordinary shares, they were to be represented on the S. & S.Y.

board. By early 1895 the company had, with a good deal of difficulty, placed £625,000 worth of 4½ per cent preference shares. Of
this figure, £125,000 had been subscribed by the M.S. & L.R. at
the price of also nominating one of the directors who represented
the preference shareholders. This decided the Aire & Calder not
to subscribe: 'Mr Bartholomew stated that he could not advise
his Board to take any shares and declined to have anything to do
with the undertaking under these circumstances.'[20] Meanwhile,
the Aire & Calder, waiting to begin the New Junction Canal, had
by an Act of 1893 got the time for compulsory acquisition of lands
extended to July 1896.

In the end, the Manchester, Sheffield & Lincolnshire nominated
five of the ten directors, though the chairman was usually chosen
from the independent members of the board. There was also
provision for arbitration between the conflicting interests on the
board.[21] The new company appointed George Welch from the
Birmingham Canal Navigations as general manager, and on 1
March 1895 took possession. It was not a good time. The Manchester Ship Canal had opened fifteen months before, having cost
much more than its estimate, and was finding it difficult to pay its
way. The enthusiasm of 1888 for waterways was over, and that of
the early 1900s had not yet been reached. Finally, tolls had been
reduced under the Railway & Canal Traffic Act of 1888.

The company started with great disadvantages. They had failed
to raise enough money to buy their waterways, and therefore had
strong railway influence upon the board. Still less had they been
able to raise working capital by selling ordinary shares to the
public. Therefore, far from being able to spend a million pounds
on reconstruction, as they had once hoped, they had no spare
money except from preference shareholders who had to be paid 4½
per cent immediately, and never managed to enlarge the waterway
beyond a 110-ton craft capacity, except for compartment boats.
Finally, the Dearne & Dove, with its continual subsidence, heavy
maintenance and declining traffic, was a financial millstone round
the new company's neck. Indeed, as early as 1906 the Worsbrough branch had had to be closed except as a water feeder, and
in 1906, due to subsidence, it was only possible to keep 4 ft 6 in in
the top end of the canal instead of 6 ft. After two more trouble-
some years, in their report of 5 April 1909, the board told their
shareholders that their practice was now to sell and lease coal
under the canal—in other words, no longer to try to mini-
mize subsidence.

The board began bravely, however, by extending the wharf, warehouse and cranage facilities at Sheffield basin, building a grain shed there, and then a 4-storey warehouse to straddle part of the basin. Their own office was also put there. Elsewhere, they dredged, raised banks and repaired along their line. Indeed, the year 1896 was something of a mirage—the only year the tonnage carried exceeded a million, the only one when they could pay 1 per cent on the ordinary shares, and the one with the highest toll earnings up to the First World War.

They were also now involved in jointly financing the New Junction Canal. In 1898 they decided to create £150,000 of debenture stock to be issued as required, to pay for their share of this, and to lengthen locks: £113,580 had been issued by 1904, when power to create £86,420 more than this by mortgages or debentures was taken, and another £50,000 in 1908.* In a period when tonnage carried was slowly falling year by year, and toll receipts were sluggish, they could do little more than finish the works at Sheffield,[22] though new warehouses were built at Rotherham and Crowle, and some other work done. Even then, their last ordinary dividend, of ¼ per cent, was paid in 1899: they were never to pay another. After 1901 they could only pay 4 per cent on their preference shares, and after 1903, 3 per cent. Yet they were brave enough to include powers to straighten the navigation at Doncaster and Sprotbrough among other improvements in their 1903 Act.

By the time the New Junction Canal had been opened, on 2 January 1905, their half share of its cost was £140,628: in the end it was almost exactly £150,000. In anticipation, they had straightened the Don below Doncaster, but minuted of the new canal:

> 'full use cannot be made of it, in connection with the working of compartment boats for Coal Traffic, till this Navigation near Doncaster and Sprotboro' has been improved by straightening'.[23]

The Doncaster straightening was opened in April: soon afterwards they let the contract for Sprotbrough, which was completed late in 1907. Even then, however, compartment boats could only be worked through the locks in threes, and therefore little improvement resulted.

The New Junction Canal, while it contributed little in direct tolls on its own length, helped over the next ten years to raise tonnage carried from 835,982 in 1905 to 961,774 in 1913, and toll

* £100,700 of 4 per cent terminable mortgages had been issued up to 1918.

Page 421 (*above*) A merchandise tug and tow, a compartment tug and train, and self-propelled craft, in Castleford cut in 1951; (*below*) the keel *Eddie* is launched at Shepley Bridge, Mirfield, on the Calder & Hebble in 1910

Page 422　The Sheffield & South Yorkshire: (*above*) eye of a needle; *Junior T*
negotiates Bacon Lane bridge on the Sheffield Canal; (*below*)
Doncaster lock about 1900

revenue from £48,981 to £53,586. In 1906, however, the Sheffield & South Yorkshire was still remarkably old fashioned compared with the Aire & Calder. A keel from Hull, carrying 100 tons and drawing 6 ft 6 in, would come up the Trent on the tide to Keadby, then sail up the canal to Thorne. Mast and sails would be taken out here or at Mexborough, and the boatman would arrange for horse-haulage to Sheffield with the horse-marines.[24] Very few motor barges appeared before the First World War (in 1906 there was only one),[25] and their use did not become general until the 1930s. The West Riding County Council, after receiving nearly 300 replies to inquiries it had made in 1907 in relation to the Royal Commission, reported that they thought the S. & S.Y. an antiquated system, insufficiently dredged, inadequately provided with wharves and cranes, and suffering from its virtual control by the Great Central Railway.[26]

The company followed the new straightenings by extending Doncaster lock in 1909 and 1910. And so, with further improvements at Tinsley, Rotherham, Doncaster and elsewhere, they reached 1914. It was the year of a keelmen's strike, a coal strike, and the beginning of a war, the first effect of which last was that the Admiralty took over many of the steam trawlers that traded to Hull and were accustomed to get their coal from the waterway, so that they now bunkered elsewhere. Here are pre-war averaged figures:

Years	Toll Revenue £	Tonnage tons	Pref. Dividend per cent	Ord. Dividend per cent
1896–1898	52,427	993,365	4·5	·5
1899–1901	47,655	902,637	4·5	·08
1902–1904	45,872	846,555	3·6	nil
1905–1907	48,899	860,703	3	nil
1908–1910	50,114	933,071	3	nil
1911–1913	51,653	938,087	2·8	nil

Meanwhile, even before the war had ended, Sheffield city council were considering a major improvement of the navigation. On 16 October 1918 they called a conference of manufacturers and another of local authorities, both of which were favourable. These were followed on 9 November by a council resolution to support an urgent improvement. Though they thought the government should nationalize the waterway and pay the costs, they were in principle willing to contribute if the navigation were to be freed from railway interference. Early the following year they com-

L

missioned a report from Sir John Wolfe-Barry, Lyster & Partners.

This firm put up several alternatives, from which on 18 March 1920 the transport sub-committee chose one, which they agreed to press upon the Minister of Transport, in the hope that the government would take over the waterway and carry it out. The plan proposed that the navigation between Tinsley and Keadby should be deepened to 8 ft from its existing nominal 6 to 6½ ft, the channel widened and straightened and bridges rebuilt. The locks, most of which only took craft some 62 ft × 16 ft, would be replaced by 18* new ones 270 ft × 22 ft with multiple gates, to take four 110 ton craft or one of up to 300 tons at once. A new basin would be built near Tinsley station, whence goods would be distributed to the eastern part of Sheffield. The rest of the Sheffield Canal would be improved, but would keep its existing locks, and Rotherham lock would remain to serve Rotherham cut and beyond. Their estimate was £1,483,426 plus an allowance for rising prices, not counting the cost to the government of acquiring the navigation from the company.[27] If the scheme had been accepted by the government, the future history of the Sheffield & South Yorkshire would have been very different. But the government had too much on its hands at a difficult time, and Sheffield, unlike Nottingham[28] in relation to the Trent, was not prepared to go ahead on its own. Simultaneously, there had been talk at Doncaster of a ship canal thence direct to Trent Falls, similar to the Ghent–Terneuzen Canal.[29]

The war ended much continental trade and disrupted that of the east coast. Costs rose, revenue fell, boats and men became scarce: 'the boats having been taken by the Government, and the men having joined His Majesty's Forces'.[30] No preference dividend could be paid for 1915 or 1916. The government took control of the S. & S.Y., as of most other canals, from 1 March 1917, and paid enough compensation to restore the preference dividend to 2½ per cent for 1917 and 3 per cent for 1918 and 1919. The war having ended, traffic offered, but many of the canal barges, and of the lighters that had worked in Hull docks, had been sunk; many more were being used:

'as Lighters and Warehouses—Shippers' Merchants and others being willing to pay very large sums per day for their use, in order to avoid paying demurrage on ships—with the result that

---

* Two new locks were to replace the four lower ones at Tinsley, while Eastwood Low and Kilnhurst Forge were to be eliminated.

Boats could not be obtained to convey traffic from the Humber ports to the Navigation, except at freights which customers refused to pay'.[31]

The rest only slowly trickled back to the Humber. Therefore money was lost and coal strikes affected traffic. In the middle of the trouble Welch retired as manager in February 1921.

Trade then revived a little, but during the inter-war period the navigation's existence was one long struggle against depression and railway, later also road, competition. In the years 1920 to 1930 only one preference dividend could be paid, 1½ per cent for 1924. Then payments were resumed, but never more than 1¼ per cent. Tonnage, 485,332 in 1924, fell to 381,727 in the general strike year of 1926, then built up to 815,329 in 1937. But this improvement was deceptive, for it marked a substitution of short-distance, low-rated traffic for long-distance movements paying higher tolls. Therefore toll revenue, £49,367 in 1927 with a tonnage of 507,833, was only £51,833 in 1937, when the tonnage was over 800,000. The company in 1923 started to pay money to a mortgage redemption reserve, and managed to keep these payments going.

Two major improvements were, however, made. In 1930 the company agreed with the Aire & Calder and the Hatfield Main Colliery Co Ltd* to lengthen Bramwith lock at a cost of some £20,000, and provide a colliery lay-by, to enable compartment boats to reach the colliery. It was opened in September 1932. In 1931, also, they agreed with Doncaster corporation for the straightening of a section of navigation there, largely at corporation expense, and the building of a new 300 ft long wharf and warehouse; they were opened on 24 July 1934. From the 1920s to the company's end they had also carried out a steady programme of bank protection, especially on the Keadby Canal, and this had greatly speeded up passage times. In 1925, also, a 2,000 ton grain silo was built at Sheffield basin by a group of millers.

The Elsecar branch of the Dearne & Dove had had to be closed in 1928 because of subsidence, and in 1934, the year the last boat went through to Barnsley, the company decided to close most of the canal, except the ⅞ mile nearest to the Barnsley Canal, which on reflection the Aire & Calder refused to take over. Coal traffic had dwindled because old and relatively small mines had been worked out, and new ones sunk further east in a better position to supply Sheffield, Rotherham and Hull, the canal used smaller barges than the main waterway, which the company thought were

* Hatfield Main is on the Stainforth & Keadby Canal.

no longer worth building, and subsidence had created great problems:

'During the last 140 years as many as three seams of coal have been worked out under detached lengths of the canal causing a subsidence of no less than ten feet, and the Company has been put to great expense to maintain the original depth of water throughout. In fact the point has been reached when it is impracticable to maintain a navigable waterway throughout with safety.'[32]

A Bill was approved at the end of 1934, but not in fact proceeded with because of expected opposition. Stainforth lock, connecting the Stainforth & Keadby Canal and the Don, was closed in 1939.

In that year came the Second World War and, in time, government control again. The canal at Sheffield was badly damaged in 1940. The banks were breached, Sheffield wharf and sheds were damaged, as were Tinsley lock and the pumping plant building. Two years later, subsidence at the Barnsley end of the Dearne & Dove ended traffic there.

After the war, the company found that oil traffic was increasing, and immediate prospects were more hopeful. In 1946, in conjunction with the carriers, they started to collect goods from works in Sheffield, carry them, and see them loaded into steamers at Hull or Goole. Financially also their position was better. Most mortgages had been redeemed, and in 1946 they decided to pay off the £16,200 still outstanding. Preference dividends, unpaid for 1940 and 1941, had been resumed with ½ per cent for 1942 and 1 per cent for 1943 and 1944. For 1945 1¼ per cent was paid, for 1946 1½ per cent. Tonnage in 1946 was 694,013.

The Transport Act of 1947 transferred the system to the British Transport Commission from 1 January 1948. Curiously, in their first year of 1895, the waterway was affected by a 15-week freeze-up, and in their last, 1947, there was another great frost. The Keadby line closed, but that to Goole was kept open. A final preference dividend of 3⅜ per cent was paid, after which the debenture stock was valued at £85 per £100, the preference shares at £22, and the ordinary shares, dividendless for over 40 years, at £5 10s (£5·50) per £100.

In 1952 a substantial remaining traffic of the Dearne & Dove, the coal and tar traffic from Manvers Main colliery at the Swinton end, ceased when the National Coal Board transferred it to road transport as part of a process reorganization. In 1961 the canal was abandoned by British Transport Commission Act except for a

¼ mile section at the Swinton end, including five of the six locks. Pumps were installed to supply this with water, and it is still in use to serve Dale, Brown & Co's glassworks and Ernest Waddington's boatyard.

In 1954 the Commission built two coal staithes at Mexborough, for loading craft to carry it to the new power station at Doncaster. The S. & S.Y. was then still dependent on coal for some 86 per cent of its traffic.

The Commission drew up and implemented a programme of improvements for the S. & S.Y. at a capital cost of £614,000. This included extensive steel and concrete piling, and also a new lock at Long Sandall. The old one, 70 ft long, had been a bottleneck between two 215 ft locks at Sykehouse below on the New Junction Canal, and Doncaster above. A new lock, 215 ft long and 22 ft wide, with 9½ ft of water over the sills, and intermediate gates at 78 ft and 137 ft, was opened on 10 July 1959, so enabling trains of 17 compartment boats to reach Doncaster wharf and Hexthorpe, 1 mile beyond. The upper gates were power operated (later the middle and lower gates were also dealt with) and the locks provided with sodium lighting.

In 1961 the B.T.C., the Sheffield Chamber of Commerce and the British Iron & Steel Federation were considering whether the main line could be enlarged to a 250 ton waterway. They envisaged an expenditure of some £3 million, including the removal of the navigation's terminus from Sheffield, where traffic was declining.[33] Work then started on modern wharves and warehouses at a new depot at Rotherham, which has since greatly expanded.

In 1963 a new deep lock was built at Tinsley to replace two old ones; it was made necessary by a new railway bridge connecting the freight terminal with Tinsley marshalling yards.

Traffic on the Sheffield & South Yorkshire in 1962 was 938,418 tons,* with a toll income of £87,078; in 1971 it was 503,504 with tolls of £32,900.

In 1966 the British Waterways Board submitted to the Ministry a £2½ million scheme for rebuilding the main line between Bramwith and Rotherham in order to carry another million tons. It proposed 10 new mechanized locks, 225 ft × 25 ft with 10 ft over the sills, to replace the 12 existing locks above Long Sandall, and make the line of the same dimensions as the Aire & Calder except for rather less clearance under bridges. It was rejected. In 1972 the

* Coal, 736,525 tons; liquids in bulk, 49,001 tons; general merchandise, 152,892 tons.

British Waterways Board, after commissioning management consultants to study the commercial traffic which could result from a £2 million improvement scheme covering the 12-mile Doncaster–Rotherham section to enable 700-ton barges to reach Mexborough and 400-ton craft to reach Rotherham, put the proposal to the Department of the Environment for sanction.

In 1969 it was decided to introduce push-towing on the Sheffield & South Yorkshire, an initial order being placed for two diesel push-tugs and nine 100–140-ton compartment boats similar to those already in use on the Aire & Calder for carrying coal to Ferrybridge 'C' power station. They began work in 1971.

At the time of the 1885 Act, a popular song ran:

> 'There will be great joy and singing
> St George's bells may crack with ringing
> This will be, I'll bet a crown, Sir,
> When Doncaster is a seaport town, Sir.'[34]

We still await the day.

Greasbrough Canal

The Newbiggin branch closed before 1900. The lower ⅝ mile of the main canal ceased to be commercially used between 1914 and 1928,[35] probably about the end of the war. The last boat into it was probably one of Waddington's to the Park Gate dry dock about 1928.

Thorne and Hatfield Moors Peat Canals

In the 1880s and afterwards, peat moss found a new market as litter for the very many horses used by public utilities. Peat cutting began again on Thorne Moor. A number of companies were founded, one of which, the Dutch Griendtsveen Moss Litter Co Ltd, built both boating dikes and tramways. In 1896 it was partially absorbed along with four others, by the British Peat Moss Litter Company. A waterway system was built, or adapted from old drains and cuttings by the Dutch company, quite separate from the older canals. It ran from the centre of Thorne Moor over an aqueduct, to the litter works, which had a short branch off the Thorne–Goole line of the N.E.R. It was used until the 1920s.[36]

CHAPTER XIX

East Riding Waterways

✦✦

Beverley Beck

THE Hull and Bridlington Railway reached Beverley in October 1846, and naturally affected the Beck's trade, though authors of the mid-1850s say the trade then still amounted to between £500 and £600 p.a.[1] In 1856 there was much local agitation when a Shipping Bill was introduced which aimed at getting rid of local dues on shipping. Beverley Beck came within its scope, and the corporation saw their revenue disappearing. However, they were not alone in opposition, and the Bill was withdrawn.[2]

Here are figures for the navigation during the century:

Year	Tonnage tons	Gross Revenue £	Profit/Loss £
1848	33,498	635	
1858	36,227	689	
1868	39,859	744	
1888	51,578	983	527
1898	56,299*	780	194
1905	101,540†	747	111 loss

* Most of this was inwards traffic: 46,669 tons was discharged on the navigation, and 9,630 tons loaded.
† Of which coal was 21,500 tons and other minerals, 4,778 tons.

Coal originating on the Aire & Calder and coming to Beverley Beck and the Hull River rose in the fifties and held steady in the sixties: 18,231 tons in 1851, 32,082 in 1861, 31,578 in 1870. But grain returning fell from 13,839 tons in 1852 and 11,087 in 1856 to 4,060 in 1866 and 3,605 in 1870. In 1870 and also in 1888 the navigation had a debt of £1,000 at 4½ per cent, but by 1898 another £2,000 had been borrowed at 3½ per cent, this to be repaid in instalments. This was to instal pumping plant to take water from the Hull River. In 1905 the plant was described as 'a steam engine and centrifugal pump fixed near the Lock Pit'.[3] In 1898 traffics were described as: 'Coal, leather, hides, tanning materials and products, artificial manure and ingredients, chalk and whiting, linseed and other seed, linseed and cotton cake and oil, wheat, bricks, tiles and sand.'[4] Under the Canal Tolls & Charges Act No 3 of 1894, consequential upon the Railway & Canal Traffic Act of 1888, the charging power of the corporation was restricted to the boundary of the municipal borough. This led, as the figures show, to a considerable fall in revenue in spite of a greater tonnage.

Craft were sometimes sailed up the Beck, more often manually hauled. In 1898 it was said that, 'A few keels are towed by a steam launch,'[5] but this soon ended. Later, traction problems were solved with the introduction of powered keels. Traffic out in 1906 included 952 tons of fertilizers, 342 of burnt ore, 1,395 of flour and 515 of scrap iron. In 1916 figures were 1,518 tons of fertilizer and 912 of burnt ore.

Grovehill lock was rebuilt in 1958 at a cost of £30,000, and takes craft 65 ft × 17 ft 6 in, with a draft of 6 ft 6 in. Barges still come to Beverley: in 1970, 28,169 tons were carried on the Beck, and £2,365 received in dues. Traffic is mainly coal, and materials for cattle food. There is still pumping plant at Grovehill lock. Near the Beck stand two public houses whose names remind us of older days, the Sloop Inn and the Mariner's Arms.

Driffield Navigation

Railways came to the Driffield area in 1845, and clearly had support among the commissioners who controlled the navigation, for when their chief official proposed in February that an additional lock should be built near the Leven Canal, the towpath extended to Hull, and inquiries made whether the proposed Hull and Bridlington railway would hinder trade by crossing the roads leading to wharves on the level, they decided it was not at present expedient to consider additional works, and that it was not 'requisite for them to interfere with the proposed course of the Hull and Bridlington Railway as they depend upon the Directors keeping a sufficient guard upon the Road to prevent accidents'.[6] This line, running through Driffield, opened on 6 October 1846: the event caused the Aire & Calder to offer a prompt drawback on coal.[7]

A year later the proposed Malton & Driffield Railway presented a worse threat because of its planned branch from Driffield to

Frodingham bridge, which would have competed directly with the navigation. The commissioners held an anxious meeting in February 1846, saying the branch would give 'facility to the Conveyance of Corn and Goods to that part of the Navigation from which the Tolls are already taken off'[8] which would so reduce their takings as to endanger the repayment of the remaining £6,139 of debt. They therefore pressed the railway promoters to make up the deficiency, and got a guarantee for four years.[9] However, the branch was never built. Perhaps the railway was discouraged by the old navigation's toll cuts of December 1846, roughly by half.

A sign of the times was the commissioners' failure to let the Hull bridge tolls in 1847. For a year they themselves collected them, until in 1848 they were let at £80 against the previous £100. But this was too much: in 1850 the figure was £65, in 1851 £50. In 1850 there were threats from the York & North Midland Railway: 'in consequence of certain proposals' made by them 'to the Cornfactors of Great Driffield',[10] the commissioners further cut grain tolls in 1 January 1851, and in 1853 bravely sent a deputation to the Aire & Calder 'to urge upon them the necessity for a reduction of the Tolls upon their Navigation'.[11]

The commissioners had now got their second wind in fighting competition, and in 1855 asked Edward Welsh to report on how best to improve the navigation. He reported[12] that the worst part of the navigation was that from Hull bridge to Struncheonhill: 'from the insufficient depths of water in this part . . . the traffic is nearly always interrupted and delayed; and these interruptions are frequently of such duration as to make the passage from Hull to Driffield occupy from four to eight days; whereas' with a spring tide 'the passage may be effected in twenty-four hours'. He suggested three alternatives: a long cut across the sharp bend near Arram from Eske to a point below the Leven Canal, and a lock on it, where the tidal effect was small; a short cut and lock above Eske; and a second lock at Struncheonhill and dredging below it, the last being much the most expensive because of the dredging required. It is likely that by now the lower lock of the Struncheonhill pair had been disused for some time:* certainly it was described in 1874 as 'fallen into decay and . . . not . . . used for many years'.[13] The first and second schemes would give the Leven Canal more water; the third slightly less. The second and cheapest plan was adopted, and a Bill introduced which also proposed to

* In 1839 the minute book refers to the lock in the singular.

amalgamate the two navigations. It was strongly opposed in Parliament by landowners who feared flooding, and had to be withdrawn, having cost the concern £730.

In 1860 the commissioners, told that a group of Driffield people were forming a company to run a screw steamboat to carry merchandise, said they had no objection so long as a speed limit of 3 m.p.h. was observed above Struncheonhill. This may have been the steam barge that was running early in the present century.[14] In the fifties and sixties coal coming on to the navigation from the Aire & Calder was steady: in 1851, 7,683 tons; in 1861, 8,367 tons; in 1870, 7,340 tons. Grain going towards the Aire & Calder system, however, was a different story: the 31,898 tons of 1852 was 24,223 in 1855 and 10,068 in 1856, while ten years later there was none at all. After that a small traffic returned.

Tolls were falling away fast: a combined average for both navigations of £889 for 1878–81 had become £450 in 1898–1901 and £444 in 1905, in which year the profit was £13. Tonnages were 35,654 in 1871, 28,818 in 1888, 24,117 in 1898 and 32,666 in 1905, the principal traffics being coal, linseed, cottonseed, wheat and flour, and later, artificial manures, carried the whole length. An average boat-load was 60 tons: the maximum, around 75 tons. The navigation was valued partly as by its very existence keeping down railway rates.

By now, the lock-keeper of the Leven Canal collected Hull bridge tolls. In spite of their finances, the commissioners were brave enough in 1898 to buy a steam dredger for £511, which they hired out when not in use, for instance to Beverley corporation and Joseph Rank. In 1910 they were told by 'several Captains' that 'the navigation is in a better state than they have ever known it before'.[15] Happily the North Eastern Railway, who at the turn of the century had been empowered to build a Beverley–North Frodingham line, did not do so. Takings in 1910 were up to £659, helped by traffic to the oil and cake mills at Driffield, and by dredger hire.

In 1922 combined receipts were £714, and profit £88. Of the original debt, £331·50 remained. Nine years later, in 1931, receipts were down to £414, profit to £11. Tonnages had fallen: cottonseed, linseed, oil and cake, 10,795 in 1922, were 4,672, though wheat was up from 1,988 to 2,606 tons. Pleasure boats yielded £7, against £1·80.

The last commercial craft to Driffield was the *Caroline* keel in 1944, to Brigham the *Ellen* in 1948.[16] Soon afterwards the line became unnavigable upwards from Struncheonhill. However, in 1970 the Driffield Navigation Amenities Association was formed to press for restoration.

Leven Canal

The canal would have been given greater depth and so benefited by the Driffield Navigation's proposal in their Bill of 1855 to build a lock below the Leven's junction with the Hull River, but this failed to pass, and no such change was made.

About the same time a description of the canal tells us that it had a considerable traffic in corn, lime, coal, etc., and that at its head, near the large and comfortable New Inn, was a commodious wharf, and the warehouses etc. of Hugh William Jackson, corn merchant.[17] In 1863 the Aire & Calder offered a one-third drawback on tolls on coal sent to the Leven Canal, on condition that 'a competent reduction' was made in Leven rates.[18] This trade must therefore have been of some importance.

The Hull & Hornsea Railway, opened in March 1864, though its line was some way from Leven, did draw away much of the canal's trade with its hinterland.

In 1888, when 4,242 tons were carried, the canal was leased to James Iveson for £110 p.a., but he relinquished it in 1891, after which it was not immediately let again. Tonnage fell to 3,765 in 1892 and 3,088 in 1893 when the tolls taken were £122, then rose again to 3,194 in 1898 and 4,546 in 1905 when the canal showed a profit of £123.[19] The improvement may have been due to the lower tolls enforced under the Railway & Canal Traffic Act of 1888. However, road traffic then increasingly competed with the waterway. From the latter part of the nineteenth century the Leven Canal lock-keeper for a commission collected the Hull bridge tolls for the Driffield Navigation commissioners, and was still doing so in 1932.

The canal was still in the hands of the Bethell family when it was closed to traffic in 1935, and sold on 30 July 1963 to Mr Frank Hopkinson of Conisbrough for £1,950. He died in 1969. In 1971 possible development as a marina and amenity park was proposed by a group of Hull businessmen.

Market Weighton Canal

Because the York & North Midland's York–Beverley line for

the time being got no further than Market Weighton, the canal benefited from the railway rather than the reverse. Even though takings fell when the North Eastern Railway completed the line in 1865, they held up well until the early 1880s. Here are averaged figures:

Years	Tolls £	Years	Tolls £
1850–54	802	1870–74	774
1855–59	745	1875–79	733
1860–64	1,077	1880–84	923
1865–69	1,010		

As soon as the sale (see p. 313) to the York & North Midland Railway had been completed, the trustees realized that navigation needs could now be subordinated to drainage if they wished, and in 1851 they asked their committee to get a report 'on the expence of converting the Canal into a warping Drain, and the advantages to be derived from it'.[20] But when they got it, they left matters as they were, perhaps because of the uncompleted railway.

The railway company, the only shareholders, were paid the balance in the navigation account annually after expenses had been met, and they authorized, or sometimes themselves did, any special engineering work. Such were the major repairs to Humber lock in 1856–8, partially financed by raising tolls. From the middle 1860s, when the York–Market Weighton railway was extended to Beverley for Hull, the section of navigation above Sod House, with little business remaining, and which under the 1784 award had been allocated as a navigation cost, because not essential to drainage, slowly silted up.

The coal trade, assuming most came from the Aire & Calder, was small. Tonnages originating on that system and entering the canal were 7,683 in 1851, 8,367 in 1861 and 7,340 in 1870.

In 1881 the trustees resolved that it was desirable to reduce tolls, presumably because the total had fallen back from £779 in 1887 to £654 in 1880, and asked the N.E.R. to reconsider them. Then the navigation had four exceptional years, for a reason not apparent in the records, taking £961, £1,137, £1,019 and £846. But the year ending 31 March 1885 saw a heavy fall to £503. Some tolls were then reduced. Instead of stimulating trade, this merely reduced takings, to £291 in 1886 and only £194 in 1892.

In 1888, with only £33 in hand, the trustees began to dredge the upper section, and asked the N.E.R. to lend enough to complete

MARKET WEIGHTON CANAL.

NOTICE IS HEREBY GIVEN,

That the Canal will be run as usual during CAVE FAIR WEEK, commencing MONDAY, JUNE 8th, and the PONDS above SOD HOUSE LOCK, will also be CLOSED from the above date for necessary Repairs.

BY ORDER.

THOS. MITCHELL,

SURVEYOR.

MAY, 14th, 1865.

WILLIAM WILSON, MACHINE PRINTER & STATIONER, MARKET WEIGHTON.

37. A stoppage on the Market Weighton Canal

the job. They refused, and in 1890–1 the balances, totalling £276, were used for this purpose. It was not enough, and in 1894 the surveyor reported that 'the canal from Sodhouse lock to Weighton end was not navigable'.[21] Finances were now very tight. No further payment was made to the N.E.R. after £60 in 1889, and in 1895 the trustees were trying to get the railway's views as the 'general liability of the Company and Trustees in maintaining the Canal'.[22] Talks and manoeuvres continued. Then the railway agreed to relinquish their rights, and Henry Williamson & Co, who used the lower part of the canal for their brick and tile making businesses around Newport,* agreed to make up annual deficiencies to a maximum of £175 p.a. for some twenty years if the 4 miles of canal nearest Humber lock were kept open.

The result was the Market Weighton Drainage Act of 1900, which gave powers to abandon the canal above Sod House lock. Takings continued to fall, and Williamson's had to make deficits good in every year, in spite of a thorough dredging of the section up to the N.E.R. bridge in 1910, using the Ouse Navigation's dredger. Little was done to the length upwards of the bridge, and there were complaints about it in 1913. The year 1910 saw the first of several annual aquatic sports meetings at Newport, 1914 a toll of 2s 6d (12½p) instituted for pleasure boats.

The war caused traffic to fall away almost to nothing, as the county War Agricultural Committee gave priority to drainage, closing the canal to navigation by order of 30 August 1917. That was also the last year of Williamson's guarantee, but the trustees told them they could continue to use the canal at their own risk. The trustees reassumed control from 31 March 1920, and got a grant from the Ministry of Agriculture for dredging. Thereafter a little navigation revived, craft with half-loads reaching the brickworks,[23] but drainage was the more important. Here are averaged figures to 1927:

Years	Tolls £	Years	Tolls £
1885–89	263	1910–14	99
1890–94	224	1915–19	29
1895–99	135	1920–24	24
1900–04	108	1925–27	71
1905–09	109		

* Newport had grown up where the canal intersected the Hull–West Riding rail and road lines.

The last craft passed the entrance lock on 31 March 1958, and by order of 1970,[24] the entrance lock was abandoned from 13 January 1971.

CHAPTER XX

Along the Ouse

The Ouse Navigation

TOLL revenue continued to fall, from the £2,038 of 1845 to the £1,540 of 1850, when the arrival of the Great Northern Railway at York forced a halving of tolls other than on coal.[1] The trustees were confident enough of this trade, upheld as it then was by Aire & Calder drawbacks, actually to raise their rate by 1d a ton. They were correct. The trade maintained itself, valuable in its own right and as keeping railway rates down, though in 1853–4 a rates agreement with the York & North Midland Railway caused the Aire & Calder to abolish the drawbacks. The navigation company reversed this policy, however, in 1865, when they reduced coal tolls to a uniform 1s 6d (7½p) a ton from all collieries on the Barnsley Canal for coal to or above York: the saving was up to 10d a ton. It did no good: tonnage from the Barnsley Canal to York, 11,443 tons in 1851 and 2,785 in 1861, was 794 in 1870. During the same period, grain traffic down the Ouse to the Aire & Calder halved, from 16,342 tons in 1852 to 7,925 in 1870.

An important initiative was taken in May 1866 when William Thompson, who owned lighters at Hull, asked that Naburn lock should be lengthened to at least 120 ft. The trustees called in W. H. Bartholomew, who reported later in the year recommending its extension to 136 ft, at a cost of £5,250, so that it could take a small steam coaster or two keels, and be similar in size to those on the upper sections of the Aire & Calder whence most of the traffic came. Returning in 1871, Bartholomew added that regular dredging was necessary below the lock, which meant that the trustees must replace their lost dredger or borrow another.

In face of the steady slide in toll receipts, itself partly the result of lack of dredging, no steam towing, and too small a lock, from £1,540 in 1845 to £1,256 in 1870, the trustees got themselves into a state of paralysis until, largely owing to the initiative of George Leeman, York's M.P. and a member of the council, the engineer Sir John Coode was in 1876 asked to report. He ambitiously proposed a new lock 140 ft × 32 ft alongside the old one, and the purchase of a dredger, the cost to be some £40,000. By this time the river had silted up to roughly the condition in which Rhodes had seen it in 1834.

Though still too nervous to build the lock, the trustees did buy a dredger, six hopper-barges and a steam tug. These helped toll receipts to climb over the £2,000 mark in 1884, partly because of Henry Leetham's rapidly growing flour milling business, founded at York in 1850. The seventies did, however, see the end of the Ouse passenger packets, no longer able to find custom once direct rail links had been built between Hull and Goole (1869) and York and Selby (1871).

However, a decisive incentive to action was given in 1886 when the War Office began a wharf at Selby for military supplies. Hoping to attract this traffic to York, A. F. Fowler was asked to prepare plans. He did so, the decision was at last taken in 1886, and on 27 July 1888 the new lock, 150 ft × 26 ft, was opened alongside the old one. Ironically, in the following year the trustees, who had read their own Acts less carefully than had the War Office, discovered they had no power to charge tolls on government stores. However, by 1896 traffic had climbed to 224,075 tons (115,532 of which was grain and flour), and receipts to £5,073. By then the corporation were working two tugs, and by 1905 were to have four.

The river was now transformed. Leetham's steam barges of up to 250 tons worked to York, and in 1908–9 the tugs towed 4,671 craft on the river. Peak year was 1904–5, when 6,765 boats passed Naburn lock carrying 373,171 tons, one-half being grain and flour. In 1888 Fowler had also proposed a lock above Wharfe mouth. L. F. Vernon-Harcourt in 1889 suggested a half-tide weir below the Wharfe, at Kelfield, to which Fowler agreed, and much the same proposal was made in 1906 by the York city engineer, A. Creer. But it was too expensive to consider seriously. The report of the Royal Commission of 1909 thought more should be done:

'the river needs much dredging, straightening of banks, training works and probably a lower lock and half-tide movable weir to keep back the warp. The profits of the traffic itself are small, and there does not appear to be on the part of the citizens of

M

York any disposition to take a large risk, with the hope . . . of making their city an inland port for sea-going vessels. The existing work on the river appears to be hardly sufficient to maintain it, even in its present condition.'

In fact, before the First World War, only minor improvements were made, the most notable being the realignment of the mouth of the Wharfe in 1912 and 1913 to lessen shoal formation.

The navigation suffered from the war. After it, as with so many others, the corporation asked the Ministry of Transport to take it over, as a means of increasing tolls above the legal limits until legislation could be passed. The request was to have an unexpected result, for the Ministry insisted that special traders' rates, notably Leetham's, should be ended. The corporation then discovered that the original agreement had been *ultra vires* under their Acts. Leetham's fought the case, and lost. In spite of a new favourable and legal offer from York, Leetham's then moved to Hull. The trade lost was never fully regained. Gross revenue, £9,624 in 1927, had fallen to £7,059 by 1938. For the year 1938-9, 202,625 tons were carried.

Since the end of the Second World War, there has been a great increase in traffic to Selby, some by small seagoing craft from the continent, some in big lighters from Hull. In 1966 some ¾ million tons moved to Selby, 88,687 to York. In 1969 the Ouse trustees began to charge cargoes in tidal waters: in 1971 the tonnage charged was 373,779, while York's trade was down to 41,766.

Derwent Navigation

From 1845 the Earl's profits fell heavily: £4,145 in 1845, they were £1,408 a year later and only £600 in 1854. In January 1844 he had cut his coal toll from 1s 8d (8½p) to 1s 4d (6½p), and two years later reduced it again to 10d (4p), soon after the Aire & Calder had given a 6d (2½p) drawback. They ended it in 1850, as part of a traffic agreement with the York & North Midland Railway which gave the latter the Derwent, Market Weighton and Driffield trade, and the former that of the Ouse to York.

The York & North Midland followed this up by proposing in 1851 an arrangement with Earl Fitzwilliam. He rejected it, saying: 'It appears to me that the effect of concluding a negotiation . . . with that Company will be to destroy the Navigation of the River Derwent, and, as I am persuaded that its maintenance is exceedingly beneficial to the country which it traverses, and

particularly to the town of Malton and my tenants there and thereabouts, I must entirely reject the proposal.'[2]
An offer of a guarantee of current receipts made in January 1852 was also turned down.

In 1852 the Aire & Calder ended their own traffic agreement with the railway, and restored the Derwent drawback: it was a year when 27,441 tons of their coal went up the river, 17,120 tons of it to Malton. But the following year they made a new agreement with the Y. & N.M.R. and Lord Fitzwilliam, and once again it was withdrawn. However, late in 1853 or early in 1854 a tripartite agreement seems to have been signed which allocated traffics and receipts. Tonnages for 1853 and 1854 (year ending 31 July) were 37,387 and 43,764 respectively, of which 23,009 (24,853) were coal and 6,351 (6,210) were grain. By now traffic to Yedingham had probably ended: tolls above New Malton are shown on a tollsheet of 1 January 1844 but not on another of 1855.

The Earl's tolls and similar receipts, £6,018 in 1845, had fallen to £2,297 in 1854. He changed his mind. John Hargreaves of the Aire & Calder, who in November 1853 had said 'my Directors prefer traffic to money', wrote again to the Earl's agent, N. C. Copperthwaite, on 28 February 1854: 'I observe by the Newspaper reports of the North Eastern Railway Meeting that Earl Fitzwilliam is in treaty with the Railway Company for some arrangement as to the Traffic of the Derwent. . . . My impression is that Navigations generally should strenuously resist all arrangements calculated to check their tonnage traffic,' and a week later: 'I note . . . that you have made a Traffic Agreement with the N.E.R. Coy on the Earl Fitzwilliam's behalf.'[3]

It soon became more than a traffic agreement. On 6 October 1854 the railway decided to open negotiations for a sale or lease of the Derwent;[4] they were successful, and on 1 October 1855 the Earl sold the navigation for £40,000, though the agreement was not signed until the following year.[5] Even before the sale, the railway had arranged for sidings to be put into river-served coalyards.[6] As the sale would have been illegal, the transaction was made not with the North Eastern Railway, but with their manager, engineer and solicitor personally, the railway company, as owners of the Pocklington Canal, then leasing the Derwent for 21 years from their own officers under the Canal Carriers' Act, which enabled one canal authority to lease a canal from another. So they gained control of the navigation against the intentions of Parlia-

REDUCTION OF DUES

ON THE

RIVER DERWENT

1st of January, 1851.

The following alterations in the Tariff of Dues payable on the River Derwent, on Vessels to and from Malton, into and from the River Ouse, will take place and be payable from the 1st of January, 1851, viz:

On Coal, Slack, and Cinders,	... ...	4d. per Ton, instead of 10d.
On Flour and Shelling,	... ...	4d. per 20 stone, instead of 6d.
On Wheat, Barley, Beans, Oats, Peas, Rye, Maslin, Malt, Line Seed, and Rape Seed,		4½ per Quarter, instead of 6d. Winchester measure.
On Bones, Cobbles, Flints, Horns, Shoddy, Guano, Nitrate of Soda, and other artificial or manufactured Composts or Manures,		1s. 6d. per Ton, instead of 2s. 6d.
On Carrots, Potatoes, Turnips, Chalk, Flags, (10 square yards) Fullers Earth, Kelp, Ling, Oils, Oil-Cake, Plaster, Pipe-Clay, Rags, Ropes, Slate, Stone, (16 cube feet) Whiting, Cement,		1s. 6d. per Ton, instead of 3s.
On Alum, Coppers, Fish, Grease, Iron of all descriptions, Lead, Tallow, Wood, Chicory,	... ...	2s. per Ton, instead of 3s.

Malton, 28th Dec. 1850.

W. ALLEN.

SMITHSON, PRINTER, YORKERSGATE, MALTON.

38. The Derwent makes heavy toll cuts in 1850

ment, though not of the Earl. When his willingness to sell became known, the local Malton newspaper suggested the town
itself might buy the navigation,[7] but this was a forlorn hope.

Traffic declined. Partly this was due to the falling away of the
internal corn trade in face of imported coal; this meant less corn
to Wakefield, and so less coal back. Much more it was due to the
railway heavily raising navigation tolls while offering favourable
railway rates, and later, to discouraging what traffic remained by
insufficient maintenance. Because they bought the river from a
private owner, no agreed clauses in a purchase Act provided for
the continuance of low tolls or even of the navigation. As regards
corn, in 1852 37,567 tons of corn from the Derwent had passed to
the Aire & Calder. In 1855, this had already fallen to 25,298 tons.
Increased railway rates brought the figure sharply down to 6,981
tons in 1856. By 1866 it was only 170 tons.

Coal had originally been charged 1s 4d (6½p) for the whole
length to Malton. Railway competition drove this down at one
time to 4d. In October 1855, when it was 1s 8d (8½p) the railway
company raised it to 2s 8d (13½p). The Aire & Calder tried to
counter this by asking coal owners to reduce their charges while
they themselves gave drawbacks on cargoes moving above Stamford Bridge.[8] However, in early 1858 they preferred to see the
trade to points above Stamford Bridge and to the Pocklington
Canal dwindle than to extend their drawbacks further and create
uncomfortable precedents.[9] Coal traffic originating on the Aire &
Calder system fell as follows:

Year	To Malton tons	To rest of Derwent and Pocklington Canal tons
1851	14,331	10,260
1861	6,482	9,501
1870	3,593	5,851

As for merchandise, the railway raised the top rate to a prohibitive
8s (40p). The 70 or 80 barges said to be working to Malton in 1855
fell away until in 1894 only one was left.

In 1871 the North Eastern Railway included a clause in their
Bill of that year to buy the navigation, still leased from their own
officers. Traders and landowners of the district, backed by the
Aire & Calder, opposed it on the grounds that it did not provide
for reducing the 'present extravagant Toll'[10] of 8s (40p) a ton, or
for effective maintenance, and the clause was struck out. As a

result, as railway opponents pointed out in 1894,[11] the lease eventually expired, and a subsequent lease or purchase would probably have been invalid because the Regulation of Railways Act 1873, s.16, made railway purchase of canals very difficult. So in theory those three railway officers and their successors continued to own the Derwent, and, opponents said, the N.E.R. thereby evaded its responsibilities under the Railway & Canal Traffic Act.

In the 1890s a Derwent Navigation Committee was formed by traders at Malton, who attacked the railway before the toll inquiries tribunal held under the Railway & Canal Traffic Act, 1888. These alleged that, because silting had reduced loads to 45 tons from 60 or more, and because the railway had raised tolls so high, trading was virtually impossible, so that only on the lower reach was any real trade left, to and from Hugh Fox's yard at Sutton with coal, gravel, lime and manure. Tonnage in 1888 was 11,799 with tolls of £565; in 1898, 8,583, with tolls of £156, and in 1905, 6,076 and £106. In 1905 the principal traffics were roadstone (1,108 tons), cave ash (536), bricks (517), manure (480), and potatoes (410).

By the time the Derwent Valley Light Railway opened in July 1913, running parallel to the lower river from York downwards past Elvington and Stamford Bridge for 16 miles to Cliff Common station on the Selby–Market Weighton railway, there was almost no river traffic.

By 1915 the N.E.R. had one barge and a lighter at Malton: there was also a float owned by the Malton U.D.C. In 1921 the Derwent was transferred to the London & North Eastern Railway until 1935, when responsibility for the river moved to the Yorkshire Ouse Catchment Board, who obtained an Order[12] extinguishing the right of public navigation.

In 1936 the Catchment Board rebuilt Sutton lock with its old timber floor, and put in a new steel upper gate. It was opened in 1937 to navigation for a short time.[13] However, in 1939 the board's report said that Stamford Bridge lock was 'no longer used for navigation', the lock cut being 'almost completely silted up'. In 1960 the last commercial barge passed Sutton lock. The Yorkshire Derwent Trust has now been formed, and has agreed with the Yorkshire River Authority that the Trust may at its own expense rebuild the Derwent locks. Sutton lock was reopened during 1972.

Pocklington Canal

When the York & North Midland Railway took over the canal in 1848, Earl Fitzwilliam offered to continue his commutation of Derwent tolls. He was asked to reduce the total, 'as the number of Vessels & tonnage of goods have considerably diminished since the opening of the railway from York to Market Weighton'.[14] The sum of £80 seems to have been accepted until the Derwent also came under North Eastern Railway* control.

In May 1850 the railway gave Swann, collecting tolls at Canal Head, notice. They did some lock repairs in 1851, whereupon some landowners suggested that the canal should be converted to a drainage channel, a tramway being laid along the towpath to carry local goods. The company liked the idea, but did nothing.[15]

Traffic fell: in 1858 the canal carried 5,721 tons and yielded the railway £617; in 1868, 3,101 tons brought in £290. By 1892 there was little traffic above Melbourne, and the whole canal only carried 901 tons, yielding £56.[16] The railway had seen little point in taking trouble with a minor waterway to a town already rail-served, and had allowed the canal to get badly silted. This meant that by 1892 it was difficult to get to the canal head loaded at all, or to carry full loads anywhere on the line. By 1905 tonnage was 1,076, bringing in £24, half of which was roadstone and manure. In 1913 the figure had risen to 1,657 tons, earning £59. Then the war came: only 50 tons were carried in 1916, in 1917 nothing at all. In 1932 the last commercial barge, the *Ebenezer*, entered the canal carrying roadstone, and in 1934 what would then have been thought the last pleasure craft.[17]

In 1948 ownership passed to the British Transport Commission, and in 1962 to the British Waterways Board. In 1969 the Pocklington Canal Amenity Society was formed to restore the canal: since then volunteers have been at work, the Board has helped, Cottingwith lock was reopened in 1972, and restoration is well advanced.

Wharfe River

A little navigation seems to have gone on throughout the nineteenth century. A directory gives two vessel owners at Tadcaster in 1861, and in 1891 William Dyson of the Britannia Inn, who

* The York & North Midland became part of the North Eastern Railway in 1854.

with a Hodgson seems to have continued to about 1914, when the last trading boat reached the town.[18]

In 1890 brewing interests at Tadcaster obtained an Act[19] to incorporate the Wharfe River Navigation Co, empowered to make the river navigable without locks for 50-ton craft thence to the Ouse. The timing may well have been consequential upon L. F. Vernon-Harcourt's proposal for a half-tide lock at Kelfield (see p. 439) on the Ouse just below Wharfe mouth. This would have backed up water on the Wharfe, and improved its navigability. Capital was to be £7,000 with power to raise £3,000 more. Power was given to act as carriers, and to build tramways from the riverside at Tadcaster to a brewery. Some work seems to have been done before the company was wound up in 1898.[20]

Foss Navigation

The opening of the York & North Midland's Scarborough line of railway on 7 July 1845 made the Foss's position hopeless. The state of the river was now a cause of concern, since it received 'in its Course the Sewage of a Portion of the City of York', which was 'not carried off, but retained in the . . . river',[21] most of it having been put there by the city's Improvement Commissioners between 1825 and 1850. A proposal to buy the navigation indeed came before York corporation that year, but was not supported by the Finance Committee, and dropped.

Early in 1848 the company commissioned a report on the problem, and in October, at the corporation's request, called a meeting to discuss the 'best plan to be adopted for cleansing the Canal and for aiding in the Sanitary arrangements of the City'.[22] After it they did try to stop some of the pollution, notably from the workhouse, general hospital and gasworks. Galvanized, they also proceeded to dredge their whole length up to Sheriff Hutton bridge to restore full depth, and, unsuccessfully, to re-let the tolls, which had reverted to them in 1845.

In July 1851 they paid what was to be their last dividend of 10s (50p) per £115 share, and then in August received an offer to purchase from York corporation. They asked £6,325 (£25 a share), but eventually took £4,000, keeping their remaining cash and investments. The sale was completed on 23 December 1852, and confirmed by an Act[23] of 1853. After paying their debts, £4,516 was left to distribute, or £17·85 per share. The city council had already in November 1852 decided that the navigation above the lower urban stretch was 'not justified on economical, sanitary or commercial grounds',[24] and in 1859 they obtained an Act[25] to abandon all but a little over a mile from the Ouse, with one lock only, Castle Mills.

For the last years of the company's life average annual receipts were:

Years	£	Years	£
1846–49	340	1850–53	230

In 1846 the paying tonnage was 14,071, and in 1853 12,691. Of the first total, 9,755 tons were coal and slack, the greater part to Sheriff Hutton. Very little of the other cargoes went above Monk bridge: of the second, 10,597 tons were coal, coke or slack.

Until 1879 the corporation let the tolls of the remaining navigation. Thereafter they took them into their own hands. In 1887 a Foss Navigation Committee was set up, followed by an agreement reached with Henry Leetham & Sons, the flour millers. Under it, the city offered specially favourable tolls, and also agreed to improve the river up to Hungate mills to give a navigable draught of 7 ft 6 in, and to rebuild Castle Mills lock to take craft 97 ft × 18 ft 6 in, carrying up to 230 tons. This was opened in July 1889 at a cost of £7,460, plant being also installed to pump water back past the lock. By 1898 tolls had risen from £294 of 1865 to £750, in which year 166,530 tons passed on the river: in 1905 it had risen to 294,142.

Rent receipts, and later tolls, taken by York corporation rose slowly through the years. Here are quinquennial average figures:

Years	£	Years	£
1861–65	305	1881–86*	455
1866–70	280	1887–92	485
1871–75	328	1893–97	697
1876–80	413		

*The total includes six months extra receipts due to a change of financial year; it has therefore been averaged to produce a comparable annual figure.

Today the Foss is less used, but traffic still passes through Castle Mills lock.

Linton Lock Navigation

When railway competition began, the navigation was in reasonable condition; between 1840 and 1842 the commissioners paid 6 per cent.[26] In 1853 about 18,000 tons were carried: here are averages for the following decades:

Years	Tons	Years	Tons
1854–63	18,329	1874–83	11,840
1864–73	14,737	1884–93	9,634

Dividends, 15s (75p) in 1869, were 10s (50p) in 1876, and 6s 6d (32½p) in 1883.[27] From 1890 onwards there were none until 1900, when 1 to 1½ per cent was often paid.

The navigation's prosperity at that time mainly depended, of course, on the Ure, and declined with it, though there was some independent income from carrying gravel and sand dredgings, and from investments. Tolls, £281 in 1895, were £330 in 1913, tonnage having risen from 15,028 to 26,249. The commissioners had joined York corporation and others in successfully opposing the Ure's abandonment in 1894 (see p. 451). Otherwise their most obvious activity was the annual outing from York by steam launch or motor boat to inspect their watery domain.

Before the First World War, the sand and gravel firm of Blundy, Clark & Co, who worked from above Milby lock on the Ure, were the principal users. However, business fell away during the war to only £42 tolls in 1916, and then slowly revived afterwards to £88 tolls and 8,318 tonnage in 1922. On 31 December 1920 York corporation leased land near the lock for a hydroelectric station. This helped the commissioners, not only in rental, but with dredging. Blundy's business then grew rapidly and Linton lock tolls benefited, rising from £190 in 1924 to £852 in 1930, then falling away to £517 in 1938. However, the money enabled dredging to be done, lock repairs to be carried out in 1929, and dividends of up to 2½ per cent to be paid in several years. By now pleasure craft were appearing, but these could not be charged toll under the original Act, though later mooring charges were to be authorized.

In 1936 there was more trouble, the lock being closed for over four months, and some also in 1937. However, in this year Blundy's helpfully agreed to take over dredging in return for a fixed annual payment. Then came the Second World War, and after 1941, when the last dividend was paid and £179 was taken in tolls, trade fell away to only £18 in 1944. By 1945 the commissioners had just enough reserves to mend two bank breaches.

Tolls then recovered, but only a little. Some lock trouble was overcome, thanks to the Inland Waterways Association bringing

LINTON LOCK NAVIGATION.

NOTICE IS HEREBY GIVEN
that the Linton Lock will be closed and remain closed from 8 a.m. on Monday, the 8th day of June, 1936, until further notice, for the purpose of carrying out the necessary repairs to the Lock.

DATED this twenty-third day of May, 1936.

BY ORDER. INNES N. WARE,

Clerk and Treasurer.

HERALD PRINTING WORKS, YORK AND LONDON.

39. A closure of Linton lock

together those concerned. The Linton Lock Supporters' Club was formed, which with the Ripon Motor Boat Club and others lent the commissioners money to help with capital expenditure. Then on 30 May 1960 a lower lock gate collapsed, and William Birch & Sons Ltd started to repair the lower gates. It became clear that the upper gates and lock walls would also have to be dealt with, at a total cost of some £5,000, of which the commissioners could only raise £1,000. After a hopeful effort to get the British Transport Commission to take over the navigation, York corporation contributed the last straw by giving notice that they would not be renewing the power station lease. It looked to be the end, and on 10 May 1962 the commissioners in accordance with the Act gave notice of refusal to act further, and many resigned.

However, Dr N. J. H. Wallis became a commissioner and later chairman, and others were appointed. On 14 October the lock was closed, and efforts made to interest the army in restoring it. These failed, but a settlement with Birch's was agreed, and an offer from the British Waterways Board to do the work accepted. The Supporters' Club and other organizations came forward with money, and in 1967 the lock was reopened. There is still some commercial traffic to the Ure, while fishing dues, mooring fees and rents bring in revenue. But the navigation continues to depend on the Supporters' Club and other voluntary bodies to help in times of difficulty.[28]

Ure Navigation and Ripon Canal

In 1844 the provisional committee of the proposed Leeds & Thirsk (later the Leeds Northern) Railway agreed with the Ure's board upon purchase of the navigation concern. The railway's shareholders confirmed the agreement in January 1845. The main motive was to get local support in and around Ripon for the railway, and so lessen Parliamentary opposition. It succeeded: the company got their Act in July 1845,[29] and in the following January the Ure company confirmed the sale at £34,577,* some £4,000 or more of which the railway reckoned the value to them of local opposition withdrawn.[30] For the ten years ending 1847 the average toll receipts had been £2,013, and profits £886 p.a.

Transfer took place on 1 July 1847,[31] £16,297 being paid in cash, the rest in railway paper. The Ure company was dissolved, the railway's Act compelling them to keep the navigation open and in good repair, and giving the Board of Trade power to regulate tolls upon complaint from the Aire & Calder. The rail line, opened in sections, was completed to Leeds on 9 July 1849. Before that, however, partial opening, together with the completion of the York & Newcastle Railway's branch from Pilmoor to Boroughbridge on 17 June 1847, had transferred most mineral traffic to rail, in spite of a cut in Ouse tolls. In 1848 the Aire & Calder arranged with the Ouse trustees for a common drawback on grain traffic to and from the Ure, and about that time they and the Barnsley Canal gave a drawback on coal. Silkstone had already asked the railway to cut Ure tolls. They refused, because they would earn more by carrying northern coal. Silkstone then cut the pithead price and the canal companies gave their drawback, whereupon the railway, still refusing to lower canal tolls, encouraged the northern colliery owners to offer a competitive price.[32]

In 1854 the Leeds Northern became part of the North Eastern Railway; they regarded canals as a nuisance, and did as little dredging or maintenance as they could. As early as 1857 owners

* Small additions raised this to a final £35,085.

of Ripon–Hull craft were complaining that the navigation had not been dredged for a long time, and was impeding full cargoes. In 1854, presumably as a result of their traffic arrangement of September 1853 with the York & North Midland Railway, the Aire & Calder told their traffic manager to discontinue their coal drawback to Boroughbridge and Ripon. However, the trade somewhat recovered in the 1860s, so that in 1869 20 boats were working in the Boroughbridge coal trade.[33] Here are some figures:

Coal originating on the Aire & Calder system

Year	Boroughbridge tons	Ripon tons
1851	3,322	4,807
1861	3,707	4,906
1870	6,847	3,175

Linton lock records give the total tonnage passing to and from the Ure as about 18,000 p.a. between 1854 and 1864.* Revenue was only a few hundred pounds a year.

By 1892 only 5,000 tons were being carried on the navigation, with a revenue of £161 and an allocated expenditure of £683. Most was wheat and coal to Boroughbridge mill: none went higher, and thenceforward the Ripon Canal was disused. There was little back carriage. Disuse to Ripon was at any rate accelerated by high tolls and lack of dredging. In 1894 the railway tried to abandon the navigation, but had to drop the proposal after strong opposition, led by York corporation, which the N.E.R. chairman described indignantly as a 'storm in a teacup'. But local people thought the navigation's survival was important to keep down railway rates, and for the Linton lock commissioners it was essential to their existence. One argument used at the time was the impossibility of getting from Swale Nab to Ripon with more than half a full cargo;[34] another, that the railway charged high tolls: to Boroughbridge 8d a ton for coal, against 4d on the Linton Lock Navigation and 2d on the Ouse from Naburn to Widdington Ings, and above Boroughbridge the statutory maxima on all goods. Defeated, the railway offered the Ure as a gift to York corporation, who refused it.

They then seem to have taken steps to prevent it being used above Boroughbridge.[35] In 1898 the tonnage was 9,001, yielding

---

* The figures given in *Canal Returns* for 1858 and 1868, totalling 9,750 tons and 5,745 tons, do not seem to be correct.

£178; by 1905 it had fallen to 3,409 tons and £71. In this year the main traffics were gravel (1,220 tons), flour (1,030) and sand (702). In 1906 it was reported impossible to reach Ripon,[36] with only one craft working regularly to Boroughbridge, carrying coal.[37] By then the Bishop Monkton Canal, disused for many years, had silted up. The following year a town's meeting at Ripon agreed that the Ure and Linton lock should be put either under a new representative trust, or amalgamated with the Ouse trustees, and George Simpson then put this idea on their behalf to the Royal Commission.[38]

About 1929 Blundy, Clark & Co Ltd, sand and gravel merchants operating from above Milby lock, brought an action against the London & North Eastern Railway, now the navigation's owners, alleging that because of neglect there was not enough water for full loads, and that Milby lock had been closed for longer than necessary for repairs. They had therefore to carry to York by rail at 2s 6d (12½p) per ton instead of by water at 3d.* Judgement was given for £2,362 compensation.[39]

In 1963, tolls were £305, other receipts £136, and expenditure £832. In 1972 there is still some commercial traffic on the navigation in sand and gravel from above Milby lock, as well as pleasure craft to Ox Close lock, the limit of navigation. Above Ox Close, the canal was abandoned by a British Transport Commission Act of 1955. In 1972, however, there were plans to restore it through to Ripon.

* Reduced from 11d in 1928 by agreement between Blundy's and the L.N.E.R.

CHAPTER XXI

Conclusion

++++++++++++++++++++++++++++++++++++++◆+++++++++++++++++++++++++++++++++

THE waterways of the north described in this book and its companion volume, *The Canals of North West England*, are very different from those of the Midlands and the south. They are based on industrial rivers: the Weaver, Mersey and Irwell, Humber, Ouse, Aire, Calder and Don, and on canal extensions of these—the Leeds & Liverpool, Rochdale and Huddersfield Canals across the Pennines. The mileage of navigable rivers and canals on the whole area was in 1800 roughly the same.

Waterways developed quickly in the north: they were mostly big, too, by the standards of the time.

Canals and Navigations in the North by Type of Waterway*

Date	Ship Canal	Broad Canal	Narrow Canal	Tub-boat or Small Canal	River Nav.	Total
	miles	*miles*	*miles*	*miles*	*miles*	*miles*
1760	—	$9\frac{1}{2}$	—	—	$243\frac{1}{4}$	$252\frac{3}{4}$
1770	—	$22\frac{7}{8}$	—	—	260	$282\frac{7}{8}$
1780	—	$120\frac{1}{4}$	—	$1\frac{1}{2}$	268	$389\frac{3}{4}$
1790	—	$131\frac{1}{8}$	—	$1\frac{1}{2}$	$278\frac{5}{8}$	$400\frac{1}{2}$
1800	$1\frac{1}{2}$	$252\frac{1}{2}$	33	1	279	567
1810	$1\frac{1}{2}$	$330\frac{1}{4}$	34	1	$285\frac{1}{2}$	$652\frac{1}{4}$
1820	$1\frac{1}{2}$	$378\frac{1}{8}$	$53\frac{7}{8}$	—	299	$732\frac{1}{2}$
1830	$1\frac{1}{2}$	$412\frac{3}{4}$	$53\frac{7}{8}$	—	$297\frac{1}{2}$	$765\frac{5}{8}$
1840	$1\frac{1}{2}$	$418\frac{3}{8}$	$53\frac{7}{8}$	—	$282\frac{1}{4}$	756
1850	$1\frac{1}{2}$	$417\frac{5}{8}$	$52\frac{7}{8}$	—	$283\frac{1}{4}$	$755\frac{1}{4}$
1900	$37\frac{1}{2}$	$401\frac{1}{2}$	$52\frac{7}{8}$	—	$231\frac{7}{8}$	$723\frac{3}{4}$
1947	36	$369\frac{7}{8}$	$32\frac{3}{8}$	—	$172\frac{1}{2}$	$610\frac{3}{4}$

* The canals and navigations included are those listed in Appendix I of this book and its companion, *The Canals of North West England*, that fall within the range of dates quoted. For classification purposes a ship canal is a canal that admitted sea-going ships; a broad canal one with locks at least 12 ft wide; a narrow canal one with locks less than 12 ft wide; and a tub-boat or small canal one taking boats carrying a

In 1820 the north had 677 miles of river and canal with broad locks, and only 54 miles of narrow canal, against 592 broad and 711 narrow in the midlands.

By 1820, the main northern waterway network was in existence, for only 33 miles were to be added later. Instead of continuing to build, capital was spent on repeatedly enlarging and improving what was there, e.g. the rebuilding of the Aire & Calder and the Don in the late 1820s and the 1830s, the enlargement of the lower Calder & Hebble after the 1834 Act, or the altering of the Barnsley Canal to take seagoing craft between 1828 and 1830. Because of these improvements, the northern waterways were better able to withstand railway and road competition, and some of them, notably the Weaver and the Aire & Calder, to develop alongside their rivals.

The northern waterways demonstrate a truth about inland waterways in Britain, and to varying extents throughout the world, that they live from the sea, from foreign and coasting trade. This trade passes up and down rivers to ports, and, where rivers do not run far enough, the water lines are extended by canals. Given good rivers running to good ports, the advantages of waterways for this branch of carrying have shown themselves through all adversities. The Aire & Calder is an example—a navigation that was making profits in 1712, and still did so in 1969/70. Originally a river navigation, then given one artificial lower section, the Selby Canal, then another, the Goole Canal; then canalized in its upper reaches both to Wakefield and Leeds, the Aire & Calder is today more canal than river. But its ancestry has enabled it to grow, and from its parent rivers comes the water upon which it lives.

In Lancashire the Weaver Navigation, opened in 1732, and still a waterway with a future, is unique. From 1760 to the present day it has been publicly owned, the sole major British example of a line whose history resembles that of most continental and North American waterways. Developing side by side with publicly owned roads, its profits paid to the public when development was unnecessary, but ploughed back and supplemented by county loans when expansion was required, the Weaver has been recon-

---

few tons each. See my *British Canals*, 4th ed. 1969, pp. 55–6 for a fuller description. For some branches I have had to conjecture the dates. Readers may like to compare these figures with those given in either *The Canals of the East Midlands* or *The Canals of the West Midlands* for the midlands area, and in *The Canals of South Wales and the Border*, *The Canals of South and South East England*, and *The Canals of South West England*.

structed again and again. Indeed, its locks, rebuilt with power operation in the late nineteenth century to take 1,000 tons of craft at a locking, are still in 1972 the largest on any inland waterway in Britain except the Manchester Ship Canal.

Each of these examples of ours sired a great waterway innovation. From the Weaver came the first modern canal vertical lift: direct but larger descendants were built in France at Les Fontinettes and in Belgium on the Canal du Centre; collateral relations, larger still, work successfully in Canada and Germany, where indeed a huge one is now being built at Lüneburg on the new Elbe Lateral Canal. From the Aire & Calder came push-towing, introduced, together with the necessary compartment boats or lighters, in the early 1860s. After spreading from its home in the United States to Yorkshire and on to the Seine, Rhine and Volga, it has now returned to Yorkshire.

Britain produced in late Victorian times three great waterway engineers: Sir Edward Leader Williams, to whom we owe the Weaver locks, the first idea of the Anderton lift, the engineering of the Manchester Ship Canal and the unique Barton swing aqueduct; J. A. Saner who later followed him on the Weaver, and on the Aire & Calder W. H. Bartholomew.

They had great forebears: engineers, of course, like Henry Berry of the Sankey Brook, William Jessop of the Rochdale Canal, or George Leather jun of the Aire & Calder. But also waterway builders. Let us think of four: first in time the little group of Leeds and Wakefield men who in 1699 got their Act to make the Aire & Calder navigable, and in five years had their line open. Then, in Lancashire, John Ashton and John Blackburn jun, who built the first modern industrial canal in Britain, the Sankey Brook Navigation, by side-stepping those who were frightened of innovation. After them, the Duke of Bridgewater, the lonely, eccentric, hard-driving, ruthless business genius who constructed canals in coal mines, was perhaps the first to introduce containers, and gave canal building in Britain an impetus that was to last for eighty years. Finally, back in Yorkshire, John Longbotham of Halifax and John Hustler of Bradford, who in 1766 called a meeting to promote the Leeds & Liverpool Canal, a barge route over a hundred miles long across England, at a time when only two modern canals had yet been built, the Bridgewater and the Sankey Brook, together totalling some 17 miles. Longer, wider, more ambitious than the Trent & Mersey, whose Act had been passed a few months before, the Leeds & Liverpool explored a

N

new dimension in transport which, against great obstacles, was carried through.

Greatness is not only in the past: it is now. Since the Second World War, thanks to far-sighted capital expenditure of some £2 million on the Aire & Calder and the Sheffield & South Yorkshire Navigation by the British Transport Commission, a basis for development was laid. The British Waterways Board carried much further what had already been done on the Aire & Calder. On the Sheffield & South Yorkshire they greatly expanded Rotherham depot, but failed to get a rebuilt waterway past the Ministry of Transport. What was first suggested by Yorkshire businessmen as in their best interests in 1885, is still, as I write, being re-considered by the Ministry's current successor. It is just as well that waterways, though officially dead, won't lie down. Indeed, they tend to survive those who forecast their demise. As I write, the Minister for Transport Services, Mr John Peyton, answers a Parliamentary question: 'Studies that have been made of the development of inland waterways for commercial purposes have not shown any case on either economic or social grounds.'* If I were given to prophecy. . . .

* January 1972.

Author's Notes and Acknowledgements

++++++++++++++++++++++++++++++++++++◆++++++++++++++++++++++++++++++++++++

I AM most grateful to all those who have helped me.

To the Archivist and staff of British Transport Historical Records at London and York for access to minute books and other records, without whom this book could not have been written, and to the House of Lords Record Office for access to Parliamentary records. Now that British Transport Historical Records have become part of the Public Record Office, I should like to acknowledge the kindness of the three successive archivists and their staffs.

To Mr J. E. Day of Doncaster, Mr J. Goodchild, curator of the South Yorkshire Industrial Museum at Cusworth Hall, Doncaster, and Dr W. N. Slatcher of Wakefield, I owe a special debt for endless help. They, along with Dr M. J. T. Lewis, and Messrs Baron F. Duckham, J. R. H. Hogwood, K. W. Newham, N. W. Nix, A. P. Voce and R. G. Walton, have kindly read portions of the manuscript in draft, though responsibility for it is of course entirely my own.

To the Town Clerk of Beverley, Mr. A. B. Anderson of the Linton Lock Navigation, and Mr L. C. Sands of the Market Weighton Drainage Board, my thanks for so kindly making records available, and to Mrs L. Skinner and Mr J. E. Day for respectively reading long runs of the York and Doncaster newspapers.

To the City Treasurer, York; the Town Clerk of Selby; Mrs A. F. Watkins; Messrs M. F. Barbey, A. D. Boddy, J. H. Boyes; Bromet & Sons, solicitors of Tadcaster; P. Burnett, H. E. Cardy of the British Waterways Board; A. Clark of Henry Williamson & Co Ltd; H. Crabtree; C. Ivan Gray; C. P. Gurrey of John

Smith's Tadcaster Brewery Co Ltd; K. Hoole; N. Hudleston; E. Paget-Tomlinson; Edward H. Pinto; K. Ramsden of the British Waterways Board; H. B. Sanders of the Ripon Motor Boat Club; J. S. Taylor; V. Waddington of Ernest V. Waddington Ltd; Reginald Wood and M. G. C. Wyatt Wheeler; my thanks for all their help.

To Mrs B. M. Brewster of the Ark Museum, Tadcaster; and Messrs John Armitage of Leeds City Museum; R. A. Innes of Halifax Museums; and R. J. Hutchings of the Waterways Museum; the archivists and staffs of the East and North Riding and County Durham Record Offices; and to the librarians and their staffs of the Barnsley, Carlisle, Darlington, Doncaster, Goole, Halifax, Harrogate, Huddersfield, Hull, Leeds, Newcastle-upon-Tyne, Scarborough, Sheffield, Sowerby Bridge, Wakefield and York public libraries, my grateful thanks.

To Mr I. Rogerson of the Gloucestershire Technical Information Service, my gratitude for quickly borrowing me difficult books; and to Mr P. G. Rattenbury, who made available the invaluable source card index belonging to the Railway & Canal Historical Society, I owe many of my references.

To Mr Richard Dean, my thanks for drawing the maps, and to Mr J. E. Day for lending me his historical maps of the Don.

My thanks are also due to the following for permission to reproduce photographs and other illustrations: British Waterways Board, Leeds, plates on pages 134 (*above*), 403; B. W. B. and Eric L. Fenton, 134 (*below*); B. W. B. and *Yorkshire Evening News*, 421 (*above*); B. W. B. and Thos Firth & John Brown Ltd, 422 (*above*); South Yorkshire Industrial Museum, Doncaster, 151, 319 (*below*), 422 (*below*), Figs 24, 37; Waterways Museum, Fig 32; Abbey House Museum, Kirkstall, Leeds, and John Armitage Esq, Fig 21; Ark Museum, Tadcaster, 337; National Reference Library of Science and Invention, Fig 31; British Transport Historical Records, York (P.R.O.), Figs 14, 27-9, 38; Goole Public Library, 404 (*below*), Fig 13; Halifax Public Library, Fig 4; Huddersfield Public Library, 49 (*above*); Leeds Public Library, 133 (*above*); East Riding Record Office, Figs 25-6; North Riding Record Office, Fig 9; Linton Lock Navigation Commissioners, Fig 39; The Editor, *The Goole Times*, Fig 33; A. D. Boddy Esq and Messrs D. T. Atkinson, 68; A. Clark Esq and Henry Williamson & Son Ltd, 338 (*above*); Harold Crabtree Esq, 404 (*above*); J. E. Day Esq, 152 (*below*), Figs 6, 7, 22, 36; J. E. Day Esq and A. J. Drury, 152 (*above*); Dr Michael Lewis, 320; the late Edward A. Pinto Esq,

338 (*below*); Alan P. Voce Esq, 67 (*below*); G. Waites Esq, 50; Mrs A. F. Watkins, Figs 12, 20; Reginald Wood Esq, 421 (*below*).

I am grateful to the City Librarian of Sheffield City Libraries for permission to publish Figs 15–17, reproduced in the Archive Teaching Unit called *The Sheffield Canal*, published by Sheffield City Council Libraries & Arts Committee, 1970; the documents are numbered Clarke Records 142 in Sheffield City Libraries Collection.

NOTES

Notes to Chapter XI

1. Don Navigation Minute Book, 9 August 1787.
2. *Doncaster Gazette*, 9 January 1796.
3. For the Sheffield Canal generally, see *The Sheffield Canal*, an excellent teaching unit produced by the Libraries and Arts Committee of Sheffield City Council in 1970, which contains teachers' notes written by C. M. Butterworth, and reproductions of 18 documents. This unit also contains material of Sheffield interest about the Don Navigation and the canal after its independence ended in 1848.
4. Surveyed by William Fairbank (Fairbank papers, Sheffield P.L.).
5. For the Chesterfield Canal, see Charles Hadfield, *The Canals of the East Midlands*, 2nd ed., 1970.
6. Don Navigation Minute Book, 6 December 1792.
7. *Derby Mercury*, 13 December 1792.
8. Don Navigation Minute Book, 26 December 1792.
9. A. E. Richardson, *Robert Mylne*, 1955, p. 151.
10. Don Navigation Minute Book, 10 January 1793.
11. *Report of Benjn Outram Engineer on the proposed Sheffield Canal*, 19 August 1793 (MD 1740/2 and 3, Sheffield P.L.).
12. Don Navigation Minute Book, 7 March 1801.
13. For the Oakham Canal, see Charles Hadfield, *The Canals of the East Midlands*, 2nd ed., 1970, p. 95.
14. Joseph Bailey to William Dunn, 22 April 1802 (MD 1740/6, Sheffield P.L.). I am indebted to Mr David Tew for drawing my attention to the Dunn letters.
15. MD 1740/9, Sheffield P.L.
16. J.H.C., 22 February 1803.
17. MD 1740/10, Sheffield P.L.
18. *Doncaster Gazette*, 4 February 1803; MD 1740/26, Sheffield P.L.
19. Don Navigation Minute Book, 17 February 1803.
20. MD 1740/26, Sheffield P.L.
21. Sheffield Canal, Miscellaneous Papers, 25–L (Sheffield P.L.).
22. For these schemes, see Charles Hadfield & Gordon Biddle, *The Canals of North West England*, 1970, Chapter XI.
23. Don Navigation Minute Book, 11 January 1811.
24. *Doncaster Gazette*, 19 October, 2 November 1810, 1 March 1811.
25. Ibid., 29 November 1811.
26. *A Plan of a proposed Canal from the intended High Peak Junction Canal at or near Padley Mill, to the River Dun Navigation at or near Tinsley*, 1813 (Fairbank papers, Sheffield P.L.).
27. *Report of William Chapman on various projected Lines of Navigation from Sheffield*, 1813 (386.1S, Sheffield P.L.).
28. Don Navigation Minute Book, 12 November 1813.
29. Ibid., 31 March 1815.
30. Prospectus of the Sheffield Junction Canal, August 1832 (Fairbank papers, Sheffield P.L.).
31. *Report on the proposed canal from Castle Orchards, Sheffield, to the River Dun below Tinsley*, 1814 (386.1S, Sheffield P.L.).

32. 55 Geo III *c.* 65.
33. *Doncaster Gazette*, 16 February, 19 July 1816.
34. Ibid., 28 June 1816.
35. W. White, *History, Gazetteer and Directory of the West Riding of Yorkshire*, 1837, p. 44.
36. *Doncaster Gazette*, 26 February 1819.
37. Ed. Alex B. Bell, *Peeps into the Past, being Passages from the Diary of Thomas Asline Ward*, p. 258, letter dated 28 February 1819.
38. Quoted from the 1820 Report in C. M. Butterworth, *The Sheffield Canal* (Teachers' Notes), Sheffield City Libraries, 1970.
39. Alan Goodfellow, 'Sheffield's Waterway to the Sea', *Trans. Hunter Archaeological Soc.*, Vol. 5, 1937–43.
40. *Doncaster Gazette*, 5 March 1819.
41. B. Baxter, *Stone Blocks and Iron Rails*, 1966, p. 170.
42. See Charles Hadfield & Gordon Biddle, *The Canals of North West England*, 1970, pp. 319–20.
43. *Map of the intended canal from the Peak Forest Canal . . . to or near the town of Sheffield*, 1824 (Fairbank papers, Sheffield P.L.).
44. Goodfellow, op. cit.
45. *Prospectus of the Sheffield Junction Canal* (see also NB 29, pp. 111–13, Fairbank papers, Sheffield P.L.).
46. *Derby Mercury*, 15 May 1833.
47. Don Navigation Minute Book, 1 May 1835.
48. SP 59. Sheffield P.L.
49. John Guest, *Historic Notices of Rotherham*, 1879, p. 546; *Doncaster Gazette*, 10 October 1834.
50. Brief, SP 59, Sheffield P.L.
51. *Doncaster Gazette*, 28 February 1840.
52. Sheffield Canal Journal, B.T.H.R., 4/1.
53. Sheffield Directory, 1845.
54. An advertisement of 1836 shows that the Humber company's fly-boats were hauled by steam tug from Hull to Tinsley, and then by horses to Sheffield, doing the trip in three days; *Doncaster Gazette*, 2 September 1836.
55. Ed. Alex B. Bell, *Peeps into the Past*, op. cit., letter of 15 February 1843.
56. Notice of meeting of inhabitants of Brightside, 9 December 1841 (Sheffield Canal, Miscellaneous Papers 35–L, Sheffield P.L.).
57. Sheffield Canal Report for 1842–3 (South Yorkshire Industrial Museum, Cusworth Hall, Doncaster).
58. *Derby Mercury*, 28 August 1844.
59. Don Navigation Minute Book, 7 July 1844.
60. Ibid., 28 August 1845.
61. George Dow, *Great Central*, Vol. 1, p. 98.
62. Ibid., p. 115.
63. Don Navigation Minute Book, 23 September 1846.
64. Ibid., 21 December 1846.
65. Ibid., 1, 29 October, 16 December 1847.
66. Ibid., 28 February 1848.
67. Ibid., 27 March 1848.
68. 11 & 12 Vic *c.* 94.
69. 12 & 13 Vic *c.* 75.
70. 50 Vic *c.* 49.

Notes to Chapter XII

1. Don Navigation Minute Book, 16 February 1770.
2. Ibid., 9 August 1792.

3. Ibid., 29 August 1792.
4. Barnsley Canal Proprietors' Minute Book, 29 October 1792.
5. A. E. Richardson, *Robert Mylne*, 1955, pp. 151-4, and J.H.C., 5 April 1793.
6. Don Navigation Minute Book, 16 October 1792.
7. Barnsley Canal Proprietors' Minute Book, 29 October 1792.
8. Printed minutes, Sheffield P.L. (EM 772).
9. *Doncaster Journal*, 3 November 1792.
10. 33 Geo III *c*. 115.
11. *Doncaster Journal*, 20 July 1793.
12. *Yorkshire Gazette*, 17 January 1795.
13. *Doncaster Journal*, 12 May 1797.
14. Ibid., 8 September 1797.
15. *Doncaster Gazette*, 7 December 1798.
16. Ibid.
17. *The Case of the Dearne and Dove Canal Company Respecting the Bill to enable them to finish and complete their Canal*, 1800 (Sheffield P.L., EM 976–78).
18. 39 & 40 Geo III *c*. 37.
19. *The Case of the Dearne and Dove*, etc., op. cit.
20. *Doncaster Gazette*, 13 November 1801.
21. Ibid., 15 March 1805.
22. Ibid., 22 March 1805.
23. Rochdale Canal Minute Book, 12 March 1813.
24. Ibid., 4 February 1824.
25. Aire & Calder Navigation Report for 1829.
26. Figures from the set of annual reports in Sheffield P.L. (EM 772).
27. *Doncaster Gazette*, 15 September, 10 November 1820.
28. Printed paper dated 26 June 1824 (Sheffield P.L., EM 772); *Doncaster Gazette*, 7 September 1821.
29. Aire & Calder Navigation Directors' Minute Book, 14 November 1821.
30. Aire & Calder Navigation papers, December 1828, brief of evidence in arbitration between Aire & Calder Navigation and Lee and Watson.
31. Don Navigation Minute Book, 29 March 1833.
32. Ibid., 5 July 1833.
33. The Witham Navigation runs from a junction with the Fossdyke (leading from the Trent) at Lincoln to the Wash at Boston.
34. Don Navigation Minute Book, 30 September 1845.
35. Ibid., 18 April 1846.
36. Barnsley Canal Proprietors' Minute Book, 1 July 1846.
37. 10 & 11 Vic *c*. 291.
38. Don Navigation Minute Book, 11 August 1763.
39. Ibid., 15 May 1772.
40. *A Report on the practicability of making a Navigation Canal from the River Dun at Stainforth-Cut, to the River Trent at Althorpe*, 28 October 1772 (Sheffield P.L., EM 772).
41. Doncaster corporation records, 14 December 1772 (Cal IV, p. 243).
42. For the Trent Navigation, see Charles Hadfield, *The Canals of the East Midlands*, 2nd ed., 1970.
43. Don Navigation Minute Book, 19 March 1782.
44. *Doncaster Journal*, 15 September 1792.
45. Ibid., 27 October 1792; Printed Report of the meeting (Sheffield P.L., EM 772).
46. Ibid., 17 November 1792.
47. 33 Geo III *c*. 117.
48. *Doncaster Journal*, 17 August 1793.
49. 38 Geo III *c*. 47.
50. *Doncaster Gazette*, 21 May 1802.
51. *Case of the Stainforth & Keadby Canal Company against the River Dun Navigation Bill*, April 1836 (South Yorkshire Industrial Museum, Cusworth Hall, Doncaster). A number of editions of this broadsheet exist, differing in details.

52. 49 Geo III *c*. 71.
53. Evidence before House of Lords Committee, 10 May 1809.
54. *Hull Advertiser*, 27 August 1803.
55. Ibid., 28 August 1818.
56. Ibid., 11 July 1818.
57. Ibid., 6 May 1825.
58. *Doncaster Gazette*, 14 July 1815.
59. Ibid., 2 August 1836.
60. *Case of the Stainforth & Keadby Canal Company, etc. ND* (*c*. 1836).
61. *Doncaster Gazette*, 14 July 1837.
62. Ibid., 29 October 1841.
63. Ibid., 26 July 1822.
64. Ibid., 12 September 1834.
65. Aire & Calder Navigation Minute Book, 27 November 1828.
66. *Doncaster Gazette*, 14 November 1828.
67. Aire & Calder Navigation Minute Book, 14 April 1834.
68. Ibid., 1 August 1836.
69. Ibid., 29 December 1836.
70. *Doncaster Gazette*, 9 October 1829.
71. *Case of the Stainforth & Keadby Canal Company*, etc., April 1836.
72. Don Navigation Minute Book, 23 May 1837.
73. Ibid., 2 June 1837.
74. Ibid., 6 October, 17 November 1837, 4 January, 26 July 1839, 3 April, 28 August 1840.
75. Ibid., 12 February 1841.
76. Ibid., 14 June 1844.
77. Ibid., 5 July 1844.
78. Ibid., 2 June 1846.
79. Ibid., 29 October 1847.
80. 12 & 13 Vic *c*. 29.
81. Aire & Calder Navigation Report for 1848, read 6 August 1849.

Notes to Chapter XIII

1. The Holderness and the Beverley & Barmston Drainage Commissioners were made responsible for dredging.
2. J.H.C., 25 February 1794.
3. Driffield Old Navigation Minute Book, 9 November 1796.
4. Ibid., 2 July 1799.
5. *Hull Advertiser*, 9 November 1799.
6. Beverley Corporation Minute Book, October 1800.
7. 41 Geo III *c*. 134.
8. George Poulson, *The History and Antiquities of the Seigneury of Holderness*, 1840, Vol. II, pp. 306–7.
9. 57 Geo III *c*. 64.
10. *Hull Advertiser*, 22 March 1817.
11. Ibid., 11 March 1825.
12. Driffield New Navigation Minute Book, 6 July 1824.
13. Driffield Old Navigation Minute Book, 2 July 1839.
14. Ibid., 11 May 1840.
15. Holderness Drainage Trustees' Minute Book, 13 May 1786.
16. *York Courant*, 27 September, 25 October 1791.
17. Holderness Drainage Trustees' Minute Book, 2 February 1792.
18. J.H.C., 5 March 1792.
19. *York Courant*, 20 August 1792.
20. Ibid., 15 September 1800.

21. Ibid., 18 August 1800.
22. For the Bethells, see J. T. Ward, 'East Yorkshire Landed Estates in the Nineteenth Century', *East Yorkshire Local History Series*, No. 23.
23. Holderness Drainage Trustees' Minute Book, 8 November 1800.
24. 41 Geo III *c.* 32.
25. J. Priestley, *Navigable Rivers, Canals, etc.*, 1831, and see the 1800 deposited plan, 'as recommended by Mr Jessop'.
26. J. J. Sheahan & T. Whellan, *History and Topography of the City of York and the East Riding of Yorkshire*, Vol. 2, 1856.
27. 45 Geo III *c.* 43.
28. E. Baines, *History, Directory & Gazetteer of the County of York*, Vol. II, p. 362.
29. W. White, *History, Gazetteer etc. of the East and North Ridings of Yorkshire*, 1840.
30. *Third Report of the Committee of Investigation into the affairs of the York & North Midland Railway*, 31 October 1849, by courtesy of Mr K. Hoole.
31. I am much indebted to Dr Michael Lewis, who spent muddy days finding the locks.
32. The artificial cut and landing is shown on the deposited *Plan of the Proposed Improvement of the Navigation of the River Hull . . .*, September 1800 (East Riding Record Office); the locks, at 054456 and 042461, cut and 'Old Coal Wharf', on the first edition of the 6 in OS plan, surveyed 1851–2.
33. William Chapman's report of 18 May 1809, Beverley & Barmston Drainage Commissioners' Minute Book (East Riding Record Office).
34. J. J. Sheahan & T. Whellan, *History and Topography of the City of York and the East Riding of Yorkshire*, Vol. 2, 1856.
35. *Hull Advertiser*, 11 December 1802.
36. Ibid., 28 May 1803.
37. *A Letter addressed to Thomas Williamson Esq . . . for the purpose of taking into consideration . . . a navigable canal between Cottingham and Hull*, 13 July 1803 (Hull P.L.).
38. I am indebted for this information to Dr Michael Lewis.
39. 14 Geo III *c.* 106.
40. *York Courant*, 28 November 1775.
41. Ibid., 20 March 1781.
42. J.H.C., 11 February 1803.
43. *Report of William Chapman, engineer, on the Drainage and Navigation of Keyingham Level*, 1797 (Carlisle P.L.).
44. For these, see Charles Hadfield & Gordon Biddle, *The Canals of North West England*, 1970.
45. *Hull Advertiser*, 30 August 1800.
46. J.H.C., 13 March 1801.
47. *Hull Advertiser*, 17 January 1801.
48. East Riding Record Office.
49. Aire & Calder Navigation Minute Book, 20 September 1792.
50. E. Baines, *History, Directory & Gazetteer of the County of York*, 1823, Vol. 2, p. 373.
51. Market Weighton Canal Trustees' Minute Book, 3 May 1825.
52. Ibid., 2 May 1826.
53. Report . . . on . . . Keyingham Level, 1797 (Carlisle P.L.).
54. 10 & 11 Vic. *c.* 216.
55. Figures from the *Third Report of the Committee of Investigation into the affairs of the York & North Midland Railway*, 31 October 1849, by courtesy of Mr K. Hoole.

Notes to Chapter XIV

1. Baron F. Duckham, *The Yorkshire Ouse*, 1967.
2. *Doncaster Gazette*, 20 October 1820.

3. Thomas Rhodes, *Report*, 1834 (York P.L.).
4. Ouse Navigation Trustees Minute Book, 27 September 1833.
5. *Report*, York P.L.
6. Duckham, *Yorkshire Ouse*, op. cit., p. 119.
7. See Charles Hadfield, *The Canals of the West Midlands*, 2nd ed., 1970.
8. J.H.C., 11 February 1796. See *York Courant*, 1 September 1795.
9. *Doncaster Gazette*, 14 January 1825.
10. B.T.H.R., DER 4/16.
11. B.T.H.R., DER 4/5.
12. *Propositions* (East Riding Record Office, DDSY 11/5).
13. Resolution of meeting of 16 December 1799 (E.R.R.O., DDSY/11).
14. Letter of William Chapman to Sir C. Sykes, 17 January 1800 (E.R.R.O., DDSY/11).
15. Letter from Thomas Ewbank to Sir C. Sykes, 9 February 1800 (E.R.R.O., DDSY/11).
16. 39 & 40 Geo III *c.* 118.
17. *Hull Advertiser*, 24 December 1803.
18. North Riding Record Office.
19. *York Courant*, 10 September 1804.
20. George Leather jun. to S. H. Copperthwaite, 27 July 1810, B.T.H.R., DER 8/1.
21. Samuel Lewis, *A Topographical Dictionary of England*, 1848.
22. B.T.H.R., DER 4/16.
23. B.T.H.R., DER 7/14.
24. Baron F. Duckham, *The Yorkshire Ouse*, 1967, p. 97.
25. B.T.H.R., DER 23/80.
26. *The New System of Uniting . . . Navigation and Agriculture* (Malton), 1806.
27. quo. Duckham, 'The Fitzwilliams and the Derwent', *Northern History, II*, 1967.
28. J. Bigland, *Description of the County of York*, 1818.
29. S. Lewis, *A Topographical Dictionary of England*, 3rd ed., 1835.
30. *York Courant*, 16 September 1793.
31. Cockshutt's report is in the Carlisle P.L. See also *York Courant*, 2 December 1793.
32. *York Courant*, 3 March 1794.
33. Ibid., 26 May, 2, 9, 16, 23 June, 7 July 1794.
34. *Observations respecting the proposed Scarbro' Canal*, 6 August 1794 (North Riding Record Office).
35. *York Courant*, 14 September 1795.
36. *York Courant*, 4 November 1793.
37. Ibid., 13 January 1794.
38. Four letters to Crosley are quoted in Basil Blackwell's sale catalogue No. 865.
39. Letter, William Plummer to Lord Egremont, 22 November 1801. B.T.H.R., POC 1/2.
40. *York Courant*, 14 September 1801.
41. Ibid.
42. Letter of George Leather jun. to S. H. Copperthwaite, 22 August 1813, B.T.H.R., DER 8/1.
43. Letter of George Leather jun. to S. H. Copperthwaite, 23 October 1813, loc. cit.
44. Broadsheet of 5 July, B.T.H.R., POC 1/3.
45. Letter of George Leather jun. to S. H. Copperthwaite, 20 September 1814, B.T.H.R., DER 8/1.
46. Broadsheet of 22 September 1814 meeting, B.T.H.R., POC 1/3.
47. Letter of George Leather jun. to S. H. Copperthwaite, 16 October 1814, B.T.H.R., DER 8/1.
48. East Riding Record Office.
49. 55 Geo III *c.* 55.
50. Letter from George Leather jun to S. H. Copperthwaite, 14 July 1815, B.T.H.R., DER 8/1.
51. *Hull Advertiser*, 15 July 1815.

52. Ibid., 11 July 1818.
53. Pocklington Canal Minute Book, 3 August 1818.
54. MS memorandum of 21 January 1822, B.T.H.R., POC 8/2.
55. E. Baines, *Directory and Gazetteer of the County of York*, 1823, Vol. II, p. 377.
56. Pocklington Canal Minute Book, 3 August 1840.
57. Ibid., 6 October 1845.
58. 10 & 11 Vic. *c*. 216.
59. B.T.H.R., DER 4/5, letter from H. Powell to W. Allen, 14 November 1848.
60. Aire & Calder Navigation Undertakers' Minute Book, 7 August 1797.
61. Mrs Brooksbank's diary, original in Helaugh papers, Leeds Archives Dept., transcripts, Ark Museum, Tadcaster.
62. *Doncaster Gazette*, 10 January 1806.
63. W. White, *History and Dictionary of the West Riding*, I.
64. Graham S. Hudson, *The Aberford Railway and the History of the Garforth Collieries*, 1971, pp. 115–16.
65. The minute books etc. are in the Guildhall, York.
66. Duckham, *The Yorkshire Ouse*, op. cit., p. 68.
67. Francis Drake, *Eboracum*, 1736, pp. 303–4.
68. *York Courant*, 16 October, 1770. See also 23 August, 4 October 1768.
69. *York Chronicle*, 17 June, 29 July, 1791 quo. Jennifer Tann, 'The Yorkshire Foss Navigation', *Transport History*, March 1970.
70. The report is printed in the *York Chronicle* for 19 November 1791.
71. J.H.C., 28 February 1792.
72. Unsigned deposited plan, North Riding County Record Office.
73. *York Courant*, 14 February 1792.
74. Deposited plan, North Riding C.R.O.
75. 33 Geo III *c*. 99.
76. Perhaps the same man who ten years earlier had been assistant engineer on the Chester Canal. I have not come across him elsewhere.
77. Foss Navigation Proprietors' Minute Book, 3 July 1793.
78. *Yorkshire Gazette*, 8 November 1794. See also *York Courant*, 10 November 1794.
79. Foss Navigation Committee Minute Book, 5 November 1794.
80. Report in back of Proprietors' Minute Book.
81. Foss Navigation Proprietors' Minute Book, 2 May 1797.
82. John Tuke, *A General View of the Agriculture of the North Riding*, 1800.
83. Foss Navigation Proprietors' Minute Book, 19 January 1798.
84. Ibid., 5 January 1801.
85. 41 Geo III *c*. 115.
86. Foss Navigation Proprietors' Minute Book, 2 January 1809.
87. B.T.H.R., DER 4/17.
88. Ouse Navigation Committee Minute Book, 1841, Returns from Naburn lock.
89. For the Scarborough branch, see K. Hoole, *A Regional History of the Railways of Great Britain: The North East*, 1965.

Notes to Chapter XV

1. Ouse Navigation Trustees' Minute Book, 26 January 1835.
2. Ibid., 30 April 1834.
3. J.H.C., 3 February 1795.
4. *York Courant*, 27 October 1794.
5. Thomas Rhodes, *Report*, 1834 (York P.L.).
6. *York Courant*, 16 March 1818, *Doncaster Gazette*, 20 March 1818: T. Langdale, *Topographical History of Yorkshire*, 2nd ed., 1828.
7. *Report of the Committee . . . of the proposed Navigation to Knaresboro'*, 1800 (Leeds P.L.).
8. *York Courant*, 20 October 1800.

9. Smithson MSS (South Yorkshire Industrial Museum, Cusworth Hall, Doncaster).
10. *Report of the Committee . . . of the proposed Navigation to Knaresboro'*, 1800 (Leeds P.L.).
11. Ibid.
12. *Yorkshire Gazette*, 4 September 1824.
13. *Report of the Committee*, op. cit.
14. Ibid.
15. *York Courant*, 8 February 1796.
16. See M. G. Butterfield, *Bishop Monkton and Environs*, ND; E. Baines, *History and Directory of Yorkshire*, I, 1822; W. White, *History and Directory of the West Riding*, II, 1838: Smithson MSS (South Yorkshire Industrial Museum, Cusworth Hall, Doncaster).
17. J.H.C., 10 December 1819.
18. 1 Geo IV *c.* 35.
19. Estimate accompanying deposited plan (House of Lords Record Office).
20. T. Langdale, *Topographical Dictionary of Yorkshire*, 2nd ed., 1822.
21. *Leeds Mercury*, 27 January, 10 February 1838.
22. Turner, *Aldborough and Boroughbridge*, 1853.
23. *Conveyance of Goods by Water to Boroughbridge and Ripon*, 1834 (Harrogate P.L.).
24. *Yorkshire Herald*, 21 February 1894.
25. Ouse Navigation Trustees' Minute Book, returns from Naburn lock.
26. Barnsley Canal Proprietors' Minute Book, 3 July 1844.
27. Ibid., 1 July 1846.
28. Newspaper report of Leeds & Thirsk Railway meeting, B.T.H.R., LNO 1/9, p. 82.
29. *A History of Harrogate & Knaresborough*, 1970, Chapter XII.
30. *Report of the Committee . . . of the proposed Navigation to Knaresboro'*, 1800 (Leeds P.L.).
31. For Telford's scheme, see *A History of Harrogate & Knaresborough*. op. cit. and *Map of the proposed Line of Navigable Canal from near the Town of Knaresboro' to the River Ouse at Acaster Sailby etc.*, 1818. (Leeds P.L.).
32. Information from Mr Baron F. Duckham.
33. R. Dodd, *Report on the Line of Inland Navigation from Stockton to Winston, by way of Darlington and Staindrop, with projected branches to Durham, Northallerton, Thirsk and Boroughbridge*, 1796 (Institution of Civil Engineers Library).
34. George Atkinson, *Report of the Proposed Great Trunk of Canal from near Boroughbridge to Piersebridge, with various Collateral Branches . . .*, 1800 (Darlington P.L.).
35. 48 Geo III *c.* 48.
36. Unidentified newspaper cutting in *Manuscript History of Canals*, p. 16 (Imperial College, Civil Engineering Library).
37. *A Fuller Report . . . on the Stockton & Auckland Canal*, 1818 (Darlington P.L.).
38. See also unidentified newspaper cuttings in *Manuscript History of Canals*, op. cit., pp. 50, 66, 67.
39. Plans of 1825, 1827 and 1828 in County Durham Records Office.
40. W. A. Brooks, *Plan for a Naval Station & Asylum Harbour at Redcar*, 1832 (North Riding Record Office).
41. W. W. Tomlinson, *The North Eastern Railway*, 1914, quoting *Durham Advertiser*, 17 July 1835.
42. Jona. Thompson, *Observations*, Newcastle, 1795.
43. R. Dodd, *Report on the line of Inland Navigation, from the City of Durham, to the navigable part of the River Wear . . .*, 1796 (Newcastle P.L.).
44. *Mr. Whitworth's Report on Mr. Dodd's projected line of Inland Navigation*, 1797 (misprinted as 1697) (Newcastle P.L.).
45. J. Phillips, *A General History of Inland Navigation*, 5th ed. 1805, p. 588.
46. Notice of 11 September 1802, newspaper cutting (Carlisle P.L.).
47. Notice of 6 September 1803, newspaper cutting (Carlisle P.L.).
48. Unidentified newspaper cutting in *Manuscript History of Canals*, op. cit., p. 25.

49. MS letter to Humphrey Seahouse, 21 October 1794 (Seaham papers, Cumberland C.R.O.).
50. R. Dodd, *Report on the first part of the line . . . from the East to the West Sea*, 1795.
51. For an account of Chapman's work on these schemes, see the 'Memoir of William Chapman' in Weale's *Quarterly Papers on Engineering*, Vol. I, 1844.
52. Dodd, *Report*, op. cit.
53. William Chapman, *Report on the measures to be attended to in the Survey of a line of navigation from Newcastle upon Tyne to the Irish Channel*, 1795.
54. William Chapman, *Report on the proposed Navigation between the East and West Seas* (in three parts), 1795.
55. Jona. Thompson, *Observations on the most advantageous line of Country . . .*, 1795.
56. *Report on the proposed line of navigation between Newcastle and Maryport, by W. Jessop, Engineer, with Abstracts of the Estimates of this Line, and also of that from Stella to Hexham, by Wm. Jessop and Wm. Chapman, engineers*, Newcastle, 1796.
57. Anon, *Considerations on the Probable Commerce and Revenue that may arise on the Proposed Canal between Newcastle and Maryport*, 1796.
58. Printed notice, 2 April 1796 (Cumberland C.R.O.).
59. J.H.C., 6 December 1796, 27 February, 9, 15, 31 March, 10 April 1797.
60. John Sutcliffe, *Report on the proposed line of navigation from Stella to Hexham*, 1796.
61. John Sutcliffe, *Report on the proposed line of navigation from Hexham to Haydonbridge*, ND.
62. Robert Whitworth, *To the Committee of the proposed canal from Stella to Hexham*, 1797.
63. Anon, *Considerations etc. now reprinted, with a preface Shewing the great National Utility of the proposed Canal*, 1802.
64. In Carlisle Public Library.
65. A Robert Dodd had worked with Ralph on the Grand Surrey Canal in 1801, but had been dismissed the following year.
66. For the Carlisle Canal, see Charles Hadfield and Gordon Biddle, *The Canals of North West England*, 1970, Chapter XIII.

Notes to Chapter XVI

1. For the Wakefield, Pontefract & Goole Railway, see John Marshall, *The Lancashire & Yorkshire Railway*, 1969, I, pp. 201ff.
2. Aire & Calder Navigation Report for 1851.
3. Aire & Calder Navigation Report for 1854, read 6 August 1855.
4. Aire & Calder Navigation Directors' Minute Book, 9 February 1855.
5. See Charles Hadfield and Gordon Biddle, *The Canals of North West England*, Chapter XVII.
6. 21 & 22 Vic *c*. 75 s. 3.
7. For the Bradford Canal, see Charles Hadfield and Gordon Biddle, *The Canals of North West England*, pp. 412–16.
8. The minute books of this company are in Goole Public Library.
9. For an account of the steamship side of the port's development, see Baron F. Duckham, *The Yorkshire Ouse*, pp. 106ff.
10. Aire & Calder Navigation Report for 1867, read 3 August 1868.
11. Aire & Calder Navigation Directors' Minute Book, 2 September 1864.
12. For an account of the Calder & Hebble under the lease, see Chapter XVII.
13. For the Leeds & Armley scheme and the building of Arches lock, see Charles Hadfield & Gordon Biddle, *The Canals of North West England*, 1970, pp. 174–5.
14. Aire & Calder Navigation Report for 1852, read 1 August 1853.
15. Aire & Calder Navigation Directors' Minute Book, 29 September 1855.
16. Aire & Calder Navigation Report for 1856, read 3 August 1857.
17. Aire & Calder Navigation Report for 1861, read 4 August 1862.
18. For the Shropshire Canal, see Charles Hadfield, *The Canals of the West Midlands*, 2nd ed. 1969.

19. For this tipping, see W. A. McCutcheon, *The Canals of the North of Ireland*, 1965, p. 71.
20. W. H. Bailey, 'Notes on Canal Boat Propulsion', Fourth International Congress on Inland Navigation, Manchester 1890 (Waterways Museum).
21. Royal Commission on Canals and Waterways, 1909, Answer No. 3,344.
22. See Charles Hadfield and Gordon Biddle, *The Canals of North West England*, 1970, Chapter XIV.
23. Aire & Calder Navigation Directors' Minute Book, 13 December 1871.
24. Aire & Calder Navigation Report for 1871.
25. See Charles Hadfield and Gordon Biddle, *The Canals of North West England*, 1970, p. 434.
26. Aire & Calder Navigation Report for 1872, read 4 August 1873.
27. Goole and Hook townships together, adjusted to the 1841 boundaries: *VCH Yorkshire*, 1913, iii, 534, I am indebted to Dr W. Slatcher for these figures.
28. *Slater's Manchester Directory*, 1882.
29. 47 & 48 Vic *c.* 161.
30. Aire & Calder Navigation Directors' Minute Book, 7 November 1881.
31. Evidence on the Manchester Ship Canal Bill, 1885.
32. Aire & Calder Navigation Directors' Minute Book, 4 February 1889.
33. Aire & Calder Navigation Directors' Minute Book, 7 December 1914.
34. Aire & Calder Navigation Report for 1892, read 8 May 1893.
35. Aire & Calder Navigation Report for 1893, read 10 May 1894.
36. Aire & Calder Navigation Directors' Minute Book, 9 January 1893.
37. 58 Vic *c.* 33.
38. 62 & 63 Vic *c.* 106.

Notes to Chapter XVII

1. Aire & Calder Navigation Report for 1847, read 7 August 1848.
2. Calder & Hebble Navigation Committee Minute Book, 7 December 1847.
3. Aire & Calder Navigation Report for 1848, read 6 August 1849.
4. Calder & Hebble Navigation Proprietors' Minute Book, 20 June 1861.
5. Calder & Hebble Navigation Committee Minute Book, 26 April 1855.
6. See Charles Hadfield and Gordon Biddle, *The Canals of North West England*, 1970, pp. 431–2.
7. Calder & Hebble Navigation Committee Minute Book, 29 July 1856.
8. Aire & Calder Navigation Annual Report for 1864, read 7 August 1865.
9. Ibid.
10. Rochdale Canal Minute Book, 11 January 1865.
11. Calder & Hebble Navigation Committee Minute Book, 21 June 1855.
12. Box 43, Frederick Walker Son & Dickie papers, Halifax P.L.
13. Calder & Hebble Navigation Proprietors' Minute Book, 17 June 1875.
14. See Charles Hadfield and Gordon Biddle, *The Canals of North West England*, p. 433.
15. Calder & Hebble Navigation Proprietors' Minute Book, 8 May 1882.
16. Ibid., 20 July 1883.
17. Ibid., 18 June 1885.
18. Ibid., 18 February 1886.
19. *Royal Commission on Canals and Waterways*, Answer 18,597.
20. For instance, see Charles Hadfield, *The Canals of the East Midlands*, 2nd ed. 1970, pp. 230, 237, and Charles Hadfield, *The Canals of South and South East England*, 1969, pp. 27, 101, 178.
21. Calder & Hebble Navigation Minute Book, 17 February 1927.
22. Ibid., 20 July 1933.
23. Ibid., 27 December 1933.
24. Information from Mr I. E. Broadhead of the Hargreaves Group, by courtesy of Mr F. Doerflinger.

25. Information from Mr Reginald Wood, son of Albert Wood.
26. For the railway-owned Huddersfield Canal, see Charles Hadfield and Gordon Biddle, *The Canals of North West England*, p. 335 and pp. 445–7.
27. *Leeds Mercury*, 10 March 1849.
28. Barnsley Canal Proprietors' Minute Book, 1 July 1846.
29. Aire & Calder Navigation Report for 1846, dated 2 August 1847.
30. South Yorkshire Industrial Museum, Cusworth Hall, Doncaster.
31. Barnsley Canal Committee Minute Book, 19 October 1854.
32. Ibid., 21 November 1854.
33. Aire & Calder Navigation Report for 1854, dated 6 August 1855.
34. Ibid.
35. Ibid.
36. Aire & Calder Navigation Report for 1855, dated 4 August 1856.
37. Barnsley Canal Minute Book, Letter of 13 July 1861.
38. John Hewitt, *The History and Topography of the Parish of Wakefield*, 1862, p. 284.
39. Aire & Calder Navigation Report for 1864, read 7 August 1865.
40. Barnsley Canal Minute Book, 4 July 1866.
41. Evidence before the Committee of the House of Commons on the 1871 Bill, 25 May 1871.
42. For the Blackhill plane, see Jean Lindsay, *The Canals of Scotland*, 1968.
43. Aire & Calder Navigation Directors' Minute Book, 4 December 1905.
44. *Lock & Quay*, August 1952.

Notes to Chapter XVIII

1. For the railway history of the South Yorkshire line, see G. Dow, *Great Central*, 1959, Chapter XVI.
2. South Yorkshire, Doncaster & Goole Railway directors' report to shareholders' meeting, 27 February 1850.
3. South Yorkshire Railway & River Dun directors' report to shareholders' meeting, 31 August 1850.
4. Information from Mr J. E. Day.
5. South Yorkshire Railway & River Dun director's report, 30 August 1851.
6. Aire & Calder Navigation Directors' Minute Book, 7 June 1856.
7. South Yorkshire Railway & River Dun directors' report to shareholders' meeting, 25 February 1853.
8. *Doncaster Gazette*, 14 December 1855. Given this newspaper statement, I do not think Dow is correct in saying the opening was to Thorne (Waterside).
9. South Yorkshire Railway & River Dun directors' report to shareholders' meeting, 29 February 1856.
10. G. Dow, *Great Central*, II, p. 200.
11. Sheffield & South Yorkshire Canal Minute Book, 20 August 1888.
12. Ibid., 22 August 1888.
13. Ibid., 27 October 1888.
14. 52 & 53 Vic *c.* 190.
15. Sheffield & South Yorkshire Canal Minute Book, 27 February 1890.
16. Ibid., 6 June 1889.
17. Sheffield & South Yorkshire Navigation Minute Book, 14 March 1890.
18. 54 & 55 Vic *c.* 170.
19. 57 & Vic *c.* 147.
20. Sheffield & South Yorkshire Navigation Minute Book, 3 January 1895.
21. For a full description, see the section on the Sheffield & South Yorkshire Navigation in the Report of the Royal Commission on Canals and Waterways, 1909. Answers 21, 768ff.
22. For an impression of the Sheffield canal and basin in 1905, see an article in the *Sheffield Weekly News*, 21 January 1905 (Sheffield P.L.).
23. Sheffield & South Yorkshire Navigation Report, 14 April 1905.

24. Royal Commission on Canals and Inland Waterways, Answer 21,843.
25. Ibid., Answer 21,885.
26. *Doncaster Gazette*, 11 October 1907.
27. 'City of Sheffield. Sheffield and South Yorkshire Navigation', April 1920.
28. See Charles Hadfield, *The Canals of the East Midlands*, 2nd ed. 1970, p. 204.
29. *Yorkshire Evening Post*, 11 January 1919.
30. Sheffield & South Yorkshire Navigation Report, 10 April 1916.
31. Ibid., 26 April 1920.
32. Ibid., 16 April 1934.
33. *Modern Transport*, 6 May 1961.
34. *Doncaster Gazette*, 25 October 1907. The song is quoted by Mr Nathan Gyles, mayor of Doncaster, as having been popular in his boyhood.
35. *Bradshaw's Canals and Navigable Rivers*, 1928 ed.
36. Information from Mr John Goodchild and Mr J. E. Day.

Notes to Chapter XIX

1. Sheahan & Whellan, *History and Topography of the City of York and the East Riding of Yorkshire*, Vol. 2, 1856.
2. *Beverley Guardian*, 16, 23 February, 1 March 1856.
3. *Canals Returns*, 1905.
4. The above information from *Canal Returns*, 1870, 1888, 1898, 1905.
5. *Canal Returns*, 1898.
6. Driffield Old Navigation Minute Book, 27 February 1845.
7. Aire & Calder Navigation Committee Minute Book, 7 January 1847.
8. Driffield Old Navigation Minute Book, 25 February 1846.
9. Ibid., 7 July 1846.
10. Driffield Old Navigation Minute Book, 31 October 1850.
11. Ibid., 5 July 1853.
12. DDX. 17/93, East Riding Record Office.
13. Driffield New Navigation Minute Book, 7 July 1874.
14. A. N. Jefferies, 'The Driffield Canal', *The Dalesman*, May 1966.
15. Driffield New Navigation Minute Book, 14 December 1910.
16. Jefferies, 'The Driffield Canal', op. cit.
17. J. J. Sheahan & T. Whellan, *History and Topography of the City of York and the East Riding of Yorkshire*, Vol. 2, 1856.
18. Aire & Calder Navigation Directors' Minute Book, 5 November 1863.
19. Figures from the Royal Commission on Canals and Waterways, 1909, and *Proceedings* under the Railway & Canal Traffic Act 1888, 1894, B.T.H.R., MT 1/22.
20. Market Weighton Canal Trustees' Minute Book, 6 May 1851.
21. Market Weighton Canal Trustees' Minute Book, 8 May 1894.
22. Ibid., 7 May 1895.
23. A. N. Jefferies, 'Canals of Character in the East Riding', *The Dalesman*, February 1966.
24. The Market Weighton Canal (Weighton Lock) (Local Enactments) Order, No. 2042 of 1970.

Notes to Chapter XX

1. For a full account of the Ouse's history, Baron F. Duckham's *The Yorkshire Ouse*, 1967, should be consulted. The following short account owes everything important to his book.
2. B.T.H.R., DER 23/80, letter of 10 May 1851.
3. B.T.H.R., DER 8/2, letters of 24 November 1853, 28 February, 8 March 1854.
4. North Eastern Railway Board Minute Book, 6 October 1854.

O

5. Ibid., 7 March 1856.
6. Ibid., 24 August 1855.
7. N. A. Hudleston, *History of Malton and Norton*, 1962.
8. Aire & Calder Navigation Committee Minute Book, 24 October 1855.
9. Ibid., 15 February 1858.
10. *Proceedings* under the Railway & Canal Traffic Act 1888, 1894 (B.T.H.R., MT 1/22), from which some of the above information is also taken.
11. Aire & Calder Navigation Report for 1870, read 7 August 1871.
12. S.R.O. 978 of 1935, The River Derwent Navigation Act Revocation Order, under the Land Drainage Act, 1930.
13. Report of the Yorkshire Ouse Catchment Board for 1937.
14. Letter from the York & North Midland Railway to William Gray jnr, 6 February 1849, B.T.H.R., POC 8/1.
15. David Silence, 'Crossroads of the Yorkshire Wolds', *Railway Magazine*, November 1965, p. 624.
16. *Proceedings* under the Railway & Canal Traffic Act, 1888, 1894, B.T.H.R., MT 1/22.
17. *The Pocklington Canal—the Case for Restoration*, 1969.
18. Information from the Curator, The Ark Museum, Tadcaster.
19. 53 & 54 Vic.
20. *Bradshaw's Canals and Navigable Rivers*, 1904 ed.
21. Preamble to 1853 Act.
22. Foss Navigation Committee Minute Book, 6 October 1848.
23. 16 & 17 Vic *c*. 56.
24. Jennifer Tann, 'The Yorkshire Foss Navigation', *Transport History*, March 1970.
25. 22 Vic *c*. 22.
26. *Royal Commission on Canals & Waterways*, 1909, Answers 19,885–6.
27. Ibid., 19,888–9.
28. This account is based on the records of the Linton Lock Commissioners, by their kind permission and that of their clerk, Mr A. B. Anderson of 8 Blake Street, York.
29. 8 & 9 Vic *c*. 104.
30. See newspaper report, Leeds & Thirsk Railway Minute Book, 31 August 1846.
31. Leeds & Thirsk Railway Minute Book, 31 July 1846.
32. Leeds & Thirsk Railway Minute Book, 27 May 1848.
33. Royal Commission on Canals and Waterways, Answer 9,869.
34. *Yorkshire Herald*, 21 February 1894.
35. Royal Commission on Canals and Waterways, Answers 27,025ff.
36. Ibid., Answer 9,870.
37. Ibid., Answers 19,993–4.
38. Ibid., Answers 27,013ff.
39. Linton Lock Commissioners Records.

APPENDICES

APPENDIX 1

Summary of facts about the Canals and Navigations of Yorkshire and the North East.

A. *Rivers Successfully Made Navigable*

River	Date of Act under which Work was begun	Date Wholly Opened	Approx. Cost at Opening £	Terminal Points
Aike Beck	None	*c.* 1800		Hull River–Lockington landing
Aire & Calder	1699	1704	£26,700[1]	Weeland to Castleford, then to Leeds and to Wakefield,[2]
				[3]
		c. 1818		Dewsbury Old Cut[4] Brotherton Staniland's
		1905		New Junction Canal[5]
		1824		Fairburn Canal
Beverley Beck	1727	1731	£1,400	Grovehill (R. Hull)–Beverley
Calder & Hebble	1758	1770	*c.* £75,000	Wakefield (Fall Ing)–Sowerby Bridge
		1828	£57,800	Branch to Halifax
		c. 1835		Branch, Fearnley Cut Dewsbury (private)[9]

[1] Capital as stabilized in 1721.

[2] In 1778 Selby became an additional terminal point when the Selby Canal was opened; and in 1826 Goole also, with the opening of the Goole Canal. In 1884 the company were also made conservators of the Ouse between 100 yd below Hook railway bridge, Goole, and Trent Falls.

[3] I have not included the short river sections by-passed by cuts, but which for a time remained open to navigation.

[4] Acquired 1878. Previously part of disused Calder & Hebble line through Dewsbury that had been by-passed.

[5] Owned jointly with the Sheffield & South Yorkshire Navigation (see Don).

[6] Present lengths, Goole–Castleford 23¼ miles, Castleford–Leeds 10 miles, Castleford–Wakefield 7⅝ miles.

Length	Greatest Number of Locks	Size of Boats Taken	Date of Disuse for Commercial Traffic	Date of Abandonment	Whether bought by Railway and Present Ownership
c. 1⅞ miles	2	40 ft × 8 ft 10 in.	c. 1850		
Weeland–Castleford 18½ miles, Castleford–Leeds 17¼ miles, Castleford–Wakefield 13 miles[6]	16[7]	54 ft × 14 ft[8]	Open		British Waterways Board
1 mile					
⅛ mile			c. 1829		
			c. 1850		
5½ miles			Open		
½ mile			c. 1849		
¾ mile	1	64 ft × 17 ft 6 in	Open	Open	Beverley Corporation
23½ miles[10]	24[11]	57 ft 6 in × 14 ft[12]	Open[13]	Open	British Waterways Board
1¾ miles	14			1942	
⅛ mile	None				

[7] On the original Weeland–Leeds–Wakefield line.

[8] Originally. Current main line dimensions are 180 ft × 18 ft 6 in.

[9] I have not included the short river sections by-passed by cuts, but which for a time remained open to navigation.

[10] Now 21½ miles.

[11] As built, omitting flood-gates and flood-locks. Subsequent changes are too complicated to summarize. There are now 27.

[12] Craft 115 ft × 17 ft 6 in to the tail of Broad Cut Upper Lock.

[13] Lower section to Thornhill power station only; last cargo to Sowerby Bridge, 1955.

River	Date of Act under which Work was begun	Date Wholly Opened	Approx. Cost at Opening £	Terminal Points
Don[1]	1726[2] 1727[3] 1740[4]	1751	£45,000	Tinsley–Fishlake Ferry[5]
Driffield Navigation	1767	1770 extension 1805 1805 c. 1770 1811	£13,000	Aike Beck Mouth–Great Driffield Fisholme–Frodingham Bridge Frodingham Bridge–Foston mills (private) Emmotland–Corps Landing
Ouse	[12]			Trent Falls–Widdington Ings[13]
Ouse (Linton Lock Navigation)	1767	1769	c. £8,400	Widdington Ings–Swale Nab
Ure and Ripon Canal	1767	1772	£16,400	Swale Nab–Ripon

[1] In 1895 a new company, the Sheffield & South Yorkshire Navigation Company, acquired the old Don Navigation and other concerns.
[2] Holmstile (Doncaster)–Tinsley.
[3] Holmstile–Wilsick House.
[4] Wilsick House–Fishlake Ferry.
[5] In 1905 the New Junction Canal was opened, from the Sheffield & South Yorkshire at Stainforth to the Goole Canal. It was jointly owned by the S. & S.Y. and the Aire & Calder.
[6] Original length to Fishlake Ferry. Now 26¼ miles.
[7] At completion to Tinsley in 1740.
[8] Except for 2¼ miles from the junction of the Stainforth & Keadby Canal to the Don River.
[9] Driffield to Frodingham Beck, canal section, 5 miles. River section 5⅛ miles.

Length	Greatest Number of Locks	Size of Boats Taken	Date of Disuse for Commercial Traffic	Date of Abandonment	Whether bought by Railway and Present Ownership
29 miles[6]	16[7]	Probably c. 54 ft × 14 ft originally	Open[8]	Open	Amalgamated with South Yorkshire etc. Rly, 1850; concern sold to M.S.L.R., 1864. Waterways transferred to S. & S.Y. Nav. Co. 1895
10⅛ miles[9] 1 mile ¾ mile 1¾ miles	7[10]	61 ft × 14 ft 6 in	1944[11]		Commissioners
51 miles[14]	1[15]	140 ft × 24 ft[16]	Open	Open	York Corporation
9¾ miles	1	60 ft × 15 ft 4 in	Open	Open	Linton Lock Navigation Commissioners
10¼ miles[17]	5	58 ft × 14 ft 10 in	[18]	Open[19]	1847, sold to Leeds & Thirsk Rly, later N.E.R. Now British Waterways Board

[10] Originally 4, one at Snakeholme, and three upwards to Driffield. Snakeholme was probably converted to a staircase pair in the 1770s. Struncheonhill was added in 1805, probably at first a single lock, which was soon also converted to a staircase pair.

[11] To Driffield.

[12] The Ouse has always been navigable.

[13] From 1884, Hook railway bridge, Goole–Widdington Ings, the 9½ mile lower stretch having been transferred to the Aire & Calder: later, to the British Transport Docks Board.

[14] From 1884, 41½ miles.

[15] Opened 1757: the tidal limit.

[16] After Naburn lock was rebuilt in 1888; before that, about 84 ft × 20 ft. Except through the lock, there are no restrictions on size other than depth.

[17] Swale Nab to Ox Close, Ure River, 8 miles; Ox Close to Ripon, canal, 2¼ miles.

[18] Above Boroughbridge, c. 1894. Below Boroughbridge, open.

[19] Except above Ox Close, abandoned 1955.

B. *Rivers with Uncompleted Navigation Works*

River	Date of Act under which Work was Begun	Money Spent £	Terminal Points Authorized	Length on which Work was Done
Bedale Beck	1767	£11,500[1]	Swale junction–Bedale[2]	Most
Cod Beck	1767		Swale junction–Thirsk[6]	Most
Derwent	1701	c. £5,000[10]	Ouse junction to Scarborough Mills	Ouse junction to Yedingham[11]
Foss	1793	c. £40,000	Ouse junction–Stillington, 16 miles	Ouse junction–Sheriff Hutton bridge, 11½ miles
Swale	1767	£11,500[15]	Swale Nab–Morton bridge[16]	Most
Wharfe	1890[20]		Wharfe Mouth–Tadcaster	

[1] Including the Swale.
[2] About 2 miles.
[3] There were to have been two locks: one, at Leeming, was probably completed. I have no evidence that it was ever used.
[4] It has not been abandoned.
[5] It was never opened.
[6] 5 miles.
[7] 5 locks were intended: one, at Sowerby, was built and probably used on one occasion.
[8] The only record of craft reaching Thirsk is in 1770.
[9] It has not been abandoned.
[10] To Malton. I do not know the cost of the Yedingham extension.
[11] Ouse Junction to Malton, 38 miles, opened c. 1723; extension to Yedingham, 13½ miles, opened c. 1813.

Greatest Number of Locks	Size of Boats Taken	Date of Disuse for Commercial Traffic	Date of Abandonment	Later Events
3		4	5	
7		8	9	
5	55 ft × 14 ft	1960[12]	1935	Sold to N.E.R., 1855. Transferred to Yorkshire Ouse Catchment Board, 1935. Now Yorkshire Rivers Authority. Yorkshire Derwent Trust now restoring locks
8	58 ft × 14 ft[13]	1859[14]	1859[14]	1852, sold to York Corporation, who still own it
1[17]	60 ft × 15 ft 4 in	18	19	
None			1898[21]	

[12] Last commercial barge through Sutton lock.
[13] Castle mills lock, 58 ft × 15 ft, rebuilt 1889, 97 ft × 18 ft 6 in.
[14] Except lower $1\frac{7}{8}$ mile, now $c.$ $1\frac{1}{4}$ mile, still open with 1 lock.
[15] Including Bedale Beck.
[16] 28 miles.
[17] Completed (Topcliffe). Five were planned, and some work seems to have been done on two others.
[18] In 1769 it was announced that the river was navigable in 'flashes' to Morton bridge: I have no evidence that any craft did the whole trip.
[19] It has never been abandoned.
[20] The river has always been navigable after a fashion to Tadcaster.
[21] Winding up of company.

C. Canals, the Main Lines of which were Completed as Authorized

Canal	Date of Act under which Work was begun	Date Wholly Opened	Approx. Cost at Opening £	Terminal Points	Branches Built
Barnsley	1793	1804	£95,000	Heath (Aire & Calder)–Barnby Basin	
Dearne & Dove	1793	1804	£100,000	Swinton (Don)–Barnsley Junction lock	Elsecar 2⅛ miles, 6 locks, 1798. Worsbrough 2⅛ miles, 1804
Emmet's	None	c. 1782		Blue Hills–Emmet's foundry near Birkinshaw	
Greas-brough	None	c. 1780		Don–Greasbrough Ings	To Sough bridge, Greasbrough c. 100 yd), c. 1780 To Newbiggin (c. ½ mile)
Leven	1801	c. 1804	c. £6,000	Hull River–Leven	

[1] After enlargement in 1881, 79 ft × 14 ft 10 in.

[2] The last date of through traffic. Last barge through Royston, 1950; through Heath lock 1952. Above Barugh disused from c. early 1870s.

[3] The 5 locks at Barugh and the 1 mile 23 ch of canal above were abandoned by an Act of 1893.

[4] Including the Barnsley junction lock.

Length	Greatest Number of Locks	Size of Boats Taken	Date of Disuse for Commercial Traffic	Date of Abandonment	Whether bought by Railway and Present Ownership
15 miles	20	58 ft × 14 ft 10 in[1]	1946[2]	1953[3]	Bought by Aire & Calder Navigation, 1875
9⅝ miles	19[4]	58 ft × 14 ft 10 in	1906[5] 1928[6] 1934[7] Open[8]	1961[9]	1846, bought by R. Dun Co; 1850, amal. with South Yorkshire etc. Rly; 1864, concern sold to M.S.L.R.; 1895, waterways transferred to S. & S.Y. Co; 1948, British Transport Commission
1 mile			c. 1815		
1½ miles	4	61 ft 6 in × 15 ft 3 in	Upper ⅞ miles and South bridge branch, 1840s. Lower ⅝ open 1918. Disused 1928. Newbiggin branch before 1900		Private
3¼ miles	1	64 ft × 14 ft 10 in	1935		Private

[5] Worsbrough branch.
[6] Elsecar branch.
[7] Through to Barnsley.
[8] ½-mile at Swinton, including 5 locks, is still open.
[9] Except ½ mile at Swinton.

Canal	Date of Act under which Work was begun	Date Wholly Opened	Approx. Cost at Opening £	Terminal Points	Branches Built
Market Weighton	1772	1782	£12,000	Weighton (Humber) lock–River Head, Weighton Common	Sir John Vavasour's Canal *c.* 1835, ¼ mile, disused *c.* 1865
Pockling-ton	1815	1818	£32,000	Derwent (East-Cottingwith)–York–Hull road near Pocklington	
Ramsden's, Sir John	1774	1776	£12,000	Cooper Bridge–Huddersfield	
Sheffield	1815	1819	£104,700	Tinsley–Sheffield	Greenland, ½ mile, 1819
Stainforth & Keadby	1793	*c.* 1802	£57,000	Stainforth (Don)–Keadby (Trent)	

[1] Weighton lock took craft 66 ft × 14 ft 10 in.
[2] The last craft through Weighton lock. The section above the next lock, Sod House, probably became disused in, or about, the 1870s.
[3] Above Sod House lock, abandoned 1900.

Length	Greatest Number of Locks	Size of Boats Taken	Date of Disuse for Commercial Traffic	Date of Abandonment	Whether bought by Railway and Present Ownership
9 miles	4	57 ft × 14 ft 2 in[1]	1958[2]	[3]	Shareholders' interest bought by York & North Midland Rly, 1850. Resold 1900
9½ miles	9	58 ft × 14 ft 3 in	1932[4]		Bought by York & North Midland Rly, 1848. Now British Waterways Board
3¾ miles	9	58 ft × 14 ft 2 in	1953	Open	1845, vested in Huddersfield & Manchester Railway & Canal Co, later L.N.W.R.; 1945, sold to Calder & Hebble. Now British Waterways Board
3 miles	12[5]	61 ft 6 in × 15 ft 3 in	Open	Open	1848, sold to Manchester, Sheffield & Lincolnshire Railway; 1849, purchased by River Don Company; 1850 became part of South Yorkshire Rly & River Dun Co's waterways; 1864, part of M.S. & L.R.; 1895 part of Sheffield & South Yorkshire Navigation. Now British Waterways Board
12¾ miles	2	65 ft × 17 ft[6]	Open	Open	1849, absorbed by River Dun Co; 1850, amal. with South Yorkshire etc Rly; 1864, concern sold to M.S.L.R.; 1895, transferred to S. & S.Y. Co. Now British Waterways Board

[4] The canal is now being restored for pleasure use by the Pocklington Canal Amenity Society.

[5] Now 11, one new lock having replaced 2 old ones in 1963.

[6] About 74 ft × 21 ft at the Keadby end.

D. *Canals, the Main Lines of which were not Completed*
None.

E. *Canals Partly Built but not Opened*
None.

F. *Canals Authorized but not Begun*
None.

APPENDIX II

Principal Engineering Works

A. *Inclined Planes*
None.

B. *Lifts*
None.

C. *Tunnels over 500 yards*
None.

D. *Outstanding Aqueducts*

Aire & Calder	Stanley Ferry (Calder)
Barnsley Canal	Barnsley (Dearne)

INDEX TO VOLUMES I AND II

The principal references to canals and river navigations are indicated in bold type

P   487

Swale Navigation and River, 28, 31, 90, 93, 96, **101–10**, 111–14, **344–5**, 348–50, 352

Swallow Wood colliery, 225

Swann, Mark, canal official, 331, 445

Swindells, H. P., canal official, 394n, 396

Swinefleet, 161, 219, 294

Swinton, 43, 78–9, 169, 220–2, 280–1, 284–5, 388, 410, 426–7; lock, 70n, 79

Sykehouse, 64, 71, 102, 377; lock, 377, 418, 427

Tadcaster, 18, 94, 100–1, 334, 337, 349, 445–6; mills, 100–1

Tallow, carried on canals, etc, 113

Tar, carried on canals, etc, 426

Taylor, Enoch, engineer, 167, 214

Team River, 116, 353

Tees Navigation Co, 350, 353

Tees River, 113–15, 343, 345, 348–50

Tees canal schemes, **113–15, 349–52**

Teesside, 115; see also Stockton

Telegraph, installation of electric, 367

Telford, Thomas, engineer, 147–8, 150, 182, 272, 315, 349

Tennant, Christopher, projector, 352

Textiles, carried by coasting trade, 22; by road transport, 195; on canals, etc, 17–22, 28, 34–5, 43, 45, 58, 95, 100, 121–3, 136, 159, 166, 173–4, 178, 189, 195, 198, 200, 203–4n, 323, 363–4, 389–90; on railways, 166, 389; see also Wool, Flax

Thackray, engineer, 214

Thirsk, 28, 93, 102, 110, 344, 347, 350

Thompson, E. & J., carriers, 195

Thompson, H. S., rly chairman, 364

Thompson, John, engineer, 78, 208, 210, 265, 281, 283, 290–2

Thompson, J., author, 116, 353, 356

Thompson, Robert, carrier, 308

Thompson, William, carrier, 438

Thomson, James, engineer, 205

Thorne, 74, 76, 80, 127n, 130, 135, 160, 209, 211–12, 216–19, 275, 290–3, 295, 373, 412–13, 423, 428

Thorne & Hatfield Moors Peat Canals, **81–2, 226, 428**

Thornes, 23, 164; cut, lock, 199, 202, 394

Thornhill, 398

Thornhill cut, 189, 200, 392

Thornton Beck, 318

Thorpe in Balne, 65, 214

Thorpe, Samuel, colliery owner, 176

Thorpe Willoughby, 32

Thrybergh mills, 78

Thurgoland, 167, 180, 287

Thwaite colliery, 35, 39; cut, lock, 20n,

33, 35, 132, 135n, 385; mill, 33n, 35, 163n

Timber, carried on canals, etc, 21, 28, 47, 70–1, 73, 75, 78, 106, 111–12, 176, 189, 198, 200, 275, 278, 286, 298, 312, 325, 327, 332, 334, 339, 354–5, 373–4, 380, 387–8, 405

Timperley, John, engineer, 132

Tindall, Richard, canal official, 298, 300

Tinsley, 64, 69, 73–5, 77–8, 80, 208–11, 215–16, 219, 265–7, 269–71, 274–6, 280, 295, 411, 414, 416, 423–4, 427; cut, locks (Don), 78–9, 215, 271, 274, 426

Tinsley locks (canal), 319, 424n, 427

Tinsley Park colliery, 272, 274

Todmorden, 189

Tofield & Co, carriers, 285

Tofield, Thomas, engineer, 98, 290

Tollerton, 112

Tolls, through, 332, 373, 375, 395

Tom Puddings, see Compartment boats

Tomroyd Wood, 180, 287

Top Pit Wood, 181, 287

Topcliffe, 101, 103, 106, 110; lock, 104, 106

Topham, John, contractor, 61

Towing, 36–7, 55, 98, 141, 146, 157, 218, 312, 323, 366–7, 423, 430; electric, 396; see also Push-towing, steamboats and tugs

Townley, Richard, subscriber, 48, 54

Towpaths, 19, 37, 55, 74, 76, 97–8, 106, 121, 195, 209, 211, 218, 291, 295, 301–2, 308, 310, 312, 315, 321, 343–4, 430

Tramroads, horse, 171, 173–4, 178, 182, 358, 445; Barnby furnace, 174; Banks Hall, 176; Barugh project, 407–8; Beamish-Fatfield 354; Brotherton, 138; Canals Junction project, 182; Co Durham, 350, 352–4; Don-Womersley projects, 137, 166–7, 214; Elsecar, 285; Fairburn, 138; Fenton's, 124n; Flockton, 55; Goole docks, 139; Greasbrough Canal, 80–1, 225–6; Heck Bridge & Wentbridge, 137–8, 166–8, 182, 214, 287; Huddersfield area, 62; Kirklees, 55; Knaresborough projects, 348–9; Lake Lock, 124–5, 148, 150, 153; Middleton, 22; New Park–Wakefield, 55; Norcroft bridge, 171, 176; Outwood-Bottom Boat, 22; Peak Forest Canal–Sheffield project, 182, 270; Sheffield area, 270, 272–3, 288–9; Sheffield–Tinsley project, 269–70; Sheffield–Wortley project, 216; Silkstone, 160, 174–6, 180, 182–5,

Wylam, 117

Yarm, 113, 115, 349, 352
Yarm & Cleveland Shipping Co, 350
Yarmouth, 128, 136, 374
Yarn, carried on canals, etc, *see* Textiles
Yedingham, 93, 98, 316–18, 321–2, 327, 441
Yeoman, Thomas, engineer, 29, 32
York, 18, 26, 28, 30, 32–3, 39–42, 64, 66, 71, 76, 83–4, 93–6, 102–3, 110–11, 123, 129, 149, 159, 165, 170, 179, 184–5, 187, 276, 313–15, 332–6, 340–4,

346–7, 350, 378, 392, 397, 399, 401, 405, 438–40, 444–6, 448, 452
York Corporation, 18, 22, 70, 93–5, 102, 334, 376, 439–40, 446–9, 451
York & Hull East & West Yorkshire Junction Rly project, 333
York & Newcastle Rly, 450
York & North Midland Rly, 156, 163, 165–6, 308, 313, 315, 325, 333, 342, 362–3, 431, 433–4, 438, 440–1, 445–6, 451
Yorkshire Derwent Trust, The, 444
Yorkshire Ouse Catchment Board, 444
Yorkshire River Authority, 444